Can I Have
a Cell Phone
for Hanukkah?

Can I Have a Cell Phone for Hanukkah?

The Essential Scoop on Raising Modern Jewish Kids

Sharon Duke Estroff

Broadway Books
New York

BROADWAY

PUBLISHED BY BROADWAY BOOKS

Published in the United States by Broadway Books, an imprint of The Doubleday
Broadway Publishing Group, a division of Random House, Inc., New York.
www.broadwaybooks.com

BROADWAY BOOKS and its logo, a letter B bisected on the diagonal, are trademarks of
Random House, Inc.

Portions of this book have appeared previously in various publications including:
About Our Children New Jersey · *Atlanta Jewish Times* · *American Israelite Cincinnati* ·
Arizona Jewish Post · *Boston Jewish Advocate* · *Broward Jewish Journal* · *Chicago Jewish News*
· *Cleveland Jewish News* · *Dade Jewish Journal* · *Dayton Jewish Observer* · *Florida Jewish
News* · *Heritage Florida Jewish News* · *The Jewish News Weekly of Northern California* ·
Jerusalem Post · *Jewish Chronicle of Pittsburgh* · *Jewish Community Chronicle of Long Beach* ·
Jewish Community Newspaper of St. Joseph Valley · *Jewish Herald-Voice Texas* · *Jewish
Independent of British Columbia* · *Jewish Journal of Greater Los Angeles* · *Jewish Leader* ·
Jewish Ledger of Connecticut · *Jewish Ledger of Western Massachusetts* · *Jewish News of
Greater Phoenix* · *Jewish Press of Omaha* · *Jewish Standard New Jersey* · *Jewish Star* · *Jewish
Voice and Herald of Rhode Island* · *Jewish Voice and Opinion* · *JT Voice of Jewish Washington*
· *Maine Jewish Community Voice* · *MyJewishLearning.com* · *New Jersey Jewish News* · *Ohio
Jewish Chronicle* · *Palm Beach Jewish Journal* · *Rockland Jewish Reporter* · *San Diego Jewish
Times* · *Sun Country Life and Style Magazine* · *Shalom Newspaper* · *Shalom Today* · *Texas
Jewish Post* · *Toronto Jewish Tribune* · *Washington Jewish Week* · *Washtenaw Jewish News* ·
Westchester Jewish Chronicle · *Wisconsin Jewish Chronicle* · *World Jewish Digest* · *Youngstown
Jewish Journal*

Book design by Diane Hobbing of Snap-Haus Graphics

Library of Congress Cataloging-in-Publication Data
Estroff, Sharon.
    Can I have a cell phone for Hanukkah? : the essential scoop on raising modern
Jewish kids / Sharon Estroff. — 1st ed.
        p. cm.
    1. Child rearing—Religious aspects—Judaism. 2. Parenting—Religious aspects—
Judaism. I. Title.
HQ769.3.E815 2008
649'.1088296—dc22

                                                                2007012238

ISBN: 978-0-7679-2544-0

PRINTED IN THE UNITED STATES OF AMERICA

10 9 8 7 6 5 4
First Edition

To Brandon, Alex, Jakey, and Emma

My source, my inspiration, my light—who so gracefully and graciously shared their mommy with a laptop computer for two and a half years

To Lee

My partner in parenting, laughter, and love, who put up with me through four human-length gestations and one elephant-length gestation, sharing in my excitement, frustrations, and dreams every step of the way

To Mom and Dad

The most loving, supportive, brilliant parents and grandparents in the universe, whose divine wisdom and insight are evident throughout this book

Contents

Contents

Preface

Five Zillion Unanswered Questions

Sure, it took a little while to get into the preschool groove, but by the time pre-K rolled around, it was essentially smooth sailing. Our kids were officially out of diapers (not counting the occasional accident), they could get dressed independently (expanding the definition of dressed to include backwards and inside out), and we'd admittedly grown attached to a few of the other preschool moms and dads.

It's not that our heads were stuck in the sand. We knew we'd eventually load our kids onto a yellow school bus and tearfully wave as they rolled away. It's just that when that day actually arrived, it felt like that cushy, comfortable rug of preschool—where we knew all the rules and our place in the circle—was being ripped out from under us.

It soon became clear that in the grade-school world, it was no longer acceptable to waltz our son into class two hours late because we both craved a lazy morning of pancakes and cartoons; or to hover clandestinely outside our daughter's classroom hoping to catch a precious glimpse of her secret school day. In the grade-school world, innocent-looking playgrounds house social hierarchies so complex they'd floor a seasoned political scientist, and children's academic strengths and weaknesses are clearly defined, evaluated, and engraved on permanent records.

Gone were the days of consulting books we'd raked in at the bris or baby naming giving play-by-play childrearing instructions for the first five years. Gone were the playgroups where fellow pre-school moms shared handy parenting tips—gone and swapped for a twenty-five-minute kindergarten open house spent filling out questionnaires, and secretly wishing that another parent would raise her hand to ask the five zillion unanswered questions bouncing around our brains. *(My neighbor says her five-year-old is reading Harry Potter, but my kindergartner has barely graduated from Bob Books—does he need a tutor? My daughter will be out of school for the bulk of September due to the High Holidays—does that put her behind the academic pack before she even pulls out of the starting gate? How many playdates should I plan to ensure my child's playground popularity? How many extracurriculars does it take to make a kid well rounded?)*

(In case you're thinking that the expertise I'd gained during my decade and a half of teaching in Atlanta public schools and private Jewish day schools—or the knowledge I'd accumulated earning the undergraduate and graduate diplomas in child psychology and education that were currently shoved in my basement under overstuffed boxes of baby clothes—enabled me to hop the hurdles reserved for parents of grade-schoolers, I can assure you that this was far from the case. As I soon discovered, no matter how professional, insightful, and levelheaded I could be regarding other people's kids, I was a mess when it came to my own.)

Alien Attack

Around the time my oldest child entered third grade, my anxiety level appeared to plateau. It's not that I'd had my five zillion questions answered or anything, it's just that I'd gotten used to the perpetual stress. But before my head had officially stopped spinning, something happened that sent it reeling all over again—Brandon turned eleven. As far as I can tell, the only way to explain my son's rapid transformation is that on the eve of his eleventh birthday, an alien snuck into his room and replaced him with a rather obnoxious version of his former self. How else can I explain why the same kid who, only weeks before, loved to cuddle with me in bed on Sunday mornings suddenly summed me up as round-the-clock eye-rolling material?

My son's alien status continued to worsen. Playdates once spent racing Hot Wheels across my kitchen floor now largely took place behind closed doors. He acquired a "screen name" (BravesFan) and would have spent endless hours sending cryptic instant messages to his friends had I not pried him away from the computer and insisted he do his homework instead. Since the other mothers were as clueless as I was about this "tweenhood" thing, I had nobody to ask whether a good parent would buy her son an iPod for his eleventh birthday. Or if a twelve-year-old was old enough to receive a cell phone for Hanukkah. Considering that the bulk of the five zillion questions I had before my son was snatched by aliens remained unanswered, I had now progressed to the next level—five zillion unanswered questions squared.

Why This Book

My personal plight as an elementary- and middle-school parent and the steady flow of Jewish mothers snagging me in the halls on my way to the lunchroom, cornering me at birthday parties, and sending scribbled notes on cereal-stained papers in my students' backpacks convinced me the five-zillion-unanswered-question syndrome was something of a parental epidemic within the Jewish community. When I began writing my now nationally syndicated

Jewish parenting advice column, I was not surprised to find that more questions came in by the droves.

Fortunately, it was about that time that I had my epiphany at the soccer field. While I won't reveal the full details of this metamorphic maternal event until Chapter 1, I will tell you this: It served as the catalyst for the liberating realization that the antidote to this parental pandemic did not entail my personally addressing each and every one of those five zillion questions, but instead helping puzzled parents clarify their big picture and sense of purpose in parenting.

It's like the Lego sets that are stuffed into my boys' closets. When you first dump the contents of the package onto the playroom floor, you feel overwhelmed and perplexed; you don't know whether you're trying to build a castle or a spaceship. It's not until you see the picture on the front of the box that all those tiny cubes suddenly take on new meaning as the building blocks of a totally cool medieval fortress. That glimpse at the final goal—while admittedly a bit daunting at first—ultimately gives us the faith, inspiration, and direction we need to begin building our Camelot.

The grade-school parenting experience is really no different from the Lego experience. Lost in the seemingly bottomless sea of expectations and the intense pressure of raising a school-age child, we feel anxious and overwhelmed. But once we figure out the big picture—what we really want for our kids—all those tiny pieces miraculously start to fall into place.

What exactly does the big picture on the front of our Jewish Parent Lego box look like? Taking into account that every parent is different (some go for more contemporary castles and others prefer more traditional sorts), it's safe to say that our picture-perfect edifices are not formed from T-ball trophies, flawless spelling tests, or multicolored karate belts. Rather, they are built from the ground up with hopes and dreams of raising resilient children who are geared to thrive despite the stresses inherent in twenty-first-century life; of *menschlich* children grounded in their Judaism and their morality; of fulfilled children confident in who they are and where they belong in the big picture of life; of empowered children capable of meeting their full potential—academically and otherwise—and one day dreaming up and building their own unique versions of Camelot.

That is the reason I have written this book: to give you an instruction manual that will focus on the big picture while providing clear and specific guidelines to help you achieve it, illuminate the infinite ways that your rich Jewish heritage can help you make all of those little daily decisions that add up to what we call parenting, and serve as a parenting ally throughout the rocky grade-school years. And, of course, to give you my trademark troubleshooting tricks to help make your life easier during your castle-building process.

By the way, my Lego castles never do quite match the one on the front of the box. But they don't have to, because our children's eyes will light up at the sight of the final product whether or not we put the flags exactly where they were supposed to go, or inadvertently forgot a window or two. Just like the Torah, which can be interpreted and applied in different ways, a good instruction manual allows for flexibility. While you are reading this book, I encourage you to pick and choose which bricks you use and the way in which you put them together.

Nu, what are you waiting for? Camelot wasn't built in a day and neither are *menschlich*, resilient, fulfilled, empowered twenty-first-century Jewish kids. So if you're ready, it's time to hit the bricks!

CHAPTER 1

The Mommy 500

When I was pregnant with my oldest child, Brandon, I traded in my red Mustang convertible for a beige Grand Caravan. Little did I know that this supersized vehicle would become my stock car for the Mommy 500—an eighteen-year race whose finish line is designated by acceptance letters to prestigious universities.

The first time I revved my engines in this marathon was two weeks into my maternal career, when I received a letter from an enterprise that I'll call Gymbananas. "It's never too early to begin thinking about college," read the primary-colored flyer, which went on to list course offerings for infants ages six weeks and up. Yes, Gymbananas had a special message for me—a sleep-deprived, hormonally challenged new mother—and it was that if I denied my baby adequate exposure to bubbles and clapping songs before he learned to roll over, I would irreparably hinder his chances of getting into Harvard. Before I could say *Oy vey*, I was giving a perky woman on the telephone my credit card number to secure my son's spot in the Wednesday-morning precrawler class.

I was at Brandon's kindergarten Rosh Hashanah celebration (my first official program as a grade-school parent) when it became painfully evident that my Gymbananas era had been but a leisurely practice lap along the Mommy 500 and I would now be putting my pedal to the metal.

"So what are Brandon's fall extracurriculars?" asked the mother sitting next to me in the apples and honey corner.

"He's playing soccer. What about Jeremy?" I replied, following Mommy etiquette to a T.

"Well, let's see," she answered, trying (unsuccessfully) to sound nonchalant. "Jeremy's fall extracurricular sport is tennis, his fall extracurricular instrument is violin, his fall extracurricular martial art is tae kwon do, and his fall extracurricular academic is science."

Before I could determine whether an extracurricular academic was an oxymoron, my wheels were racing. I spent the rest of the morning signing Brandon up for an array of extracurriculars, and trying to figure out how I'd managed to walk out of the kindergarten Rosh Hashanah celebration indelibly inscribed in the Book of Stress.

A Message from Bubbe

"And vy should you be inscribed in the Book of Stress?" my bubbe asked as I explained why I'd arrived so *farklempt* to Shabbat dinner. "If a race is making you *meshuga* then drop out of the race!"

She clearly doesn't get it, I thought to myself. And how could she get it? How could someone from a simpler generation even begin to understand how it feels to have everyone from Gymbananas executives to media moguls to the other moms in the carpool line reminding me that if I don't fuel my kids up with everything from pinch potting to pitching lessons, they'll be left in the dust come college application time. And then there's that whole overachievement thing. I mean I grew up at the height of the women's lib movement—raised to be strong and in charge, driven and successful. How could my ninety-five-year-old grandmother possibly see that I'd put every bit of that energy and determination into my life choices, my education, my career—and I wasn't about to drop the ball when it came to my kids?

And so I plugged ahead, dutifully devoting every afternoon and weekend to schlepping my family from activity to activity in the name of achieving perfect children (perfect defined as academically gifted, athletically exceptional, musically prodigious, socially popular, and self-esteem-saturated).

Then one day, many years and laps around the Mommy 500 track later, I had the epiphany I mentioned in the preface. It was the annual soccer registration day and my three boys and I (Baby Emma in tow) were—for the eighth year running—spending a steamy July afternoon waiting in line to ensure they made it into the most prestigious league in the area. Finally at the registrar's desk, I grabbed the applications and began filling out the elaborate forms. First Jake, then Alex, then Brandon . . . Wait a minute! Where was Brandon's age group?

Certain the absence of my oldest son's division was a misprint, I pointed out the mistake to the check-collecting registrar. "Sorry," the woman told me, "Metro Soccer doesn't have a middle-school division."

"But what am I supposed to do?" I said. "Brandon has played soccer every fall since he was three. How will he spend his Sundays?"

"My kids like the lake," she said. "It's much less crowded in the fall. The beach isn't too far either."

Before I could reply that going to the lake seemed like a silly waste of time that could otherwise be spent fine-tuning soccer skills, Brandon chimed in. "You know, Mom, that does sound kind of fun."

"What sounds fun?" I asked, glancing back at the sea of anxious parents, fingers itching for those golden application forms.

"Going to the lake."

"And the beach!" added Jake.

"Yeah!" said Alex. "I could finally use the new boogie board I got for Hanukkah two years ago!"

Suddenly, I felt myself entering a transformational spin, like Lynda Carter on the old *Wonder Woman* TV show, fueled by the realization that the check-collecting registrar—and Brandon, Alex, and Jake—were absolutely right. It *would* be fun to spend Sunday afternoons at the lake rather than at the soccer field for a change. In fact it would be *more* than fun, it would be positively liberating.

I could finally see that I'd been paralyzed by the inflated expectations of our overachieving, anxiety-filled culture; that I'd been basing the decisions I made for my children on what other people thought rather than on what I knew in my heart to be true. I at last understood that my ultimate goal in parenting was not to raise spelling bee champions, prom queens, and soccer stars but to bring up fulfilled, resilient, empowered, *menschlich* kids (see preface).

With this newfound insight, I discovered the strength and courage I needed to take my bubbe's advice to heart and step out of the race for kiddie perfection. I was able to ease up on the pressure, scale back the extracurriculars, and begin enjoying my children for who they were today (not who I hoped they would be at high school graduation).

I'm not going to lie to you. Steering clear of the Mommy 500 has not been easy, especially with all those other racers whizzing by me on the track! But I've managed to do it, and so can you. All it takes is some good, dependable AAA roadside assistance. That's right, AAA: Accept, Avoid, Accentuate—all the tools you need to keep your family safe, grounded, and miles away from the race lights.

The Social, Emotional, and Physical Price of Achievement-Oriented Parenting

So you're still waiting for it to happen, huh? You know deep in your parent gut that dropping out of the Mommy 500 is the right thing to do for yourself and your kids, but you've yet to undergo that Wonder Woman–style tranformational spin. To start you whirling, here are some harrowing trends researchers are uncovering at alarming rates in overscheduled, stressed-out twenty-first-century kids:

- Lack of independence and self-reliance due to having virtually every aspect of their lives planned in advance by a third party.
- A need for constant stimulation and an intolerance of boredom resulting from a childhood devoid of unstructured moments.
- Deteriorating parent–child relationships caused by never having time to be together without a purpose and destination.
- Loud, aggressive, or impulsive behavior resulting from excessive input and need for an emotional outlet.
- Early burnout from an overload of extracurriculars and academics.
- Increased incidence of teen suicide, drug use, eating disorders, and depression.
- Physical/psychosomatic complaints (e.g., headaches and stomachaches) caused by stress.
- Orthopedic issues (knee, joint, foot problems) linked to still-developing bodies being pushed beyond their limits via organized sports.
- Failure to notice and appreciate the simple joys of life due to spending the majority of one's childhood strapped into an SUV.

AAA Tools for Steering Clear of the Mommy 500

Accept Imperfection

If you try really hard, you might be able to remember the honeymoon period of parenting. Okay, so it may not have felt like a honeymoon—with its 3 A.M. feedings, projectile vomiting episodes, and mountains of dirty diapers—but it was. After all, during those early months of our kids' lives we could appreciate them for exactly who they were—burping, barfing, pooping, perfect little beings.

With every year that passed, however, we saw that definition of who and what our kids should be constrict a bit more. It was no longer enough for our child to be a part of a Little League team; he needed to be the star of the Little League team. It wasn't enough for him to be accepted into an exclusive private school, he needed to be at the top of the class at that exclusive private school. And before we knew it we were caught up in the blur of the Mommy 500 chasing down the very perfection we'd once found in our little one's every breath.

Speaking of breath, take a deep one, because we are about to embark on a mental journey. (And I'm giving you fair warning; it's not the kind of mental journey that will land you on a beach chair in the Caribbean sipping a piña colada.)

Think about something you really enjoy doing. No, not shopping! Something like working as a pediatrician, managing the school carnival committee, or playing tennis on a breezy spring morning. Now picture yourself taking part in this activity: how fulfilled you feel when you are successful (not necessarily "the best" kind of successful, but successful in your own terms) and how it leaves you feeling stronger, empowered, and energized. Okay, hold that image.

This time, think about something you—quite frankly—really stink at. Something you have very little, if any, desire to do. (I, for example, might think about golf. I'm lousy at golf. My three-year-old beats me at putt-putt. I find golf boring and—my apologies to my husband—a total waste of six good hours.)

Now picture yourself being forced to partake in this activity at least once every weekend and a couple of nights a week just for practice; and every time you do (here's the clincher) there is an audience watching. An audience that cheers, yells strategic pointers from the sidelines, and appears genuinely disappointed when you inevitably screw up. Now, keep that image in the forefront of your mind while we take a brief side trip to the Jewish Community Center gymnasium (where I happen to have spent the bulk of last Sunday afternoon watching my three boys play basketball).

It's the championship game in the second-grade basketball league and you are having a hard time concentrating on the game due to all the yelling. (No, not from the players, from the parents!) Here are a few of the comments you can't help but overhear in the stands:

Daniel's dad to his son: *What are you doing? I showed you how to dribble the ball. Wait a minute . . . you're going the* wrong direction!

Daniel's dad to fellow fans: *You should see him on the baseball field. He owns the baseball field!*

Evan's mom: *Daniel, pass the ball to Evan!*

Andrew's dad [after his son scores a basket for the other team]: *How could he do that? What was he thinking?*

Evan's mom: *Andrew, pass the ball to Evan!*

Benjamin's mom to her son: *Wake up out there, Benjamin!*

Benjamin's mom to her fellow fans: *I knew I shouldn't have let him go to his best friend's slumber party last night!*

Evan's mom: *Benjamin, pass the ball to Evan!*
Jared's dad: *Way to go, Jared! You did just what I told you to do and you got that shot! See I told you I knew what I was talking about!*
Evan's mom: *Jared, pass the ball to Evan!*

Finally, imagine what it feels like to be Daniel, Andrew, Benjamin, Jared or Evan—to be expected to perform masterful basketball moves in front of a whole bunch of people when all you really want to do is play around with your friends on the court and eat a yummy snack afterward. Think about what it must be like to have your stomach all scrunched up in knots because you just let down Mom, Dad, and Coach . . . again.

Okay, now it's time for some Yom Kippur—caliber self-reflection.

Do you find it a bit ironic that we parents have no problem whatsoever accepting our own weaknesses and imperfections? I, for example, am completely at peace with the fact that while I may be an effective writer, I would make a terrible accountant. You've probably come to terms with the reality that you don't stand a chance in an Olympic pole-vaulting competition. If we can accept these truths for ourselves, why can't we do the same for our kids? Maybe our child is an average math student. No learning disabilities, just not particularly adept at crunching numbers. Does that mean she needs twice-a-week tutoring after school every week? How many lessons in pole vaulting do you think it would take to shape you into Olympic gold medal material?

There's no better time than right now, my fellow former Mommy 500 racers, to grant our children their God-given right to be good at some things and downright lousy at others. To give ourselves permission to take pride in our kids even if they are shy, klutzy, and average. There's no better time than right now to remember what it feels like to rejoice in our children's utterly imperfect perfection.

Avoid the Self-Esteem Parenting Trap

For all intents and purposes, the modern parental psyche exists in a chronic state of contradiction. On one hand it has us obsessively pushing our kids toward a societally driven definition of perfection. On the other it has us dousing them with empty accolades in an attempt to convince them they've already achieved it.

I know what you're thinking: What could be wrong with boosting a child's self-esteem? Doesn't my little *bubbeleh* need to feel good about himself?

Of course we want our children to feel good about themselves! But creating a parentally fabricated reality by misleading our kids about their performance and abilities (i.e., *You are the smartest boy in the whole school! You are the greatest soccer goalie ever!*) is not a viable means of achieving this objective. In fact it's liable to have just the opposite effect.

Take the case of Hannah, a precious second-grader I once had the privilege of teaching. Hannah was quick as a wink, sharp as a tack, and cute as a button. She was also a dreadful artist. Every bunny she drew turned out like a blob, she smeared all her stick figures, and she couldn't color in the lines to save her life. But at home—thanks to her mother's fear that learning the truth about her shortcomings might cause irreparable damage to her self-esteem—Hannah learned she was a gifted artist. Each time Hannah's mother praised her blobs and extolled her stick figures, Hannah's self-esteem went soaring (wouldn't yours if you could so effortlessly produce such artistic masterpieces?).

One day in class, Hannah joined a group of students in putting together a presentation about toucans. Although capable of writing a killer paragraph, Hannah insisted on being the group's designated artiste, promising to adorn the poster with the same lovely birds that were plastered all over her refrigerator at home. But when the other members of the group returned from doing toucan research in the library and saw the rainbow-beaked blobs Hannah had smeared across their poster submission, they were horrified (and told her so). Hannah was heartbroken, and the self-esteem that Hannah's mother had painstakingly worked to heighten was history.

In her famous song "Al Kol Eleh" Naomi Shemer, Israel's late beloved songwriter, wrote of the inseparability of the honey and the bee sting. In order to enjoy the sweetness of the honey, we must also accept the pain of the bee sting. All parents want their kids to feel confident, but as Hannah's story demonstrates, shielding our kids from their shortcomings by creating a parentally fabricated reality only sets them up for future disappointment.

Hannah's mother would have served her daughter far better by acknowledging that everyone has strengths and weaknesses and praising her creativity and determination, rather than her artistic prowess.

Each and every child has wonderful things to offer. Our job as Jewish parents is not to earn ourselves a spot in the Winner's Circle at the Mommy 500 by raising kids who are universally talented—or at least believe they are thanks to buckets of empty praise. It's to help our children discover and nurture their true strengths, facing up to their limitations while they're at it. We can rest assured that when they do, their self-esteem will—at long last—legitimately go soaring.

Accentuate Your Child's Unique Set of Gifts

The final third of our AAA formula is by far the most fun of the three. After all, while the previous two discussions focused largely on coming to terms with what our children *can't* do, this one is all about enjoying what they *can* do! The following suggestions for creating an environment that accentuates your kids' unique array of talents and gifts can help illuminate their essential place and purpose in God's universe.

Redefine success. Getting A's and scoring soccer goals aren't the only ways kids can be successful. Studying extra hard for a spelling quiz (even if it only yields a B) and supporting teammates during a game should be considered equally (if not more) valuable. By expanding the narrow societal definition of achievement, we open a world of possibilities in which to uncover our children's true gifts.

Walk a few blocks in their sneakers. We parents expect our children to fit into our world—to sit quietly at restaurants and keep their shirts tucked in at synagogue. But rarely do we take the time to familiarize ourselves with their world. By making an effort to experience life from our kids' perspective—whether it means sitting with our daughter through her 800th viewing of the Disney Channel tween cult movie *High School Musical* or asking our son to give us a tutorial in Pokémon card trading basics—we come to understand and appreciate our children in a brand-new light.

Take an extracurricular siesta. While extracurricular activities in moderation (more on this in Chapter 6, "Extra, Extra, Extracurriculars") can play an important role in our children's lives, an occasional season-long siesta from organized activity affords us the opportunity to spend time with our children in a comfortable and relaxed way. Let your kids take turns deciding how to spend your newfound family time by planning activities that reflect their individual interests (e.g., biking, Rollerblading, tie-dying T-shirts, or making family friendship bracelets).

Hang out with them. Sure it seems embarrassingly obvious, but given the pace of modern family life, we rarely get around to just cuddling up on the couch with the kids and jabbering about nothing. Our children are only five once, or six or seven or eight . . . Before long they'll consider hanging out with Mom right up there with wearing saddle shoes on the uncool scale. So seize the opportunity to snuggle when you can (and no sneaking in trips to the laundry room!).

CHAPTER 2

Weathering the Storms of *Yetzer Hara*

Do you remember the old Calgon commercial? You know, the one where a stressed-out suburban mom who's up to her eyeballs in mouthy, misbehaving kids yells, "Calgon, take me away!" and miraculously lands herself in a luxurious bathtub flanked with candles and flowers? It doesn't work. Even the most desperate primal scream you can muster won't land you in a Calgon bathtub. But I'll bet you already knew that, because you've probably tried it too. After all, disciplinary struggles are as sure a part of the parenting experience as Cheerios and Pampers.

This is not to say, of course, that children are inherently horrible. They're precious, delicious, and wondrous! But they can also be unruly, defiant, and nerve-racking. Still, if we were being perfectly honest we'd have to admit that we don't *really* want our children to be as docile and tranquilizing as a Calgon bath. I mean, there's nothing exhilarating or rewarding about shaping a perfectly round bath bead into a perfectly round bath bead! Part of the thrill and challenge of parenting is taking a child who is oozing with what the Talmudic rabbis referred to as *yetzer hara*, or impulse for evil, and helping him or her grow into an independent thinker with the confidence, backbone, and sense of right and wrong to make appropriate behavioral choices.

How exactly do we facilitate such a monumental metamorphosis? By following the lead of a worthy parenting role model. No, I'm not talking about Dr. Phil! I'm talking about a botanical wonder known as the palm tree.

A palm tree! You may be thinking. Now you've totally lost me. How could a kitchy plant that adorns cocktail napkins at seedy beachfront bars help me get my kids to behave and make wise moral choices?

It is true that in recent years the palm tree has been typecast as a backdrop for partying and sipping piña coladas. But there's so much more to this remarkable plant than plastic leis and hula skirts. In fact, when it comes to weathering the nasty storms of *yetzer hara*, the palm is the shining star of the forest.

What gives the palm tree this remarkable record of resilience in the face of blustery behavior? As I see it, the secret lies in two of its defining characteristics: unfailing flexibility and embrace of *derech eretz*. In the remainder of this chapter I'll elaborate on both these highly effective storm survival strategies, and outline how they can help you gracefully ride out the storms of *yetzer hara* that inevitably lie ahead for your grove.

Palm Tree Storm Survival Strategy #1:
Flexibility

Objective: Empowered, adaptable, reasonable children

Shortly following the birth of my first child, a friend gave me a piece of advice that I've used every day of my life since. It goes like this: When it comes to parenting, *it's either bend or break, baby!* The palm tree knows this truth as well. When hurricane-force winds roll through, it doesn't remain absolutely rigid. It opts instead for the flexible route, bending in the direction of the storm, but never surrendering to it.

Generally speaking, the storms of *yetzer hara* that most obviously call for parental flexibility fall under two umbrellas: circumstantial storms and power struggle storms. What do ya say we put on our galoshes and go splash around in each of them?

The Circumstantial Storm

During the circumstantial storm, our child's unruliness comes not from within, but from an extremely frustrating or annoying situation that has upset him or her.

The precursor to a circumstantial behavioral storm might be a three-hour traffic jam that prompts our kids to play a round of tackle football in the back of the SUV, or a nasty cold that hurls our normally easygoing daughter into meltdown mode over a few spilled Rice Krispies. It could be a never-ending runway delay that has our son rolling up and down the aisle like a giant *kishke,* or the last-minute cancellation of a Cheetah Girls concert that leaves our daughter in a foul mood to beat the band.

The purpose of parental flexibility during a circumstantial storm may be summed up in two words—damage control. Take the following example:

After referring to 14 different Best Family Resorts in the World lists and scouring the Internet and travel guidebooks for months, you've booked the ultimate family escapade at a blissful Caribbean resort. Your week in paradise promises activities galore for your fun-seeking crew, from water-skiing to parasailing to swimming with the dolphins. You've even gone so far as to enroll your kids in a two-day tennis camp so you can spend quality time with your spouse sipping frozen daiquiris poolside.

Unfortunately, even rose-colored sunglasses can't keep the storm clouds at bay, and the minute your plane lands on the runway, the skies open up like the Red Sea in the Book of Exodus. Suddenly, your fantasy of spending a week of paradise in the Caribbean sun with one big happy family gives way to the reality of spending a week of torrential weather in a claustrophobic hotel room with a band of restless natives.

If you crack like a rigid oak when you meet with such literal and metaphorical stormy weather, you can bet your kids will follow suit. But if you can manage to make like a palm tree and bend in the blustery winds, you'll keep the sopping situation from taking its toll on your children's behavior and your sanity.

Sure, it's not parasailing, but by putting that three-hundred-dollar-a-night hotel room to good use as a venue for a family charades marathon (interspersed with a round or two of the quiet game) you sidestep a behavioral blowout while enjoying a perk that promises to last longer than two free rounds of golf: the replacement of your pulverized fantasy of the picture-perfect family vacation with something really worth fantasizing about—an image of your children many years from now, once again stuck in a torrential downpour in a Caribbean resort, showing your grandchildren how a bit of flexibility can turn lemons into luscious lemon daiquiris.

The Power-Struggle Storm

Remember when our little *bubbeleh* spoke her very first sentence? "Me read book" seemed worthy of a bat-mitzvah-caliber celebration. But somewhere over the next half decade or so, that same *bubbeleh* learned to string together sentences like "You can't *make* me read that book!!!" which sounded more like giant cymbals being pounded together by Godzilla than music to our ears. Such are the seeds of the power-struggle storm—a surge of turbulent behavior that originates not with an unfortunate circumstance but with your child's torrential attitude. Fortunately, a bit of parental flexibility can mitigate the impact of even the most tempestuous of power struggles.

Take the following, ahem, hypothetical situation:

It's Game 4 of the World Series between the Red Sox and the Cardinals and Boston is poised to win the title for the first time in eighty-six years. Our ten-year-old—let's just call him Alex for argument's sake—is an ardent Boston fan who just happens to have a major math test the next day. It's already 9:30 (an hour after Alex usually crawls into bed amid the Red Sox banners, bobble heads, and autographed baseballs) and he's yet to crack open his math book. When we not so subtly suggest that he Tivo the game as he had done for the rest of the pennant race, number crunch for fifteen minutes, and then march his red-socked feet up to bed, he looks at us as if we'd suggested he clean the bathroom with his toothbrush and flat out refuses to budge off the couch.

Do we take the inflexible approach, grabbing the remote control from under the pillow where our baseball-obsessed son has futilely tried to hide it, push the off button, and command him to hit the books pronto? Do we go to the opposite extreme and immediately tumble to his demands? Or do we channel our inner palm tree, letting our son stay up to watch his beloved team finish out the Series under the condition that he wake up extra early the next morning to practice long division?

True, opting for the latter approach may leave our son a tad tired the next day, but he's bound to be no worse for wear in the long run. Besides, in being flexible, we've given him something far more valuable than a good night's sleep—the empowering message that his mom respects and understands just how important that game truly is to him, and that he has the ability (within limits) to make a difference.

Clearly, we should explain to our little Boston fan that he should not expect such leniency until next time the Sox make it to the Series, but chances are he already knows our flexibility is the result of an extenuating circumstance. Besides, if we want our kids to be flexible and accommodate our requests, we must occasionally be flexible and accommodate theirs.

Okay, you may be thinking, I see the point about allowing our child to watch his favorite team win the World Series, but does being a flexible palm tree mean giving in to my kids' every whim and fancy?

Of course not—we aren't trying to raise Green Monsters, here!

What we must understand about the palm tree is that while it may be unfailingly flexible, it's no pushover. To the contrary, the palm tree is a tree with a spine! (In fact, the *lulav* we shake during the annual Sukkot march around the synagogue that's meant to represent our spines is actually part of a palm tree!) The palm's strength in the face of the storms of *yetzer hara* lies in its ability to achieve an intricate balance between firmness and flexibility—just enough give to keep from toppling over, just enough might to remain rooted in its resolve.

Here's a more everyday example, to illustrate how the firmness/flexibility tactic can help us weather power struggles in a more run-of-the-mill scenario:

Our six-year-old's room looks like a tornado blew through, but it's our in-laws who are actually due to blow through in a few short hours. When we ask our daughter to clean up the damage immediately, she responds with a sassy "You can't make me!"

Do we emphatically reply, "Don't you dare talk to me like that, young lady—you are in major trouble!" and proceed to cancel tomorrow's playdate as retribution? Do we try the strategy we read in that parenting magazine last week and repeat the request over and over again until our willful daughter submits? Or do we offer to let her finish playing her game before getting started on the mess, requiring the task be completed within a reasonable time frame? (Knowing, of course, it means we'll have to devote the next ten minutes to hanging out in her room and enforcing our edict.)

The latter suggestion shows our willingness to compromise without compromising our authority. If she doesn't follow through on her end of the bargain, a consequence is certainly in order, but it needs to be directly linked to the crime. Instead of randomly canceling our daughter's plans, we can tell her that she will not be allowed to have a playdate until she cleans her room. That way we remain firm with our request, impose a reasonable consequence, and leave her feeling empowered all the while.

The Tevye Rule

A critical point regarding the all-important palm tree attribute of flexibility is that there are certain situations that are not appropriate venues for flexible parental boundaries—ever. Safety and morality, for example, should never be sacrificed in the name of flexibility. And then there is what I call the "Tevye Rule" based on the classic Sholem Aleichem character in *Fiddler on the Roof.*

As you may recall, Tevye, the tradition-loving milkman, assumes that his daughters will be eager to employ the services of the village matchmaker when they prepare to marry. His daughters, however, being modern Anatevka girls, have different plans—one by one asking their papa to bless their personal choices of husband material.

Tzeitel, the oldest daughter, is the first to throw the fiddler off balance when she informs her father of her wishes to marry Motel the tailor. Tevye reasons:

> *On one hand, what kind of match would that be for my Tzeitel, with a poor tailor?*
> *On the other hand, he's an honest hard worker.*

Tevye goes back and forth in this fashion—from hand to hand to hand to hand—until he agrees to bend the rules and offer his blessing to Tzeitel and Motel.

A similar scene plays out when Tevye again wills himself to bend his paternal boundaries and offer daughter number two his blessing in her marriage to the revolutionary student. But when Tevye's youngest daughter goes off and gets hitched by a priest to a Russian youth and asks for her father's postmarital blessing, the milkman passionately announces, "This time there is no other hand!"

Every parent has areas that offer no room for fudging and only you know exactly what yours are. What I will say here is this: if in your efforts to be flexible, you find that you've run out of hands, consider it a message from your inner Tevye that in this particular situation, the oak approach is the way to go.

Jewish Parent 911

Using Flexibility to Steer Your Kids Toward Good Behavioral Choices

Pick your battles. If you argue with your kids over every small potato, it will be harder to get them to cooperate in the case of a fully loaded spud. By limiting your demands to those that really matter, you'll significantly up the odds of your kids heeding them.

Stick to your guns. When you do put your foot down, don't give in. Tell your child that whether he asks you once or he asks you a hundred times your answer is going to be the same, so he may as well save you both the trouble and stop asking now.

Set a timer. Rather than demanding that your child start her homework "this very second" or else, set a timer to go off in ten minutes and tell her she can begin her homework anytime between now and then. If she fails to comply, be prepared to impose a reasonable consequence.

Palm Tree Storm Survival Strategy #2:
Embrace Derech Eretz
Objective: Independent, menschlich, *self-disciplined children*

The Talmudic Laws of *Derech Eretz*

When Brandon was in first grade, he returned home one day in a huff about a new boy at school. Although Brandon had yet to officially meet this new kid, word on the blacktop had it he was a bona fide brownnoser! How else could you explain why all the teachers were bragging about him?

"Do you know this boy's name?" I asked my son.

"It's Derek," Brandon seethed, "Derek Eretz."

Derek Eretz, Brandon's teacher informed me, was actually *derech eretz*, a Hebrew phrase that translates literally as "the way of the land," but is most commonly associated with the act of showing polite, respectful, and thoughtful behavior to people and the environment. Just prior to Derek's debut, it turns out, my son's Jewish day school kicked off a formal educational program drawn from the Talmudic laws of *derech eretz*.

Upon hearing this news, I could swear I was being doused with Calgon bath waters. Not because Brandon would never have to worry about meeting Derek Goody-Two-Shoes Eretz in the flesh, but because I knew that from that point forward, my husband and I were not alone in our quest to civilize our children. We had just discovered a formidable parenting ally, and his name was Derek Eretz.

Okay, so maybe the Talmudic laws of *derech eretz* were written a couple of thousand years ago. But that doesn't mean they're obsolete. To the contrary, they're timeless rules of decency—written in the context of Jewish values—that are just as relevant today as ever before. And the best part is we didn't write them. So the next time our child gripes over having to visit Great-aunt Gertrude in the nursing home, we simply explain that showing respect for the elderly is a prime rule of *derech eretz*, and if she has a problem, she can take it up with the Talmudic rabbis!

In the Talmudic laws of *derech eretz* we twenty-first-century parents have far more than a collection of antiquated rules of etiquette. We have a parenting ally with a multimillennial track record of success, a blueprint for raising respectful, self-disciplined, *menschlich* kids, and a Jewish child's guide to appropriate, decent behavior. Not bad for a brownnosing new kid named Derek.

The following tips will help you incorporate Talmudic *derech eretz* into your parenting game plan and have your kids walking the way of the land in no time:

Outline the rules. *Derech eretz* is a vastly broad and inclusive concept. We can help ensure our children understand its meaning by breaking it down into bite-sized chunks. Here are some fundamentals principles to cover:

Treat parents and teachers with respect.
Treat others the way you would like to be treated.
Respect the elderly.
Be kind to animals.
Be respectful to nature and the environment.
Use good manners and be polite.

Model derech eretz. Although it may seem like our kids never pay attention to us, we can rest assured they pay plenty of attention to us (even when we wish they wouldn't). We are their role models, and they are constantly looking to us for direction. This is not to say that if we aren't as virtuous as Queen Esther we're parental failures. Everyone messes up now and then, and it's healthy for our kids to see that we do, too. Still we owe it to our children to at least aspire to model *derech eretz*, and to use our inevitable slipups as a means of teaching the art of owning up to—and learning from—our mistakes.

Catch them being good. Sure, we ultimately want our kids to follow the rules of *derech eretz* because they know in their hearts it's the right thing to do, but in the meantime occasionally rewarding respectful, *menschlich* behavior is certainly appropriate. Make a *derech eretz* chart and put a sticker on it whenever your child goes above and beyond the basic requirements for civility (i.e., washing the dishes without being asked). Go out to a movie to celebrate when he reaches the end.

Talmudic *Derech Eretz* in Action

I asked some first-graders to share examples of how they've followed the laws of *derech eretz*. Here are a few of their responses:

"When my brother went on a sleepover, I fed his pet lizard."—Cole

"When my dad couldn't see, I helped him find his glasses."—Noah

"I went to a place where old people live and played violin for them."—Sabrina

"I helped my mom water the flowers."—Jack

"When my friend was sick, I called him to say I hope he feels better."—Izzy

"I helped my teacher clean the classroom."—Rebecca

Nature's Laws of *Derech Eretz*

Sounds good, you may be thinking but I'm not quite seeing the connection between the Talmudic laws of *derech eretz* and the palm tree thing.

A mighty fine point, indeed, because the Talmudic definition of *derech eretz* doesn't have much to do with the palm tree at all. Luckily, good old Derek is a versatile chap and his literal translation has everything to do with it.

As I mentioned before, the term *derech eretz* translates literally as the "way of the land." Although rabbis and scholars have argued for centuries over the true meaning of this ambiguous phrase, I take it as referring to the fundamental cause and effect relationships that exist between living organisms and their environments.

As we established in the flexibility discussion, the wise palm tree is a master at recognizing the interconnectedness between actions and outcomes. The palm knows that stubborn trees that refuse to bend in the face of hurricane-force winds are destined to become firewood. It knows that plants that need plenty of sunshine to grow should spread their roots in tropical climates.

You might say that while the Talmudic laws of *derech eretz* are all about respect and decency, nature's laws of *derech eretz* are all about Darwinian survival. Take the case of the stick bug of the rainforest.

The stick bug is a bug that looks a whole lot like a stick. (Hey, I'm not claiming to be an entomologist here!) When the stick bug was just a baby he would waltz his wooden legs anywhere he darn well pleased. But one day, during a leisurely stroll across a hot pink bromeliad, that carefree stick bug had a terrifying, yet enlightening near miss with a hungry harpy eagle. Empowered with a newfound understanding of the ways of the jungle (namely, when bugs with sticks for legs make themselves easy targets for flying predators, they risk being eaten for lunch), the stick bug devised the ingenious, life-saving strategy of camouflaging himself on a tree branch and refraining from moving a muscle for the majority of his long, blissful life.

Of course it wasn't easy for Mama and Papa stick bug to let their little one risk life and limb learning the lessons of *derech eretz*, but they knew that only in doing so would they prepare him to one day face the jungle on his own.

Unfortunately, we human parents haven't been quite as willing as the rest of the plant and animal kingdoms to let *derech eretz* have a go at our young. In fact many well-meaning modern parents have gone so far as to position themselves as human shields between their kids and the natural consequences of their actions. Consider the following:

Example A: Leah worked superhard on her spelling homework last night. She dotted every i and crossed every t—except one, that is. She forgot to put her homework in her backpack. The next morning, after Leah's carpool drives off, her mom notices her homework on the kitchen counter. Not wanting her daughter to get into trouble, Mom hightails her way to school and delivers the spelling assignment safe and sound before the first-period bell.

Example B: Ben wants to play catcher for his Little League team. He thinks the equipment is really cool and he's not at all interested in playing his current position in right field. Unfortunately, Ben has a habit of goofing off at practice and has yet to develop the skills he needs to be a good catcher. The coach gently explains to Ben that if he works hard and concentrates during practice, he'll likely be ready to take a whirl at the coveted position by midseason. Later that evening Ben recounts the story to his parents, proclaiming he has the "worst, most unfair coach ever!" Upon hearing this emotional plea, Ben's dad calls the coach and implores him to let his son play catcher during the next game.

Sure, Leah's mom and Ben's dad had *warned* their kids that failing to take responsibility for their homework and goofing off at Little League practice could yield undesirable outcomes. But the reality remains that no matter how many times we tell our kids not to touch a hot stove, or academic tutors or piano teachers tell our kids not to touch a hot stove, or baseball, soccer, and tennis coaches tell our kids not to touch a hot stove, the only way our kids will really learn not to touch a hot stove is by trying it—and finding out that it hurts like heck!

No, I'm not suggesting that we allow our children to go around getting third-degree burns for the sake of a learning experience! That was only a metaphorical example. The point is that only by loosening the reins and letting our kids have some firsthand contact with the way of the land, will they truly come to understand the impact of their actions and the importance of making thoughtful, appropriate choices.

Admittedly, it's not always easy to let our children take a fall, but we need to keep our eye on the prize and give them room to stumble nonetheless. How about a quick practice round?

The school bus is scarcely minutes away from your house and your first-grader just spilled an entire glass of chocolate milk on his favorite Power Ranger T-shirt. After scrambling to find a dry, stain-free alternative you are met with steadfast resistance by your pint-sized breakfast companion. You begin weighing the alternatives.

Do you yank the soiled garment over your son's extra-hard head, forcing him to slip on a clean shirt and dragging him kicking and screaming to the bus stop? Or do you take a deep cleansing breath, hurry him out the door, and allow him to board the bus in his chocolate-coated condition?

The wise palm tree—having full faith in *derech eretz* and the potency of natural consequences—would undoubtedly advise us pick the latter. After all, it knows that the moment our stubborn kid enters the classroom wearing his breakfast on his Power Rangered chest, his peers will ensure that he never makes such a foolish choice again. It also knows that the clean T-shirt we tucked in our son's backpack will be put to good use before the recess bell rings. But most importantly it knows that having just come in contact with a metaphorical hot stove, our son learned a lesson more powerful than hours of being nagged by Mom could have ever afforded him.

So you see, nature's laws of *derech eretz* are not a malevolent force from which we must obsessively shield our offspring. They are—like their rich Talmudic counterpart—a formidable parenting ally. An ally who guarantees that stubborn kids who refuse to wear jackets to school learn a lesson while freezing their tushies off at recess. An ally who ensures that children who ignore parental reminders to study for spelling tests receive poor grades. An ally who reassures us that in letting our kids take an occasional fall, we ultimately teach them to stand up, brush themselves off, and rejoin the game . . . wiser and stronger. And an ally who reminds us that our mission in parenting is not to raise children who fly because we tell them when, where, and how to flap their wings, but because they have the confidence, competence, and stamina to soar independently.

The Logical Consequence (Giving the Natural Consequence a Kickstart)

That's all well and good, you may be thinking, but what happens when the natural consequences of my kids' unwise actions don't pan out the way I want them to?

A wise point indeed, because the reality is that sometimes our daughter will turn in a sloppy homework assignment, and the teacher won't say a darn thing about it. Or our son will make fun of his sister's outfit and she'll start bawling just like he'd hoped she would. When nature's laws of *derech eretz* are not quite doing the job on their own, it's time to impose the logical consequence: a multitasking punishment that simultaneously reflects a natural outcome of the crime, teaches a lesson, and involves a meaningful act of retribution.

For example, our daughter who is counting her lucky stars because her sloppy paper sailed by the teacher: don't you think it would be nice for her to rewrite the assignment nonetheless, throwing in a note written in her neatest handwriting apologizing for her carelessness? And our son who was mercilessly mocking his sibling's clothes: don't you think folding and putting away all his sister's clean laundry for the week would be an ideal means of expressing his remorse?

I have to be honest here—orchestrating a logical consequence is liable to take a lot more thought and effort than simply exiling your kid to his room for the night. But in taking the time to transform a punishment into a learning experience, we grant our children both the burden and the blessing of being ultimately responsible for the choices they make and the places they go.

Jewish Parent 911

Utilizing Logical Consequences

Make a game of it. Play the "if/then game" by throwing out hypothetical situations and then having your kids say what the outcome may be. For example, *If* you forget to set your alarm in the morning, *then* . . . or *if* you forget to do your homework, *then* . . .

Let your kids help determine their own consequences. Sit down with your child and decide together on a logical consequence for his wrongdoing. If he comes up with a blatantly lenient suggestion, explain that you can either arrive at a reasonable consequence together or you will determine one independently.

1–2–3 . . . logical consequence. If you are going to use the old "counting to three" strategy (a miraculously effective tactic), be prepared to impose a logical consequence should you happen to reach a full count.

Say "This is the last time!" and actually mean it. Clue your child in that this is the last time you will be reminding her to do her book report. If she chooses not to take your advice at this point, she should be prepared to face the natural consequences of her decision. Trust me, she'll be cracking out that paper and pencil in no time.

The Democratic-Assertive Parenting Style

Excuse me? you're probably thinking, could you please run that subheading by me one more time? "The Democratic-Assertive Parenting Style"? The last time I read words like that was during a 2 A.M. cram session for an 8 A.M. poli-sci exam!

Okay, I'm with you on that one. But trust me, you can't skim over this part or you'll be jumping off the train before we pull into the station! Besides, once you get the logical punishment thing rolling, you're well on your way to achieving a consistent democratic-assertive parenting style, so you might as well find out what the heck it is!

A parenting style is the primary approach we consistently employ when interacting with our children. Researchers have determined that the vast majority of our individual styles will fall into one of three inclusive categories:

The authoritarian style: This parenting approach has been promi-
nent for the majority of Western history. The general idea of the authoritarian philosophy is *Do it because I said to do it and if you don't do
it you're in trouble.* While these parents obviously love their kids, they
spend much of their parental energy outlining rules and consequences rather than sharing warm fuzzies.

The permissive style: In the spirit of the hippie movement, this approach blurs the line between parent and child. The polar opposite
of authoritarian parenting, the permissive relationship is essentially a multigenerational friendship. The permissive parenting
style is still popular today, mainly as a result of the self-esteem
movement, rather than lingering flower-child principles.

The democratic-assertive style: The palm tree gives this parenting
style—which revolves around a basic appreciation of natural consequences—two fronds up as the best choice for raising resilient kids
in the twenty-first century. Children growing up in a democratic-
assertive household know that their opinions are valued and re-
spected, but that adults are ultimately in charge of the game (the
good old firmness/flexibility balance). Democratic-assertive parents make sure their kids feel the full impact of their poor choices,
supplementing natural consequences—when necessary—with their
own logical consequences. It is the democratic-assertive parenting
style that researchers tout as helping kids learn to accept responsibility, make wiser choices, and better cope with change. And hey,
you've go to admit that at the end of a long hard day, a houseful of
empowered, *menschlich,* resilient kids beats a Calgon bath any night
of the week.

Spotlight on Sibling Squalls

How did Mike and Carol Brady do it? I mean, with the exception of Jan's fleeting bouts of older-sister envy, an unfortunate incident involving Peter's football and Marcia's nose, and some healthy card-house-building competition, the Brady kids lived in a perpetual state of sibling nirvana. No random spurts of violence in the back of the wood-paneled station wagon; no vying for Alice's undivided attention; not even a passing jab about ill-fitting bell-bottoms.

We non-Brady parents, on the other hand, hang out on a different channel—a channel where brotherly battles and sisterly squabbles occupy prime-time slots, and peaceful coexistence among siblings seems less likely than a Florence Henderson cameo on *Desperate Housewives.*

But just because the closest our brood will ever get to Bradyesque sibling bliss is watching Nick at Nite, that doesn't mean we should check ourselves into the Parental Hall of Shame. After all, brothers and sisters have been going at it since the days of Cain and Abel. In fact, many experts, like Nancy Samalin, author of *Loving Each One Best: A Caring and Practical Approach to Raising Siblings,* see sibling squabbles as natural and as integral building blocks in childhood social development, ultimately helping kids effectively manage conflict on the schoolyard and into adulthood.

Okay, you're probably thinking, brothers, sisters, and bickering go together like bagels, lox, and cream cheese. Are you implying I should watch from the sidelines while my kids beat one another to a pulp? I'm not suggesting that at all, because there is a fine line between healthy and hurtful sibling quarreling. Our role as parents is to give our children enough breathing room to reap the underlying social developmental benefits of sibling rivalry, while still establishing and enforcing clear boundaries and parameters. The following suggestions will help you strike this tricky yet crucial balance.

Outline the rules of the game. During a moment of relative peace, sit your kids down and discuss the difference between fair and unfair fighting. Bickering over which cartoon to watch on Sunday morning, for example, is normal and acceptable, but becoming physically aggressive or making cruel and degrading remarks are outright fouls.

Nix the play-by-play refereeing. Rather than jumping in the moment your kids start going at it, take a deep breath and give them a chance to work things out themselves (calling fouls if necessary). You may be surprised by how adept children are at resolving conflict independently.

Offer up a Plan B. If, perchance, squabbling sibs cross over to the dark side, it's time to intervene. When emotions are running high, however, a parental plea to "stop fighting this instant!" is unlikely to do the trick. Rather parents need to provide kids with a viable alternative. Exile them to their rooms to blow off steam, or send one to the front yard and one to the backyard. When my boys were younger, they had preassigned corners in the family room. If kicks and punches started to fly, I'd call "corners," and they'd report to their respective domains to cool off.

Hindsight is 20/20. If your children have a blowout that requires adult intervention, take some time after the smoke clears to discuss what they could have done differently, and how they might avoid such a situation in the future.

Try reverse psychology. Telling your kids they *can't* play with one another for the next half hour may be just enough to remind them how much they really do appreciate one another and get them to reel themselves back in.

Consider their perspective. To help parents understand the sibling plight, Samalin recommends imagining your spouse returning home one day with a new, younger, cuter husband or wife and announcing he or she will be living with you from now on. Would you feel compelled to love and adore this person? Or to strangle him or her?

Who cares who started it? When children argue, the parental knee-jerk reaction is to try to tap an instigator. This practice is both unnecessary (you can bet your bottom Yu-Gi-Oh! card that neither party is completely innocent) and counterproductive (placing blame on one party only fosters additional animosity between clashing kids). Rather than worrying about who started it, therefore, let your kids concentrate their efforts on ending it.

Have family meetings. Head off possible sibling conflicts by establishing regular family meetings. During these weekly gatherings, sit down with your crew to discuss any issues that may be brewing and brainstorm possible resolutions.

Put a lid on it. Encourage *shalom bayit* (peace in the home), as well as cooperation among brothers and sisters, with a marble jar. Every time your kids successfully avoid or resolve a conflict without parental intervention, place a marble in a jar. When it's filled to the rim, take the whole crowd out to a movie to celebrate.

Keep perspective. Think of the act of raising siblings as an old-fashioned roller-coaster ride—simultaneously scary, thrilling, dizzying . . . and bound to be over far too soon.

CHAPTER 3

Countdown to Kindergarten

The Kindergarten Readiness *Shpilkes*

To those unfamiliar with the kindergarten readiness *shpilkes*, you may be wondering why on earth anyone would waste time worrying about whether or not a kid is ready for kindergarten. I mean, it's kindergarten for heaven's sake! But if you are a parent, you probably know what I'm talking about. The story goes something like this . . .

Once upon a time there was a whimsical land of make-believe, dress-up, and fingerpainting. A magical place where "work" was a four-letter word, "elemenopee" was still one letter, and you couldn't spot a math fact for miles. They called it Kindergarten.

One dark day (after the royal superintendent concluded that Kindergarten's whimsical ways were partially to blame for the kingdom's lackluster standardized test scores) everything changed. Stuffed animals and dollhouses were replaced with math manipulatives and spelling tests. Wooden blocks and Play-Doh gave way to rigorous core curriculums and palace-mandated standards.

Once word got out about Kindergarten's abrupt metamorphosis, the parents of the kingdom started to worry that it would take more than five candles on a birthday cake to prepare their children to enter this playroom turned pressure cooker. In fact some decided it would take at least six candles!

Now the royal superintendent had a whole new problem on his hands—with so many children entering Kindergarten at age six, he needed to up the difficulty level. So he did. Now the parents were even more worried, especially in the case of boys whose birthdays fell precariously close to the cut-off date. And that's how the kindergarten readiness shpilkes *came to be.*

(By the way, if you're wondering what happened to that once carefree land of dress-up and make-believe, it now has a new name. They call it preschool.)

Having managed to deliver all four of my kids a stone's throw from the illustrious school cut-off date, I'm a member in good standing of the "Late Birthday" Parents Club. So you know I speak from experience when I tell you that the worrying kicks in the instant the ultrasound technician assigns our baby a due date between Passover and Rosh Hashanah (or Rosh Hashanah and Hanukkah, depending on your local kindergarten entry cut-off date). Double the worry if the ultrasound technician also reveals our baby to be a boy. We then proceed to fret for the next five years. One minute we are all but certain our kid will be able to handle the demands of the modern kindergarten curriculum (a.k.a. the former first-grade curriculum) despite being a "young" five, and the next we are convinced that if we don't give him the "gift" of an extra year we'll hopelessly doom his academic career. But even a final verdict can't free us from our misery, as every academic or social glitch our child experiences over the next twelve years will leave us wondering whether it could have been prevented had we only made a different choice about kindergarten.

The Real Scoop on Retention

So you're ready for the bottom line, huh? You want to know if it's better to delay or not to delay kindergarten entry for late-birthday children. Unfortunately, as of publication time, it still has no answer.

And it's certainly not for lack of trying. Mounds of research have been collected in hopes of revealing the real scoop on retention, only to conclude that there is no scoop. Dr. Lorrie Shepard, for example, a professor of research methodology at the University of Colorado at Boulder, reviewed sixteen studies on the long-term effects of delaying kindergarten and found no significant difference between kids who had been retained and those who hadn't.

In fact, just about the only decisive result that's emerged from the retention research at all is that roughly 15 percent of children entering kindergarten nationwide have been held back, and that the vast majority of these late starters are Caucasian, male, born in the second half of the year, and come from rather affluent homes.

The lack of conclusive evidence, however, hardly implies that kids can't profoundly benefit from an extra year (many do). Or be hindered by one (some are). In fact the ambiguous evidence likely results from a relatively even match between the pros and cons of delaying kindergarten. Take the example of Ben and Josh, two boys I taught as second-graders, who had exactly the same birthday (August 15), had been retained for presumably the same reason (poor fine-motor skills), yet saw very different outcomes from their extra year.

By the time Ben arrived in my class at the age of eight (his birthday was the first day of school), he was at the top of his game. That extra year of pre-K had been just what the doctor ordered. Ben had kicked off kindergarten cutting and coloring with the best of them, and it was hardly a struggle for him to write in his daily journal or do other seatwork. Ben emerged from kindergarten confident, proud, and positive about school and remained on that track for the long haul.

Josh was a different story, as round two of pre-K scarcely made a dent in his list of fine-motor issues. Josh, it turned out, would need far more than 365 extra days to clean up his coloring act—he would need years of occupational therapy (complicated by his being shut out of a prime early intervention window while his parents and teachers eagerly waited for that extra year to work its "magic"). Making matters worse, Josh had been intellectually ready for kindergarten at age five. He was an introspective child who lapped up learning. Because the repetition of the pre-K curriculum left Josh bored and frustrated, he started acting out in class, ultimately being labeled as a behavior problem. By the time I met Josh in second grade, he'd already decided he hated school.

What we learn from Ben and Josh is that there is no such thing as a one-size-fits-all answer to the kindergarten dilemma. We owe it to our kids to shy away from blanket assumptions about age, gender, and readiness, and take the time to make a careful, thoughtful choice based on their individual academic, social, and emotional profiles in combination with the pace, expectations, and philosophy of the school they will be attending. Don't try to make this decision alone. Consultation with teachers and pediatricians, as well as private educational testing, can help you determine whether retention is a good choice for your child.

In the end what matters most is that you believe in the direction you've chosen for your child and remain strong enough in your resolve not to second-guess your decision. Sure you'll encounter some rough spots along the way, but chances are that your child will be just fine—retention or not—as long as you and the school are there for guidance and support throughout the journey.

Jewish Parent 911

Solving the Kindergarten Dilemma

Trust the preschool teacher. Educators see your child daily in a classroom setting and can compare his degree of readiness to that of other children his age, so it's important to take their input seriously.

Delay making the decision as long as you possibly can. Preschoolers can change enormously during the course of the year. A child who doesn't seem ready in January may be raring to go by May.

Think beyond kindergarten. While a six-year-old may have a seemingly sizable advantage over a five-year-old classmate when it comes to forming letters or sounding out words, this discrepancy is likely to be short-lived. By the second or third grade, just about every child can read and write, and age no longer remains a formidable factor in determining academic success. Still, if your child is the type to be easily discouraged, struggling in the beginning can have a lasting impact.

Weigh social and emotional factors heavily. While older and younger children tend to even out academically in the early elementary years, it can take much longer for a child to catch up in the social, emotional, and physical arenas.

Know the signs of readiness. While every child has his or her own unique developmental timetable, experts say that most will demonstrate the skills and accomplishments listed below and will most likely develop the others during the kindergarten year. Here are some general kindergarten readiness markers adapted from *The Educated Child* by William J. Bennett and colleagues:

- *Personality*: He exhibits an avid curiosity about his environment and is eager to learn. He is confident in his ability to succeed and independent enough to do certain things for himself (or at least give it the old kindergarten try!).
- *Social skills*: She doesn't need to be a social debutante, but she should be able to integrate into a group, relate to new children and adults, and adapt to new routines. A willingness to take turns and share is helpful, too.
- *Motor skills*: In the large-motor arena, he should be able to jump, run, hop on one foot, throw, catch and kick (balls, that is, not other kids). On the small-motor side, he should handle a crayon or pencil comfortably and be in the process of developing potty-friendly skills like snapping, unbuttoning, rebuttoning, and zipping.
- *Language skills*: She needn't be capable of giving the Gettysburg Address, but she should be able to communicate effectively with adults and other kids.
- *Attention and focus*: Five- and six-year-olds are naturally jittery, but most kindergartners can listen to a story or participate in a discussion for ten to fifteen minutes. He should also be keen on finishing the majority of projects he starts.
- *Other cognitive skills*: From a math and reading readiness standpoint, she should be able to name numbers and count, identify letters, and understand letter–sound relationships. Most kindergarten-bound kids can also compare various objects using relative terms (i.e., bigger, smaller, heavier, lighter, more, and less).

Look out for red flags. Before I even begin discussing the potential signs of kindergarten "unreadiness," I want to be sure you understand that they should *only* be considered red flags if they are present en masse and with great frequency. Okay then. Here they are:

- A general lack of impulse control and tendency to settle disputes by hitting or biting instead of using words.
- Excessive anxiety over separation from parents.
- Difficulty sitting still long enough to listen to a short story.
- A tendency to jump from one activity to the next, rarely completing tasks.
- Developmental delays in a particular area, such as language or gross- or fine-motor skills.

School Shopping

Once you've decided *if* your child is going to kindergarten, it's time to decide *where* your child is going to kindergarten. No pressure here, but selecting an elementary school for your son or daughter is a huge decision! Not only are you entrusting your child's academic, social, and emotional well-being to this institution, you're picking a parenting partner for at least the next six years.

It may well be that for your family, tapping that perfect school is a no-brainer. Perhaps you moved into a neighborhood with the specific intent of sending your child to the sweet public elementary school down the street with fabulously high test scores. Or your kid is a fifth-generation legacy at an exclusive prep school (his great-great-grandparents' portraits are hanging in the lobby) and has been enrolled at the school since he was a zygote. Maybe your town or county has a wonderful charter school or magnet program. Or you want to send your child to a Jewish day school and there's only one in town that fits the bill. If you fall into one of these categories, you should use the upcoming information to confirm that your school of choice is indeed everything you believe and hope it to be. If, however, you are uncertain about where to send your child to kindergarten, it's time to do some school shopping.

School Shopping Step #1:
Assess Your Needs

Let's say you need to buy a dress for your nephew's bar mitzvah party. What's the first thing you do? You look at the invitation and figure out what kind of dress you need. Will you be attending a black tie, semiformal, or dressy-casual event? What will the weather be like where you are going? Similarly, your first step in selecting a school is to identify your child's and family's needs. Here are some key questions to consider:

Your child's needs:
- Is your child most likely to thrive in a more or a less structured environment?
- Are you looking for a school that heavily stresses academics? Creativity?
- Does your child need individualized attention or have special learning needs?
- Is your child likely to feel overwhelmed by a large school? Become stir crazy in a small one?
- Does your child have any special interests or talents like music,

art, or athletics that you would like to see the school's curriculum address and develop?

- Do you want your child to go to school with children she already knows?

Your family's needs:

Philosophical and Financial

- Do you want to send your child to a local public or charter school?
- Would you prefer a private school setting? If so, do you want a Jewish day school or secular private school? Are you willing to consider non-Jewish parochial schools?
- What are your financial constraints? If you do opt to go private, what sacrifices may need to be made?

Logistical

- Are you willing to have your child bused? If so, how far?
- If you will be driving your child to school, how far are you willing to travel?
- Would you like to be part of a carpool with families that live nearby?
- Do you need a school that offers after-hours care?

School Shopping Step #2: Narrow Your Options

Perusing every store in the mall in search of a party dress would be a waste of valuable shopping time and energy. The next phase in your school shopping process, therefore, is narrowing your scope to a few worthy candidates. There are numerous resources that can help you do this:

Education Guides

Many local newspapers and magazines release education issues in the fall and winter months (peak school shopping season since private school applications are generally due in January or February). These special editions usually include a few general educational tips flanked by oodles of ads for schools in your area. While school-paid promotions offer an admittedly subjective picture, they can give you a sense of an institution's overall philosophical approach. If a school's ad spotlights its academic record, for example, you can expect a college prep flair. If it mentions educating the "whole child," you may find a hippyish, free-spirited ambience.

Local Departments of Education

If you are considering the public school route and want to learn more about your neighborhood school, contact your district's department of education (you can find the number in the blue government pages of your phone book) and request test scores and other vital stats like student–teacher ratios. You may also want to inquire about available charter or magnet school programs. Similar information should also be available at your local library in school reference resources or archived education guides.

Other Parents

Your parental peers are a primary source of school scoop, so let the schmoozing begin. Track down parents at the playground, the supermarket, and the swimming pool. Ask them where they send their kids to school. What do they like about the school? What do they dislike? How would they describe the parent and student population? (Bear in mind that different parents experience the same school differently, and be tactful and noncommittal in your discussion.)

The Internet

The Web offers an endless supply of useful information as you work to hone in on the right school for your child and family.

Here are some websites worth visiting:

- http://nces.org.gov—The U.S. Department of Education's National Center for Education Statistics can provide information on every school in your area—public and private—from size to student–teacher ratio to racial/ethnic makeup to standardized test scores. If you are researching private schools be sure to check accreditation status.
- www.privateschoolreview.com—This stocked website will give you the brass tacks on a wide range of private schools. You'll also find maps to the schools and links to their websites.
- www.maven.co.il—Maven Search is a Jewish search engine that offers a comprehensive list of Jewish day schools throughout the United States along with links to their home pages.

Should You Consider Jewish Day School?

We can't very well have a discussion about school options for Jewish children without mentioning Jewish day school. After all, somewhere in the neighborhood of 200,000 Jewish children are currently enrolled in one of roughly seven hundred U.S. Jewish day schools. If you live in a major metropolitan area with a significant

Jewish population, chances are you have multiple day school choices. There are Orthodox, modern Orthodox, Conservative, Reform, and nondenominational community day schools. The breadth of American Jewish day school options is as diverse as the American Jewish population itself.

A day school education offers numerous benefits. It reinforces and builds on the core morals, ethics, and values we want to instill in our children. The intertwinement of Judaism with daily school life fosters a strong Jewish identity and a sense of continuity and communal belonging. Most Jewish day schools employ well-trained teachers and have involved parent populations. From a logistical standpoint, day school parents can strike Hebrew school off their lists of afternoon destinations.

Jewish day school also has its drawbacks. The cost can be prohibitive, especially in cases of multiple tuitions (although many day schools offer financial aid). Clearly, the day school student population is more homogeneous than that of a public or even a secular private school and can leave kids sheltered. (When I was teaching in an Atlanta Jewish day school I asked my fourth-graders to estimate what percentage of the U.S. population is Jewish. Their guesses ranged from 85 percent to 97 percent. The actual percentage? 1 percent.)

Some parents worry that spending half a day engaged in Judaic studies (a traditional Jewish day school schedule) will leave their children underprepared academically. Is this a valid concern? In a strict sense, I don't believe it to be. Many day schools compensate for the half-day schedule by kicking up the intensity and pace of the general studies curriculum and utilizing a slightly longer school day. We also shouldn't assume that just because a lesson falls under the Hebrew umbrella, it doesn't develop critical academic preparatory skills; many aspects of the Judaics curriculum (i.e., learning a second language and analyzing Torah text) foster essential higher-level reasoning abilities in kids. Most Jewish day schools boast high educational standards, excellent standardized test scores, and impressive alumni acceptance records to secondary schools and universities.

That said, some students have great difficulty juggling Judaic and general studies. They may have language-based problems that make it tough for them to learn in English, much less in Hebrew. They may have attentional issues that leave them wholly overwhelmed by the dual curriculum. They may have specific learning disabilities that require a special type of learning environment. Fortunately, more and more Jewish day schools are supplementing or reworking their programs to accommodate students with varying learning needs. If you are concerned that your child may struggle in a traditional Jewish day school structure, talk to the individual school or consult your local Jewish Family and Children's Services for additional information and guidance.

The following resources can provide you with valuable information on Jewish day schools in your area:

- PEJE (Partnership for Excellence in Day School Education; www .peje.org)
- Association of Modern Orthodox Day Schools (www.amods.org)
- Solomon Schechter Day School Association of the United Synagogue of Conservative Judaism (www.uscj.org)
- PARDES (Progressive Association of Reform Day Schools; www .pardesdayschools.org)
- RAVSAK (The Jewish Community Day School Network; www .ravsak.org)

School Shopping Step #3:
Becoming a (Sneaky) Tourist

You would never buy a dress for your nephew's bar mitzvah without first taking a trip to the fitting room; since selecting a school for your child is exponentially more important, you can't proceed to the checkout without investigating firsthand whether or not it's a good fit. This is the purpose of the school tour. But buyers beware. The school tour is, by its very nature, a skewed version of reality.

Chances are that your tour guide will take you to visit only the *best* teachers' classrooms, introduce you to only the most *impressive* students, and adjust the route to showcase the facility's crown jewels (i.e., freshly donated gymnasiums, state-of-the-art computer labs, or Broadway-worthy auditoriums). Of course, it was plenty of thoughtful research that landed you at this school in the first place, so it's unlikely to have major skeletons in the closet (though I've yet to encounter a school that is skeleton-free); but you won't have the full scope of information you need to make an educated decision until you figure out what really goes on within school walls.

No, I'm not suggesting you sneak in late at night and install nannycams in the classrooms! The truth is you can find out everything you need to know during the course of an impossibly perfect school tour if you know where to look. The following suggestions will assist in your snooping:

Schedule your tour during the school day. While tours may be offered on the weekend or in the evening, your undercover investigative potential is exponentially reduced when the kids are missing. So, if at all possible, put in for an extended lunch break and visit the school during working hours.

Bring your spouse along. Two pairs of eyes are better than one. Besides, a decision of this magnitude should most definitely be a joint one.

Arrive early. Show up for the tour before the first bell rings and check out the atmosphere as students enter the building. Do they seem happy to be there, or do they look like it's the last place they want to be on earth? Are the teachers in the classrooms when the children arrive? If so, do they greet the kids warmly?

Scope the hallways. What's the atmosphere in the corridors? Are the kids walking single file under threat of life and limb? Are they totally out of control? Are there students wandering aimlessly? Do you see other parents around the school? Do they appear to be volunteering—or hovering?

Check out the bulletin boards. What kind of work is displayed outside the classrooms? Does it appear kid-done or does it look like the teacher cleaned them up with an eraser and Wite-Out? Do many of the assignments demonstrate free expression or were they cranked out in cookie-cutter fashion. Do you see a wide range of subject areas covered? Are any subjects overrepresented? Underrepresented?

What's up in the classrooms? Pay attention to the classroom environment (bearing in mind that you are likely observing the school's instructional pride and joy). Does it seem competitive? Nurturing? Boring? Are teachers encouraging students to analyze information or just regurgitate facts? Are the kids superglued to their chairs or do they move about the room learning in various ways? Are kids working in small groups or do the classrooms seem like lecture halls?

Take a head count. Regardless of what the reported student–teacher ratio is, do some calculating of your own in the classroom. If the ratio is off in one room, the extra teacher may have just made an emergency run to the bathroom. If you find the number of staff consistently coming up short, she may be a figment of the school's imagination.

Take a good look at the facility and amenities. Do the classrooms have computers? How many? Is there a technology lab on campus? What about a science lab or art studio? Is there a gymnasium? If so, does the equipment look safe or prehistoric? Ditto for the playground. Does the school have a clean, functional cafeteria? Are the bathrooms hygienic and unscathed by graffiti? Is the water coming out of the water fountain water-colored?

Pay attention to the older students. Psychologist Wendy Mogel suggests that even if your child is only entering kindergarten, you hone in on some fifth- or sixth-graders. Do they seem happy and empowered or stressed out and miserable? A peek at these older kids will give you keen insight into who you can expect your child to become at this school.

School Shopping Step #4:
Surviving the Kindergarten Interview

Under normal shopping circumstances, the fortuitous discovery of the perfect dress is generally followed by a mad dash to the cash register to buy it. If your school shopping has revealed a public school as the perfect fit for your child, this basic principle applies and you are free to proceed to the checkout. If, on the other hand, you have your heart set on a private school, you likely have one more hurdle to jump—the kindergarten interview.

True, the very thought of the kindergarten interview sends chills up our spines—I mean, having some stranger judge whether our precious, perfect child is worthy of admission to her school? But try to look on the bright side: You don't want to send your child to a school where he may not succeed, and the kindergarten interview provides a safeguard against this. Just as different stores cater to different fashion tastes and body types, a school's educational approach and teaching style will gel better with some kids than it will with others. The interview process can provide a school with valuable insight into whether a child will succeed under its roof. It's your real child who will be going to school every day, so you should feel good about sending your real child (albeit a scrubbed-up, well-rested version) to the interview.

Should a dreaded rejection letter show up in your mailbox following your child's interview, consider it a reprieve from a potentially costly mistake and move on. Don't worry about how your child is going to handle the news; the truth is that to the vast majority of five and six-year-olds, a kindergarten classroom is a kindergarten classroom is a kindergarten classroom. The only way your kid will be devastated by a rejection letter is if she sees that you are. If your child asks for an explanation, use the good fit/bad fit analogy. Some dresses fit you perfectly and others are tight, itchy, and just no fun to wear. Which would you rather walk around in for the next six to thirteen years? (Note: This advice also holds true in cases of older children changing schools due to moves, reevaluation of needs, and/or unexpected itchiness on the part of your original choice.)

Most importantly, never lose sight of the fact that the best school for your child isn't the one with the best test scores or the most societal clout. It's the school that comes closest to fitting your child and family—academically, philosophically, socially, and emotionally.

Helping Your Kid Kick Off Kindergarten with Confidence

Mazel tov! Your school shopping spree has been a smashing success and your little *bubbeleh* is eagerly counting down the minutes until her first day of kindergarten. Now it's time to get cracking on your next order of business—preparing her to make her elementary debut. But wistfully tracking down the coolest Barbie or Batman backpack on the market is only a fraction of the assignment.

Visit the school. A summertime sneak preview of the school, kindergarten classrooms, and playground will help minimize fear of the unknown and make your child more comfortable during her first days of school.

Get into the kindergarten swing. A week or so before the start of school, begin easing your child into the school-year schedule. That way he'll be bright-eyed and bushy-tailed on his first day.

Play down your own mixed emotions. Rather than rambling on about how you can't believe your baby is growing up, emphasize how excited you are that she's going to kindergarten.

Send a security object. The promise of being able to bring a favorite blanket or stuffed animal—albeit stashed safely out of sight in his backpack—will be worth its weight in lunch money in building your growing kindergartner's courage.

Celebrate. Boost your child's excitement about school with a special celebratory dinner the night before he starts kindergarten. Use colorful school supplies to decorate the table for the occasion. (Just don't go overboard on the sugar!)

Talk about your first-day-of-school experiences. Psychologists believe that sharing family stories is one of the most effective ways for parents to strengthen their children emotionally. During your celebratory dinner, take turns sharing first-day-of-kindergarten stories.

Ease into after-school care. Many children's after-school situations change with their entrance to kindergarten. If your child will be attending a Jewish Community Center or other day-care program after school, see if the facility offers a camp and enroll her there for a week or so over the summer; that way she'll be settled in when school kicks off in the fall. If you'll be utilizing the school's after-school care program, talk to your child about where she should go, who's in charge, and what to expect there.

Make sure she has a familiar face at school. Having at least one friend on the first day of kindergarten can make all the difference to a child, so call the school over the summer, ask for the names of a few of your child's future classmates, and arrange a playdate or two.

Read all about it. There's nothing like an uplifting story about another kid in the same boat to help build a kindergartner's confidence. Here are some worthy choices:

Annabelle Swift, Kindergartner by Amy Schwartz
Kindergarten Rocks by Katie Davis
Miss Bindergarten Gets Ready for Kindergarten by Joseph Slate
The Night Before Kindergarten by Natasha Wing and Julie Durrell
Look Out Kindergarten, Here I Come! by Nancy Carlson
The Kissing Hand by Audrey Penn

Finding Your Place in the Kindergarten Circle

So our child is at last happily plugging away in kindergarten. Good work, indeed! But don't think for a second that we're done. To the contrary, our work has just begun. Researchers have determined that the one constant factor for students who do well in school is *parent involvement*. While I'll go into more detail regarding the parental role in a child's education in the next chapter, here are four ways you can help ensure your little slugger's rookie year is a grand slam.

Be Prepared and On Time Every Day
Being a mother of four, nobody knows better than me how hard it is to get the troops dressed, fed, and out the door to school every morning. And nobody knows better than me how receiving a tardy slip or showing up stag to the teddy bear picnic can ruin a kid's whole day. Fortunately—barring unforeseen morning disasters—a few simple proactive measures can preclude such slipups. Before your child goes to bed, have him lay out his clothes, including socks

and shoes (you can't imagine how many late arrivals are attributed to lost sneakers). Help him check his backpack to make sure it's stocked with everything he needs for school the next day and hang it on a designated backpack hook. Keep a calendar in the kitchen with important dates and school events circled in marker. (Some organizational goddesses I know use a different color for each child.) For the especially morning-challenged, try hanging Post-it note reminders on the bathroom mirror (use picture cues for nonreaders). Assuming your crew remembers to brush their teeth, this technique can jog even the sleepiest of memories.

Encourage Independence

Kindergarten is all about being independent; but it is a complex independence, because our kids can only achieve it with our help. The role of the kindergarten parent, therefore, is to act as something of a stagehand, stealthily setting the scene for our children to be self-reliant. If your kid has yet to master the art of unbuckling and buckling, for example, don't risk a potential potty disaster by sending him to school fully belted. Outfit him in elastic waistbands for the time being and practice his buckling skills on weekends. If it takes your child twenty minutes to open a package of string cheese, don't make her spend her lunch period struggling. Have her open the package at home, seal the string cheese in a ziploc bag, and place it in her lunchbox.

Volunteer in the Classroom

Kindergarten is a monumental leap. You can help ease the shock for your child and yourself by helping out in the classroom. Start by being patient. Most kindergarten teachers don't want parents anywhere near their class for the first weeks of school to allow students time to acclimate and prevent unnecessary bouts of separation anxiety, but once the school year is in full swing it's fair game. Begin by calling or e-mailing the teacher and asking how you may be of assistance. If she doesn't bite, make some suggestions. Perhaps you play guitar and can come for a musical interlude between learning centers. Maybe you're a superb chef and can make Hanukkah cookies with the class. If you work during the day, ask if you can read a book to the class first thing in the morning, or bring in a special snack in the afternoon. If it's difficult getting to school during regular hours, ask the teacher if she needs help cutting (kindergarten teachers always do) and let your child see you clipping away for her classroom at home.

Build a Bridge Between Home and School

One of your primary means of ensuring your grade-schooler's long-term academic success is fostering a fluid connection between home and school. It won't take a teaching degree to accomplish this goal, but it will take some persistent fishing. Every night at dinner, ask your child what she learned at school and use her response as a springboard for conversation. ("You learned about food groups? What is your favorite food group? Mine is carbohydrates.") If your child insists she learned nothing, scrounge around in her backpack for clues. ("I see you drew some clouds and a sun today. Are you learning about weather? Let's go outside and see what the weather is doing right now" or "I see you are practicing writing the letter *B*. Let's see how many things we can find in the house that start with *B*.") If your backpack excavations indicate your kindergartner is learning to add and subtract, make up problems at the breakfast table. ("You have two doughnut holes and I give you two more, how many do you have now?") Or during dinner. ("You have four chicken nuggets and eat one, how many are left?") Once you get in the mind-set, you'll find opportunities for making home—school connections everywhere you look (especially if you look in the next two chapters, where I'll kick this discussion up a notch).

CHAPTER 4

School Rules

When my kids were in the throes of the terrible twos, I had a blissful image of how life would be once they started elementary school. They'd return home from a day chock full of learning, jabbering away about their adventures in academe. I'd trade them a plate of freshly baked cookies for a pile of A+ papers. They'd gobble, I'd gloat. That's it.

I never considered the parental ulcer potential of a book report. Or the emotional charge of parent–teacher conference night. It didn't cross my mind that the reality of orchestrating my children's academic existence would make the terrible twos seem like a spa treatment.

Fortunately, I've since learned that when it comes to the grade-school parenting experience, my fantasy (seeing my kids thrive and succeed academically) and my reality (enduring anxiety beyond my worst PMS nightmares) were in fact only steps—not worlds—apart. I learned that by making three simple, yet monumental, parental moves, I could simultaneously alleviate my stress and put my kids on the road to realizing their full academic potential.

The Three Parental Steps to (Almost) Stress-Free Grade-School Success

1. Form a solid partnership with the teacher.
2. Understand and embrace your child's unique learning profile.
3. Create a healthy homework environment.

Parental Step #1
Form a Solid Partnership with the Teacher

Making Nice

Chances are that your child's teacher spends as much—if not more—time with your kid as you do. She is truly your parenting partner and your first line of defense in ensuring your child's academic success. It's crucial, therefore, that you build a formidable and amicable relationship. Here are some insider's tips toward ensuring your spot on the teacher's good side:

Do lay the groundwork for open, amicable communication by telling the teacher you are excited that your child is in her class and you are looking forward to a successful year of working together.

Don't kick off the season with a boastful or heavy-handed tone ("Noah learned all his multiplication facts this summer—clearly he will require math enrichment"). Instead, sit tight and show your trust in the teacher to accurately assess your child's needs.

Do make sure your son or daughter is prepared for school each day with homework and other necessary materials.

Don't call the teacher at home unless it's a life-or-death emergency. (There's no faster way to the teacher's doghouse than calling her in the middle of a family dinner to discuss your kid's grade on the latest math test.) If you want to talk with her, e-mail or phone in a message at school requesting a time to chat.

Do stay on top of what's going on in the class and important upcoming events by reading the teacher's curriculum letters or website postings.

Don't hit her up at open house or school assemblies with personal questions about your child. ("How's my little Rachel doing in math?") Not only do such requests put her in an uncomfortable position, she's got way too much going on to give you a thoughtful answer.

Do send the teacher occasional cheerful notes telling her how much you appreciate her, using specifics if possible. ("Sam really enjoyed making slime during science yesterday.") Double the brownie points if you cc the compliment to the principal.

Don't ask the teacher to go light-years beyond the call of duty (i.e., asking her to send home a daily page-long written narrative about your child's performance and behavior).

Do volunteer to help out in the classroom—or make copies, laminate, and do other really boring teacher tasks—whenever your schedule permits. (If it's difficult for you to get to school during working hours, offer to make phone calls, cut materials, etc., from home.)

Don't bad-mouth the teacher to—or within earshot of—your child. Even if you think she's the Wicked Witch of the West, you need to present a united front.

Do fill the teacher in on any issues at home that may impact your child's mood or functioning at school.

Don't go above the teacher's head (i.e., to the principal) with classroom concerns before addressing them with her first.

Do be understanding of the difficult job a teacher faces—balancing the academic, social, and emotional well-being of a roomful of students . . . and keeping their parents happy to boot!

Beyond the Apple . . .

Hanukkah Gifts and Midyear Goodies Every Teacher Will Appreciate

While you don't want to come across as a complete brownnoser, sprinkling the teacher with occasional inexpensive tokens of your appreciation is a surefire way to keep your relationship with her (not to mention her relationship with your child) in tip-top shape. Don't think of it as bribery, think of it as maintenance.

- Most teachers have very limited classroom budgets and tons of items they'd love to purchase if only they had the means to do so. A gift card to Wal-Mart, Target, or a book or office supply store—even if it's only for five or ten dollars—will help her improve the classroom.
- There's nothing like a bunch of freshly picked flowers from your backyard garden to brighten a teacher's desk and day.
- Teachers never have enough places to keep things like paper clips, thumbtacks, pencils, and the like. Take your child to a do-it-yourself pottery place and let her decorate a box or small bowl for the teacher to stash her odds and ends.
- Teacher's lounge coffee is notoriously the pits. A gift certificate to Starbucks or other posh coffeehouse will let your child's teacher get her daily helping of caffeine in style!
- For lack of a better way to put this—kids are germy. They don't cover their mouths when they cough and sneeze, they forget to wash their hands after they go to the bathroom, and they don't use tissues nearly enough. Any teacher would appreciate some

luxuriously-smelling antibacterial gel or lotion—and some
sudsy kid-friendly soap for her students—to help give her im-
mune system a fighting chance.
- Of course the best gift you can possibly give the teacher doesn't
cost a penny: A handwritten note from your child expressing
his gratitude and adoration as only a child can.

Making the Most of Parent–Teacher Pow-Wows

From the teacher's perspective, parent–teacher conferences represent a revolving door of anxious moms and dads. From the parent's
perspective it's our big chance to find out everything we need to
know about our child's school existence! Here's how to make the
most of your kid's fifteen minutes in the spotlight.

Arrive on time. There's no such thing as being fashionably late to
a parent–teacher conference. Even a five-minute delay on a parent's part can throw off a teacher's carefully synchronized schedule
for the rest of the evening. If you are late due to unforeseen circumstances, cut your losses by offering to finish up your chat via phone
call later.

Open the meeting on a positive note. ("Your bulletin boards look
great." "I really enjoyed the written piece Jake brought home from
school today.") This will help set an amiable tone for the rest of the
conference.

If—or should I say *when*?—the teacher brings up concerns (conferences rarely comprise a teacher soliloquy singing a student's
praises), don't feel like you're the only parent in the classroom
whose kid has an issue. The truth is that every child has a *shtick* of

some sort. Some kids' *shticks* just happen to be more obvious in a school setting.

If the teacher shares an observation regarding your child that differs from your take (i.e., "Emily doesn't seem to understand what she's reading"), ask for specific examples. If you still believe the teacher to be off base, don't tell her she's wrong. Say something to the effect of "Emily often tells me about the books she's reading at home. Perhaps she feels a bit more distracted or anxious at school. I know how busy you are, but would you mind doing a short one-on-one assessment of Emily's reading comprehension whenever you get a chance?"

If your child is experiencing a problem at school—academic, social, or behavioral—it's important to form an action plan. What is the teacher going to do on her end? What should you do on yours? Provide a quick recap to ensure everyone's on the same page. ("Just so I'm clear, Mrs. Smithberg, I'm going to buy a pack of flashcards today and start working with Daniel on his math facts at home. You are going to include him in small-group math reinforcement opportunities at school. If he doesn't show improvement by Passover, I am going to look into having him tutored. Did I forget anything?") If your child's difficulties are too complex to address in a short conference, don't hesitate to request a separate meeting with the teacher and other school professionals to discuss the situation in depth.

When the teacher turns the floor over to you to share questions and concerns (which she most probably will, but if she doesn't jump in and take it anyway!), don't waste time talking about issues that the teacher can't change. ("I can't stand this math book!") Bring up issues that are within the teacher's realm of control or at least repackage them so they can be. ("Sam has a hard time understanding the instructions in the math book. I'd really appreciate it if you could take a moment to go over them when assigning homework pages.") This is also the time to fill the teacher in on anything going on at home that could impact your son or daughter in the classroom.

If you're concerned your child is not being adequately challenged academically, it's important to present your case tactfully. First and foremost, never play the "bored" card. ("Hannah keeps complaining that school is boring. Obviously the work is too easy for her.") Not only do teachers who work overtime planning exciting learning experiences for their students find such statements offensive, the reality is that kids can find school boring for a million different reasons. They may have attentional difficulties, learning problems, or just want to go outside and play. Rather than focusing on the fact that your kid considers this teacher's class to be snooze city, say something like "I noticed Hannah got all A's in math this term. If you feel it would be appropriate, we'd love for her to have a few additional challenges in class."

Just prior to wrap-up time, the teacher will probably ask if you have any other questions. While a truthful answer would likely be "Why, I do have a few zillion questions. Thanks for asking!" A single inquiry is all that is socially appropriate at this point.

Don't waste your final question on something inconsequential like "When are the gift wrap orders due?" Make it a doozie with plenty of bang for your buck. My personal favorite: "Could you give me a general idea of where Alex falls academically in the context of the class?" Teachers have a relative understanding of our child, and a perspective on his place in the academic pack, that we parents don't. It's important for us to know the answer to this question, not from a Mommy 500 competitive standpoint, but from a standpoint of helping and understanding our child as a learner. (We'll dig deeper into this topic later in the chapter.) Once you have your answer, thank the teacher for her insight and hospitality and be on your way.

Finally, don't lose sight of the fact that the parent–teacher conference is a touchpoint—not an annual summit meeting. Our children's teachers are among the most central and influential figures in our kids' lives. It's vital that we communicate with them regularly, effectively, and respectfully.

Teachers from the Black Lagoon

It's a scene straight out of the worst-case scenario parent handbook. Our child—a normally happy student—lands the Teacher from the Black Lagoon. She's evil, he tells us, shaking in his Air Jordans. Not to mention out to get him. How can he possibly be expected to learn when his teacher is the scholastic version of Attila the Hun?!

Suddenly our primal parental instinct kicks in. The same adrenalin-fueled impulse to protect our young that once had us lunging for our toddler milliseconds before he stuck his Barney fork in the electrical outlet is now prompting us to grab his fourth-grade teacher by her ruffled collar and command her to keep her claws off our kid. Or else.

But we can't relapse into our primal maternal fury yet, my fellow Jewish parents. Not before we take a good, hard look at the split screen. You know, like when important news breaks out during a major television ratings event like the Academy Awards, and they split the screen between Halle Berry's acceptance speech and an oil spill on the interstate. Just like that. Only different, because this screen is split between our kid and, well, our kid.

(65)

On one side we see our moppy-topped nine-year-old, with freckles that tug at our heartstrings, imploring us to free him from the wrath of the evil Mrs. Xstein. On the other screen we see him again. But this time he's all grown up—and he seems to be saying something about quitting yet *another* job. Mean boss, he tells us. Out to get him. How can he possibly be expected to perform at work when he's forced to put up with the corporate version of Attila the Hun?!

Taken aback, we begin to refocus and then the picture changes. It's still our son on that second screen and he's still all grown up, but he seems different this time—empowered, resilient, *menschlich*. Mean boss, he says. What can you do? Sometimes you get to work with nice people; sometimes you have to work with cranky people. That's just the way life is.

It was a lesson he'd learned way back in fourth grade when his mom insisted he march his Air Jordans straight into that swamp monster's classroom and hold his head high. For hurt her as it might, she believed in her heart that moppy-topped nine-year-olds who muster up the courage to tough out a whole school year with the Teacher from the Black Lagoon emerge from those murky waters resilient, empowered, moppy-topped *mensches*. That's just the way life is.

By the way, what that boy didn't know is that once his mom took control of her primal urge to strangle the swamp monster, she continued to watch her son carefully for weeks and months to come. She knew that if her son's complaints persisted or worsened or he started to show signs of extreme stress (i.e., stomachaches, sleeplessness, depression, or anxiety), she would march her *tuchas* right into that school and have a serious chat with the teacher—and maybe even the principal after that. But that didn't happen. (In fact, while

Mrs. Xstein never quite turned into the warm fuzzy that the boy and his mom hoped she would be, she wasn't *really* the Teacher from the Black Lagoon . . .)

Jewish Parent 911

Helping Kids Cope with Difficult Teachers

Share your own "Teacher from the Black Lagoon" stories. By telling our children about our childhood experiences with mean teachers, we give them a perspective they may not otherwise grasp. I often tell my kids about my sixth-grade Hebrew teacher, a hulking, bearded rabbi who threatened to sit on any students who talked during class. Such tales help them understand that having difficult teachers is a highly survivable, universal experience.

Be a sounding board. Do you know how sometimes you just need to get together with your girlfriends, eat a gallon of cookie dough ice cream, and gripe? You don't really want your friends to offer solutions ("You know, you could solve your bathing suit problem by going on the South Beach diet"), much less intervene on your part ("I'm going to call your boss on Monday and tell her to stop overworking you this instant!"). It's often the same when our kids complain about mean teachers; they just need to vent. Rather than making a beeline for the principal's office after your child reports his teacher forced the class to have a silent lunch period for doing absolutely *nothing*, respond with an empathetic "That's too bad. I'll bet you missed talking to your friends."

Help your child see the future. Explain to your child that throughout life, she is going to have to deal with people who are grumpy, unreasonable, and insidious. While spending a year with a mean teacher may seem like a dreadful chore now, it will teach her that she can succeed with even the most difficult of people—a lesson that will ultimately make her life easier, not harder.

Get involved only as a last resort. According to Dr. Charles Fay, a school psychologist and coauthor of *Love and Logic Magic*, parents should intervene on behalf of their child only when it is clear that the teacher is so incompetent or negative that even the best-behaved student would find it impossible to adapt. Fortunately, such educators are few and far between.

Parental Step #2:
Understand and Embrace Your Child's Unique Learning Profile

There's a line in the Book of Proverbs (Parsha 22 to be exact) that says, "Educate a child according to his way." Never has this sliver of wisdom rung truer than it does today, when cramming kids into societally constructed Harvard-bound boxes has become parental sport.

In her book *Blessing of a Skinned Knee*, Wendy Mogel writes, "We should think of our children as packages of seeds that came without a label. We can't tell what season they'll bloom, or what kind of flower we'll get. Our job is simply to pull the weeds, provide the water and step back and wait."

In other words, helping our children fulfill their potential does not entail turning perfectly average students into valedictorians. It means cheering them on as they take their own shape as learners, providing them support should they struggle and enrichment should they shine. But mostly, it means nurturing them, nourishing them, and watching them flourish, into the one-of-a-kind flowers God designed them to be.

Eight Different Ways to Be Smart

Let's just admit it. We want our kid to be tapped for the talented and gifted program. But just because our child has yet to reveal himself as a brainiac in the strictest sense of the word doesn't mean he isn't super smart. In fact according to Harvard professor of education Howard Gardner's highly acclaimed, positively ingenious theory of multiple intelligences, human beings show at least eight distinct types of intelligence of value to society—eight different realms in which to discover and illuminate sparks of genius glowing within our kids. Here is an overview of each of these intelligences and the ways they often manifest themselves in children:

- *Linguistic intelligence*: Kids with linguistic intellect generally excel in reading and writing; they may be aces at crossword puzzles and get lost in books for hours on end. They enjoy telling jokes and stories and can argue their point to a fault. Writers, lawyers, and English teachers tend to have linguistic intelligence.
- *Logical-mathematical intelligence*: Children with logical-mathematical strength get a kick out of patterns, categories, relationships, strategy games, and experiments. They are savvy math students. This type of intelligence teams up with the linguistic realm to form the traditional definition of intellect. Accountants, scientists, and economists tend to exhibit logical-mathematical intelligence.

- *Spatial intelligence*: Children with spatial smarts enjoy solving mazes, doing jigsaw puzzles, and drawing. They love building things out of Legos and wooden blocks. They are excellent map readers and may have a propensity for daydreaming. Architects, interior designers, and photographers often have high levels of spatial intelligence.
- *Bodily-kinesthetic intelligence*: Agile and physically coordinated, these kids may excel in athletics, martial arts, or dance. (They can also have a tough time sitting still.) Choreographers, actors, and physical therapists tend to have bodily-kinesthetic smarts.
- *Musical intelligence*: These kids are natural singers or instrumentalists. They have a good ear for tunes and lyrics and may be discriminating listeners. Music teachers, songwriters, and Broadway performers have musical intelligence.
- *Interpersonal intelligence*: Interpersonally intelligent children have smarts in the social arena. They may be natural leaders, or have strong communication skills and a keen awareness of the feelings of others. They have the ability to pick up subtle social cues and generally don't like to be alone. Psychologists, doctors, and teachers often show interpersonal intelligence.
- *Intrapersonal intelligence*: Kids with this type of intellect are introspective and have a strong sense of who they are. They are not easily swayed by what's "in" and "out" with other kids. They play well alone and may keep journals. They can come across as shy or stubborn. Entrepreneurs, rabbis, and activists tend to exhibit intrapersonal intelligence.
- *Naturalistic intelligence*: This is Gardner's most recently added intelligence. It refers to an ability to recognize and classify elements of the natural world. Naturalistic kids may be animal lovers and show an interest in all things botanical. They enjoy

hiking, camping, and gardening. Veterinarians, marine biologists, and landscapers are apt to have naturalistic intelligence.

Finally, if you've concluded that your child is not a budding Marie Curie, Pablo Picasso, Emily Dickinson, Jacques Cousteau, or Albert Einstein, rest assured you're in good company. At the end of the day most of our kids are, well, regular old kids—good at some things, not so good at others, and counting on us to love and support them in all their wonderfully regular-kid glory.

Deciphering Standardized Test Scores

While standardized test scores are admittedly given far more hype and weight than they deserve, they can—when interpreted correctly—give us important insight into our child's academic profile and learning needs. Unfortunately, they can also rank right up there with hieroglyphics on the unreadability scale. The following information will help you cut through the jargon and decode the true meaning and implications of your child's standardized test results.

The most important thing to understand about standardized tests is that they are norm-referenced. This means the scores reflect a student's ranking relative to other children at the same grade level who took the same test. Norm-referenced results are usually communicated as follows:

Percentiles: A score in the 76th percentile means a child's performance equaled or surpassed that of 76 percent of the students who took the test (not that 76 percent of the questions were answered correctly).

Stanines (standard nines): This is a method by which each student tested is assigned to one of nine groups based on a bell curve formed by their scores (lots in the middle and fewer at the extremes). Though this scoring is sometimes criticized as too broad, extreme stanine scores (1's and 2's or 9's) can be indicative of specific problems or talents.

Grade equivalencies: These commonly misunderstood scores work as follows: If a fifth-grade child received a math computation grade equivalency of 9.5, this means she obtained the same score as a typical ninth-grade student in the fifth month of school taking the *same* test. This does *not* mean she's ready to skip the next three years of math instruction; there are many critical ninth-grade skills that are not evaluated by a fifth-grade standardized test.

It's also important to be aware of the ways your child's scores will be used. While some schools place more emphasis on standardized test scores than others, all are likely to use the results in some combination of the following ways:

- To compare individual students or groups of students to some national or local standard.
- To track individual progress.
- To evaluate the effectiveness of instruction.
- To identify students who might benefit from enrichment or remediation.

If you are concerned about your child's scores, schedule a meeting with the teacher to review the results and discuss whether they reflect your child's school performance. Ask to see your child's answer sheet along with the original test, if available. Sometimes lower scores result from stray marks, incomplete erasures, or the error cascade that follows a misplaced answer. Children with attentional and organizational problems may also score in ways that don't reflect their true academic aptitude.

On the flipside, don't assume high test scores undermine academic concerns expressed by your child's teacher. Multiple-choice test formats don't address skills of recall, memory, written expression, or organization, all or which are critical to daily school functioning.

Finally, keep in mind that while standardized test scores can be valuable tools, they don't mean nearly as much as how a child does in school every day.

Learning Styles

Just as children vary in their areas of intellectual strength, they also differ in the ways they are best able to acquire, process, and retain new information. This is called their *learning style.* In recent years, learning styles have made their way to the forefront of cutting-edge educational thought. Consequently, increasing focus is being placed not only on *what* kids learn, but on *how* they learn. Here is a brief explanation of each of the three primary learning styles.

Auditory learners learn best by listening and talking. They need to hear information so they can remember it. Auditory learners perform maximally when a teacher presents material verbally. Your child may be an auditory learner if he enjoys telling and listening to stories, talks to himself, hums and asks lots of questions, becomes distracted by having too many sounds at once, or enjoys talking about what he's learning.

Visual learners learn by watching. They need to see the information in order to retain it. Visual kids respond best when teachers present material using chalkboards, overhead projectors, handouts, charts, and graphs. Your child may be a visual learner if she notices details, has a vivid imagination, is keenly aware of similarities and differences, enjoys art and drawing, or has trouble remembering verbal directions and messages.

Kinesthetic learners process information through movement and physical manipulation. They need to actually be in motion in order to learn. Kinesthetic kids learn best through hands-on experiences like field trips and science experiments. Your child may be a kinesthetic learner if he prefers showing you things to telling you about them, seems to be in constant motion, has a short attention span, or taps his pencil and fidgets while doing his schoolwork.

Why is it important for us to have a grasp of the way our child learns? Because research shows a student's academic performance can suffer significantly if she is not taught according to her learning style. If our child is a visual learner, for example, and her teacher is a lecture queen, she's only going to process a fraction of the information presented in class. If our kid is a kinesthetic learner and the teacher gets frustrated every time he bounces his knees and taps his pencil, he's liable to be jumping out of his skin by the end of a long, drawn-out verbal lesson (not to mention missing the bulk of the material).

The kids with the hands-down advantage on the school front are the auditory learners—it is estimated that 80 percent of academic instruction is delivered verbally. Unfortunately, only 10 percent of grade-schoolers are auditory learners. In other words, as many as

90 percent of kids may be performing below their academic potential as the result of a mismatched teaching style.

On the bright side, progressive schools nationwide are now working to accommodate their curriculums to meet the needs of all learning styles. Still, most have plenty of ground yet to cover in adapting their programs. If you suspect that your child is not receiving ample instruction in accordance with his learning style, it's time to schedule a meeting with the school.

Here is a list of proven strategies for maximizing learning for each of the three learning styles. By employing these techniques with our children at home and encouraging the teacher to do the same in the classroom, we can help ensure that they receive ample opportunity to cash in every last one of their intellectual chips:

Effective Strategies for Auditory Learners:
- Having material read aloud when they study so they can hear the information
- Studying with a partner and talking out ideas and solutions
- Reading material to be learned out loud with a parent
- Taking part in verbal drills or spelling bees
- Making an audiotape of lessons at school (with permission, of course!)

Effective Strategies for Visual Learners:
- Using flashcards to help them memorize information
- Highlighting key words and phrases
- Using charts to organize information
- Drawing pictures about what they learn
- Having verbal instructions written on the blackboard
- Using an assignment book and taking notes

Effective Strategies for Kinesthetic Learners:

- Working with math manipulatives (beads, cubes, counters)
- Turning information into a skit and presenting it
- Keeping hands busy by taking notes or drawing diagrams about the material
- Keeping a stress ball, Silly Putty, or Play-Doh in the desk to help them get their "fidgets" out
- Allowing them to stand in the back of the class during a lesson
- Taking plenty of stretch breaks while studying

Raising Little People of the Book

Reading is at the very heart of education. It enriches the imagination, builds vocabulary, teaches grammar, and makes students better spellers and writers. If our kids are going to thrive and succeed in our fast-paced, achievement-oriented society, it's important that they become proficient readers. How can we ensure our children gain the reading skills they need? Perhaps the philosopher Epictetus put it best: "If you wish to be a good reader, read." There never was and never will be any other way. Here are some suggestions for igniting a love of reading in your child:

Give reading a prime-time slot. Regardless of how much kids like to read, they won't read if they haven't any time to do so. By setting aside twenty minutes or so every day (right before bedtime usually works well), we provide our kids ample reading opportunity while sending the message that it's an activity worthy of their precious time.

Check the reading level. When children take on books beyond their proficiency level, they can rapidly become disheartened. To determine whether a book is too hard for your child, have her read the first page aloud to you. If she stumbles over more than five words, put it back on the shelf and help her make another selection.

Enlist Hollywood. Seeing a story on the big screen (or a small one) can provide just the spark kids need to pick up the book version. Flicks like *Lemony Snicket's Series of Unfortunate Events, Matilda, Stuart Little,* and, of course, the Harry Potter movies, are sure to have your little stars hitting the library in no time.

Gear them up with glossy pages. Kids needn't peruse classics to reap the benefits of reading. Magazines that zero in on children's passions—from skateboarding to fashion—can inspire even the most reluctant readers to start flipping pages. Techno-savvy kids can pull up favorite magazines online at sites like Sports Illustrated Kids (http://www.sikids.com) and Time for Kids (http://www.timeforkids .com/TFK).

Create a library on wheels. Propensity toward carsickness aside, keeping a supply of books in the car will turn all those idle hours in traffic into valuable reading time.

Turn them on to books on tape. Listening to a book on tape while following along in the real thing gives struggling readers (or those who simply want to tackle a book that's beyond their reading level) an opportunity to enjoy the story without getting bogged down by difficult words.

Money talks. In addition to your child's regular allowance, provide a small allotment exclusively for reading material. Even if all your kid can afford is a paperback book or magazine, you've helped your cause along.

Start a parent–child book club. This hot new trend in book clubs offers benefits galore ranging from heightened reading skills to multigenerational bonding. Find out everything you need to know about organizing your own parent–child group at: http://www.pbs.org/parents/readinglanguage/articles/bookclubs/main.html.

It's in the bag. Stash some books in a tote bag and pull them out whenever you and your kids get caught in a holding pattern. Whether waiting at the doctor's office or a restaurant, your children will be thankful to have books to bust their boredom.

Add "book night" to your Hanukkah traditions. Reserve one night of your Festival of Lights this year for family members to exchange hot reads. Spend the rest of the evening enjoying your new books together. Make your gift last all year long by making Family Reading Night a weekly tradition.

Read to your kids. For kids who are learning to read—and even those who are old pros!—it's always a treat to listen to a book. Be expressive and vary your intonation as you read to encourage your kids to do so on their own.

Parental Step #3:
Create a Healthy Homework Environment

Homework, huh? The bane of every grade-school parent's existence. I'd say this juicy topic requires a chapter all its own . . .

CHAPTER 5

Surviving Homework

Back in my B.C.E. (Before Children Era), I believed homework was safely tucked away with my textbooks, term papers, and diplomas. I never imagined that by my year 6 A.C.E., homework would again be an albatross around my neck, its weight and magnitude trumping anything I'd known in my own school days.

It didn't start out that way. In the beginning, it was heartwarming to watch my boys proudly plug away at a page of homework as if it were an official proclamation of their big kid status. But before long the novelty had worn off, the difficulty level had kicked up, and homework assignments had become the bane of my weeknight existence.

Many years later, I finally realized that the source of my after-school misery was not the homework itself, but the fact that my children were completely dependent on me to organize, orchestrate, and execute it. Furthermore, I had created this beast by making every parental homework mistake in the book, mistakes that—I've since discovered—circulate through the modern Jewish parent population like dreidels at Hanukkah. In the name of restoring peace and sanity to Jewish homes everywhere (at least between 4 and 8 P.M. on weeknights), here are the most common and counterproductive Jewish parent homework mistakes.

Homework Mistake #1:
Becoming Overly Involved in Our Children's Homework

I know what you're thinking: What could possibly be wrong with being involved in my kids' homework? I mean, it's got to be better than watching *Oprah* every afternoon and staying out of the homework picture altogether.

It is true that parental involvement in homework contributes to kids' long-term academic success. But you know what they say about too much of a good thing—research shows that excessive parent involvement on the homework front can be just as bad for kids as inadequate parent involvement.

It's like teaching your child to ride a bicycle. If you take the underinvolved parent route (hanging out on a lawn chair yelling for him to hop on the bike and start pedaling) your kid is sure to wipe out and bust his butt a millisecond later. But taking the opposite approach (holding on to the bike with a white-knuckle death grip) isn't going to get your child riding either, as he'll never have the chance to learn to balance without your support.

Of course, a bit of white knuckling is only natural in the beginning, but then we need to take a step back from our kids' schoolwork. How far back, you ask? Far enough to allow our children to feel the inevitable bumps along the homework road, but not so far that we can't jump in should they pop a tire, skew off course, or start spinning out of control. In achieving this critical middle ground, we afford our children the precious opportunity to develop the skills and confidence they need to successfully pedal their way through homework—and life—independently.

Homework Mistake #2:
Pushing for Homework Perfection

Among the most counterproductive moves we modern parents make regarding our children's schooling is taking a Mommy 500 approach to their homework. Not only does insisting on homework perfection fan the flames of academic burnout; it can set them up to fall flat on their faces in the classroom. Take the following scenario:

David is having a heck of a time with his fractions homework. He's got his numerators and denominators confused and doesn't understand for the life of him how one-eighth could be smaller than one-fourth. As David struggles through his assignment, his mom (who regularly sits a paper football flick away while he's doing his homework) alerts him to every mistake he makes, forcing him to rework each botched problem. Before long, David is in tears. That's when David's dad steps in with a lengthy tutorial about the way they taught fractions in the "good old days." Two excruciating and emotional hours later David and company are finished with their homework. The following day David turns in his immaculate assignment—and proceeds to bomb a pop quiz on fractions.

As David's story demonstrates, our role in the homework process is to recognize—not camouflage—our children's academic struggles. It's certainly appropriate to provide technical support now and then. But if your child is incapable of doing her homework *without* your support, it's time to tack a note on the homework page informing the teacher that it was completed with help, and asking her to please review the material with your child in class the next day. We can rest assured that if we do so, the teacher will think more—not less—of us as parents.

Homework Mistake #3:
Doctoring Our Kids' Homework

A close cousin to Mistake #2 is the covert homework clean-up attempt. Now don't go acting like you don't know what I'm talking about. We've all done it! We tiptoe downstairs after our child has gone to bed and ever so carefully fish his *Mouse and the Motorcycle* book report out of his backpack to do a little tactful touching up. We correct his misspelling of *motorcycle*. We separate out a few run-on sentences. We even embellish his illustration of the mouse with a pair of chic rodent-sized sunglasses. Then we carefully return the sparkling book report to our child's school bag.

Okay, you may be thinking, so I've done a bit of homework doctoring in my day. Is that so terrible? It wasn't like I was doing my kid's homework for her while she was playing video games in the other room. Besides, what if the teacher decides to hang up the assignment on the bulletin board for the whole world to see? Shouldn't I want my kid to be proud of her work?!

Of course we want our kid to be proud of her work. But the reality is she will only be proud of her work if it actually is her work. I know, I know, you only used a little bit of Wite-Out. Still, even the most discreet of parental homework refinements sends a neon message to our kids that we believe them incapable of doing bulletin board–worthy work without our help—a message that is sure to prove more detrimental to our child in the long run than having to face up to drawing a mediocre mouse.

The Magic of the Homework Portfolio

It's a classic parental catch-22. Our child returns from school with a backpack full of graded homework and piles it sky high on the kitchen counter. Faced with this overwhelming onslaught, we weigh our options. We could take the quick and easy route, slyly tossing the tower of papers into the recycling bin. But such a clean break hardly feels comfortable as our child put plenty of time and effort into completing all that schoolwork. Besides, how could we possibly do away with her *Tales of a Fourth Grade Nothing* book report when she'll never be in fourth grade again?!

We could try the packrat approach, stuffing the teeming stack into supersized Tupperware containers and sealing it off for posterity. But adding on an extra room to the house for the sole purpose of storing old homework seems a bit extreme. Besides, what exactly is posterity going to do with an airtight box of crumpled worksheets?

Or we could find the answer to our decluttering prayers in a handy system called the homework portfolio (a system that just happens to come with a fringe benefit of teaching kids to recognize and take pride in their academic achievements).

Here's everything you need to know to take back the kitchen counter and get the homework portfolio working for your family:

First things first—you can't implement a homework portfolio system without a homework portfolio! Depending on personal preference, you can create the vehicle for this plan using a real artist's portfolio, a scrapbook, an accordion folder, or even a specially decorated box. Personalize the portfolio with your child's name, grade, and academic year.

The next step is blocking off some time to help your child scour the homework stockpile for pieces that make her feel especially proud and/or happy (making sure to drive home the point that an assignment needn't receive stellar scores to be a source of pride). Should your child determine that a) all of her work is portfolio worthy or b) none of it is, do a bit of modeling. "I really like this story you wrote about your pet alien," you might say. "It uses lots of great describing words and the surprise ending is fun." Or "Oh, here is that long division homework you worked so hard on last month. I know you didn't get everything right, but you got most of them, and I'm so proud of the effort you showed."

Every now and then, try to drum up a homework portfolio audience to ooh and ahh over the impressive assemblage. Grandparents are always eager for the job, as are empty-nester friends and relatives. You can even turn it into a mitzvah project and let your child show off her prized works to residents of a nursing home.

Finally, head off future schoolwork deluges by kicking off each new academic year with a fresh homework portfolio. Whenever your child returns home with a bursting backpack, have her lay out her work, add any extra special pieces to her collection, and recycle the rest . . . for posterity.

Homework Mistake #4:
Answering Kids' Questions Too Quickly and Directly

Don't get me wrong here. I'm not suggesting we leave our kids high and dry when they have questions. But offering up a steady flow of answers on a silver platter is not the solution either. To help establish why this is the case, I'm going to take you on a mini-mental journey.

Imagine you are about to host your first ever Passover Seder. You're feeling nervous and excited, harried and hopeful all at the same time. Sensing your *shpilkes*, your mother offers to accompany you to the grocery store to "answer any questions you may have" along the way. And answer your questions she does!

"I'd definitely go with the Manischewitz marble cake mix over the yellow cake mix," she tells you, "and don't forget to underbake it just a tad." "Of course, only kosher for Passover marshmallows are kosher for Passover . . . the other kind aren't even kosher when it's not Passover!" "No, matzoh meal and cake meal aren't the same." The question/answer pattern continues until you've loaded your cart with everything you need for matzoh ball soup to Passover brownies with nuts.

At the end of the shopping trip you thank your mother for coming along. And you mean it, being all but certain you never could have pulled off your first official shopping trip as a Jewish matriarch alone. But what happens next year when she's in Florida for the month?

Similarly when we answer our kids' homework-related questions in too timely and direct a manner, we ultimately keep them from gaining the confidence and competence they need to do it on their own. So how do we make sure our kids get all the answers they seek without compromising their budding homework independence? By putting a new spin on an old school-yard poem: *I'm rubber and you're glue. Anything you ask bounces off of me and sticks to you!*

The following scenarios demonstrate how you can bounce your kids' questions right back at them, fostering critical homework autonomy that will stick for years to come:

Scenario 1:

Child: *I don't understand this homework sheet. What am I supposed to do?*
Parent: *Did you read the instructions at the top of the page?*
Child: *I already did. I still don't get it.*
Parent: *Why don't you read the directions out loud this time, and try to explain them to me in your own words.*

Scenario 2:

Child: *What does 16 divided by 4 equal again?*
Parent: *Remember that division is the opposite of multiplication. Can you think of what number you multiply by 4 to make 16?*
Child: *No. C'mon, just tell me!!!*
Parent: *I have an idea: go grab sixteen Froot Loops and divide them into four piles. Then you'll have your answer.*

Scenario 3:

Child: *Did I make any mistakes on my vocabulary paragraph?*
Parent: *I see four mistakes that you made, can you find them?*
Child: *I can only find two. Where are the other ones?*
Parent: *I'll give you a hint. One mistake is in the first sentence, and the other is in the third sentence.*

Scenario 4:

Child: *How do you spell* independent?
Parent: *How do you think you spell* independent?

(One final hint: If your kids continue to pile on the questions, set a limit on the number of inquiries they can make during a given homework session. Keep track of their questions with tallies and close up shop once they've maxed out. This technique teaches children to weigh out whether they really need help before asking for adult assistance.)

Homework Help
Courtesy of the World Wide Web

Reinforce academic skills while fostering independence by steering kids toward homework help websites. Here are some of note:

http://school.discovery.com/homeworkhelp/bjpinchbeck/ BJ Pinchbeck's homework helper is nothing short of a mecca of helpful homework tips and information. Part of Discovery.com.

http://www.timeforkids.com/TFK/hh/rr The Time for Kids (as in *Time* magazine) homework helper helps kids independently answer their homework questions by linking them to the "smartest sites on the Web."

www.factmonster.com This great site features an almanac, atlas, dictionary, and encyclopedia compiled especially for kids. It also features a homework help center that caters to all different subjects and grade levels.

www.cogcon.com/gamegoo/gooey.html Game goo has tons of fun, animated, yet educational games. Plays like a video game, works like a homework reinforcement book.

www.enchantedlearning.com This site caters to the preschool and elementary set and features everything from picture dictionaries to dinosaurs to geography games.

http://mathforum.org/dr.math/ No need to ask Mom when you can ask Dr. Math at this award-winning website.

www.coolmath.com This site looks like a video game, but don't be fooled—it's really number crunching in disguise.

Homework Mistake #5:
Resorting to Threats and Punishments

Let's be honest, we've all taken the low road at one time or another. After all, there's no faster way to get a homework evader to hit the books than threatening to ground him until his iPod is obsolete. But nothing transfers the responsibility of homework from child to parent faster than an adult-controlled threat.

Sure, you may be thinking, that sounds just peachy on paper, but my kid *only* responds to threats and punishments where homework is concerned! What am I supposed to do, smile pretty and hope he complies?

Good point, indeed! The reality is that while some kids are just naturally conscientious students, many need to feel the presence of consequences to entice them to do their homework. Fortunately, when it comes to homework we've got nature's laws of *derech eretz* on our side (see Chapter 2), as an AWOL assignment is almost certain to yield a consequence in the classroom. Still, as we also discussed in Chapter 2, natural consequences sometimes require a subtle parental kick-start to get the job done effectively. How do we kick-start a consequence without stooping to threats and punishments?

By making an ever so subtle semantic alteration that magically transforms our statement from a *threat* to a *choice*.

Rather than saying, "Finish your book report or I won't let you go to Ari's house later," change your wording to "You have a choice: either finish your book report and play with Ari, or don't finish it and stay home later to work on it." Or try "Do you want to rewrite your sloppy paper at home, or should I send a note to the teacher asking her to have you do it in class?"

The "you choose" approach will help you remain threat-free through all kinds of sticky homework situations.

Homework Mistake #6:
Using Positive Reinforcement Incorrectly

As long as we're in a fessing-up kind of mood, we may as well come clean about occasionally bribing our kids to do their homework. ("If you finish your homework you can stay up late and watch *American Idol*. If you get an A on your spelling test I'll give you a dollar. If you finish all your work before we light the Hanukkah candles tonight you get double presents!")

Well I've got good news and bad news. First the bad news. Studies show one of the fastest ways to snuff out any glimmerings of intrinsic motivation and conscience in kids is to offer up *constant* rewards for doing the right thing. Now the good news. Studies also show one of the fastest ways to capitalize on any glimmerings of intrinsic motivation and conscience in kids is to offer up *occasional* rewards for doing the right thing.

How can this be true? Just ask B. F. Skinner. You know, the

world-famous behaviorist who spent his entire life hanging out with rats trying to get them to press down on a metal bar with their little rat feet. Well, anyway, what Skinner found was that if he *never* gave the rat a treat when it pressed the bar, the rat didn't press the bar very much at all. If he gave the rat a treat *every* time it pressed the bar, the rat pressed the bar a whole lot—but the second the treats stopped coming the rat stopped pressing. But when Skinner gave the rat a treat *occasionally* upon pressing the bar, the rat kept pressing that bar over and over again.

No, I'm not implying our kids are like rats! But the reality is that Skinner's findings have been replicated infinite times in people as well as rodents. In fact I've personally witnessed them replicated in my own students and children time and time again. Sure there are some who will fight me on the suggestion that rewards could ever have a place in the homework cycle. But I'm sticking to my guns on this one: Positive reinforcement, when used *appropriately*, is the spoonful of sugar that helps the homework go down.

So where do we draw the line between appropriate and inappropriate positive reinforcement? Keeping in mind that different parents will have different ideas and degrees of comfort regarding this issue, here are some general parameters:

· Giving kids an M&M every time they finish a math problem is *not* appropriate. Giving kids a sticker to place on a chart each night they finish their homework independently, then offering up a trip to the movies when the chart is full *is* appropriate.
· Slipping kids a quarter every night after they finish their homework is *not* appropriate. Slipping a marble in a jar each night after they do so and letting them have a few friends over for a slumber party when the jar is full *is* appropriate.

- Throwing a weekly homework party to celebrate children's homework success is *not* appropriate. Having a seasonal homework party to celebrate children's homework successes and budding independence *is* absolutely appropriate.

Homework Mistake #7:
Expecting Our Kids to Be Able to Do Homework Anytime and Anywhere

Having spent over a decade in the classroom, I can tell you firsthand that kids do homework in the darnedest places: on the sidelines at soccer practice (during water breaks); in a fast-food restaurant (on a fast-food bag); in the car on the way to piano (with a broken crayon); in front of the television (watching Nickelodeon). I even had a student do his homework while getting a cast in the emergency room (using his good arm).

The trouble is that kids have busy little minds. They often find it difficult to concentrate under the best of circumstances. How can we possibly expect them to focus on long division with *Fairly OddParents* blasting in the background? We owe it to our children to give homework a clear time and place in their hectic lives. Here are some pointers on how you can do so.

Setting the Homework Routine

Kids are creatures of habit. They like knowing what to expect and when to expect it (even when all they have to expect is doing homework). Given the pace of modern family life, it's virtually impossible to create a homework routine that will work every night of the week. The objective, therefore, is to establish a routine that works with the ebb and flow of your crowd.

If your daughter has Hebrew school from 5:30 to 7 on Tuesdays and Thursdays, for example, she should probably get plugging on her homework right after school. If she has gymnastics at 3:30 Wednesdays, she'll need to crack the books afterwards. If she has soccer on Tuesdays at 5, she should do a bit of work on either side of practice. (By the way, should you find a surplus of extracurriculars makes it virtually impossible to plan consistent homework times for your child, something's got to give—and it's not going to be the homework. Find tips on how to go about lightening your extracurricular load in Chapter 6.)

A child's individual style and needs should also be taken into account when outlining a homework schedule. Some kids require a fifteen-minute break after school in order to get into a homework mind-set; others need to get started pronto or their fifteen-minute break turns into an evening siesta. Some children must stretch their legs at regular intervals to maximize performance; others need their tushies superglued to the chair for the duration.

A further consideration is the parent's individual schedule and preferences. Some parents like to chat with their kids about their day before setting the homework machine in motion; others want to get the tough stuff out of the way and save the schmoozing for dinner. Some working parents want their kids to complete their homework with the babysitter or at after-school care; others prefer that their children wait until they return home before hitting the books.

When you do set a viable homework schedule for your family, increase the chances of it being followed by posting it prominently on the refrigerator or bulletin board. Finally, remember what they say about the best-laid plans, and be ready to exercise occasional flexibility.

Creating a Homework Space

If we left it up to our kids, they'd set up homework shop at the kitchen table, smack dab in the center of the household hustle and bustle. Unfortunately, many kids are unable to concentrate in such a hopping environment. This is the reason that in addition to setting regular homework times, we need to provide our kids with a homework-friendly space.

Keep in mind that an ideal homework environment for one child might not be so for another. Some kids need a little background noise to concentrate, others require complete silence. Some children work best sitting in an upright chair; others are most successful when sprawled out on a rug or sofa. Test out several scenarios to see which work best for your child before tapping an official homework spot.

Once you decide on the location, park a supply of sharpened pencils, loose-leaf paper, rulers, crayons, markers and other homework necessities nearby. Make sure the area is well lit and free of televisions, video games, iPods, cell phones, and other distracting electronics. Finally—as we discussed earlier—while you don't want to be center stage in your child's homework space, you should park yourself firmly on the periphery.

How Much Homework IS Too Much?

Truth be told, homework has been on the upswing since Sputnik. Still, research shows the pendulum to have picked up speed at an alarming rate in recent years, leaving already overscheduled modern kids stressed out, burned out, and wiped out.

Just how much homework *is* appropriate for a grade-school child? The National Association of Educators (NEA) and the National PTA recommend that nightly homework last approximately ten minutes per year of school. In other words, second-graders should have about twenty minutes a night and fourth-graders about forty.

If your child's homework time regularly exceeds this ballpark range, you've got some homework of your own to do—as your child's advocate. Ask other parents in the class if their kids are spending tons of time on homework too. If the answer is yes, try to round up a crowd and present your case to the school. And don't think a few parents can't make a big difference. Thanks to parents lobbying for less homework for their children, a school board in Piscataway, New Jersey, created a formal policy limiting the amount of homework teachers may assign each night.

If, however, you find that your child is spending far more time on her homework than her classmates are, you have a different problem on your hands—determining why it is taking your child so long to get through her assignments. Your first stop is ruling out any Jewish parent homework mistakes (particularly #3, pushing for homework perfection, and #8, expecting kids to be able to do homework anywhere and everywhere) as causative factors. Next, schedule a meeting with the teacher to discuss possible homework problems and solutions. Perhaps your child is having a hard time settling

down and would benefit from a timer being set. Perhaps she is placing too much pressure on herself to complete perfect work and
needs to be encouraged to loosen up a bit. Maybe your child is struggling with the material and needs additional academic support; or
is simply an inherently slow worker who would benefit from having
her assignments modified accordingly (i.e. only completing odd
numbered problems rather than the full page). If your child continues to spend an excessive amount on her homework even after
measures have been taken to increase her speed, an evaluation by
the school counselor or other professional may be in order.

Homework Mistake #8:
Not Knowing How to Handle the Big Ones

It never fails. Just when we've almost gotten the homework thing
under control, the teacher assigns a big one. They come in many
forms: tri-fold science fair displays; multifaceted book reports;
biographical essays to be accompanied by life-sized likenesses.
Name your poison, the reality remains: When the big ones hit, the
rules change. In other words, while fostering homework independence is still a primary goal, gargantuan, long-term assignments
require significantly more parental support and guidance than run-
of-the-mill homework.

This is not to say, of course, that we should go overboard by personally fashioning a plaster of paris bust of Junie B. Jones and trying
to pass it off as our child's work. But we should accept that not all
homework is created equal and adhere to the following parental
steps for managing the mega-assignment:

Step 1: Figure out your role. Some colossal assignments are meant to be a bonding opportunity between parent and child, others specifically call for minimal parent input. It's important to be clear on what our role is in the assignment from the get-go.

Step 2: Clarify the objective. Take a few moments when the project is first assigned to help your child understand the precise nature of the task. My son was once given an assignment to create a book report mobile, and it wasn't until he was halfway "finished" with the project that he asked me what a mobile was. If your child is having difficulty understanding his ultimate goal, ask the teacher if it might be possible to show the class a completed project from a previous year.

Step 3: Break it down. If the prospect of completing a long-term, multifaceted assignment can seem daunting to adults, it can feel positively mountainous to kids. We can help keep our kids from feeling overwhelmed by breaking down the project into small manageable tasks. Let's say your child is supposed to create a book report consisting of a three-paragraph summary and a three-dimensional diorama (a book report in a box, for all you rookies out there). It might be divided into the following subtasks:

    a. Read the book, taking notes of important events.
    b. Write a rough draft of the summary.
    c. Write a final draft of the summary.
    d. Obtain the box and materials for the diorama.
    e. Lay out the diorama without the glue.
    f. Glue down the diorama.

Step 4: Make a timeline. Even breaking down an assignment into manageable steps isn't enough to keep a procrastinator from waiting until day twenty-nine to get cracking on a monthlong project. The most effective way to avoid such chronological catastrophes is to pull out the calendar immediately upon completing Step 3 and set a deadline for each of the subtasks (taking into consideration, of course, that reading the book will take longer than gluing down the diorama).

Step 5: Pull out those cheerleading pom-poms. When an assignment drags on and on, it's easy for kids to get disheartened. We can help keep our kids feeling positive by offering up plenty of encouragement and deserved praise along the way.

Homework Mistake #9:
Having a Negative Attitude about Homework

Kids hate homework. And why not? It's difficult, time-consuming, and often downright boring. Still, when we parents join our children in complaining about their homework (or worse yet, bad-mouthing the teacher for assigning it in the first place), we only make the situation that much more torturous. If, on the other hand, we can muster a thumbs-up attitude about homework, studies show that our kids will be more internally driven to do their assignments and more successful at school in general.

Sure, you may be thinking. That sounds good in theory, but how can any reasonably sane person possibly achieve a positive attitude about homework?

Hey, even homework has a silver lining!

Homework provides the practice and repetition our kids need to solidify skills, while helping teachers monitor their progress. It arms our children with critical life skills—like organization, time management, and independent problem solving—while teaching them about hard work, personal responsibility, and accountability. By recognizing the purpose and inherent value of homework and approaching it with the right attitude, we'll help ensure our children reap its well-disguised benefits.

Jewish Parent 911

Reinforcing School Skills over the Summer

During the school year, academic skills are reinforced constantly via homework. Summertime is a completely different story, as most kids hardly pick up a pencil for the entirety of June, July, and August. No wonder studies show that students forget as much as 80 percent of what they were taught the previous year during the hot summer months.

So how do we help keep our children's hard-earned school skills fresh over the summer? By disguising academic reinforcement as summer fun and games!

Reinforce math skills using . . .
A deck of cards. The card game "War" provides an ideal means of solidifying basic facts. Begin by removing all face cards and placing the pile face down on the table. Players pick two cards each, then add,

subtract, or multiply the two numbers together (depending on the skill you're practicing). The high scorer collects all played cards.

A soccer ball. Use a permanent marker to randomly fill the hexagonal sections of a soccer ball with the numbers zero to ten (repeating the numbers until the ball is covered). Throw the ball to your child and have her add, subtract, or multiply the numbers closest to each thumb. See how many times you can toss the ball back and forth without making a mistake.

A basketball hoop. Get basic math facts in all-star shape with a slam dunk competition. Every time your child answers a math question correctly let him take a shot. Offer a prize when he reaches a designated number of points.

Beads and string. Fractions can make a fashion statement when kids string necklaces with colored beads. Challenge your child to make a necklace that is half blue or one-quarter red.

A calculator. Kids love anything that involves a race, so they're all over "The Calculator vs. The Brain" game. Assign a "caller," a "calculator," and a "brain" at the start of each round. The caller states a math problem; the "calculator" manually punches the problem into his number-crunching device (even if he already knows the answer), while the brain solves the problem mentally. The first player to offer the correct answer wins the round. Keep switching roles. (Hint: you'll know this game is working when kids start begging to be the "brain.")

M&M's. Give your child a math story problem and have her "act it out" using the colorful candies (i.e., "I had six M&M's and my mom gave me eight more. How many do I have now?"). I'll have to admit to favoring subtraction story problems when M&M's are involved (for obvious reasons).

Loose change. Have children grab a handful of loose change, estimate the value, and count out the true amount. Offer a 10 percent prize for close guesses.

Reinforce language arts skills using . . .

A wooden block. Write the words *who, what, where, when, why,* and *how* on the faces of a block. After reading a book or chapter with your child, take turns rolling the block and asking and answering story-related questions beginning with the word on top (i.e., *who* are the characters in the story? *where* do they live?).

Magazines and comic books. Even kids who cringe at the thought of reading a book cover to cover jump at the chance to flip through comics and magazines. Sneak in extra reading practice by stocking up on kid-friendly periodicals.

Shaving cream. Cover a tabletop with plastic wrap and make a gooey shaving-cream palette where little fingers can practice letters, spelling words, and handwriting.

Mad Libs. These wacky fill-in-the-blank activities provide a fun and effective way to reinforce parts of speech. (And remember, "booger" is a noun.)

A timer. Designate a few times a week as family D.E.A.R. (Drop Everything and Read) time. Set the timer for twenty or thirty minutes of silent literary bliss.

Index cards. Write the letters of a mystery word on blank index cards; scramble them up and have kids try to decode the secret word.

CD player. Round up the whole family to participate in "musical stories," an adaptation of musical chairs. All participants sit around a table with paper and a pencil in front of them. When the music starts, they begin writing a creative story, stopping when it ceases. Participants then stand up and move to the chair at their left, leaving their story behind. When the tunes resume they add to the story at their new seat. Keep going until players are back where they started and can see what became of their original tales.

Sidewalk chalk. Writing your spelling words on plain old paper may be snooze city, but scrawling them across the driveway is a totally different story. Chalk up the mess to academic advancement and let the rain take care of the cleanup!

CHAPTER 6

Extra, Extra,
Extracurriculars

I haven't told you a story since way back in the kindergarten chapter.
I'd say it's high time for another . . .

Howie and Goldie

*Once upon a time on a Wednesday, before chess club and after tennis team, two
Jewish children named Howie and Goldie decided to go on an afternoon walk
through the woods. They were so eager to commence their journey they didn't even
complain when their parents made them practice piano for thirty uninterrupted
minutes and have a brief kid-on-kid soccer scrimmage in the backyard before
they left. As soon as their mom gave them the go-ahead, Howie and Goldie
grabbed the rolling backpacks full of matzoh balls she'd packed for a snack,
kissed the mezuzah, and began their excursion.*

*Unfortunately, amid the exhaustive preparations the kids inadvertently left
their cell phones on the kitchen table. With no way to contact their parents for
navigational support they needed an alternate strategy. Luckily, Goldie, who
had just completed a six-week extracurricular enrichment course in critical
thinking and problem-solving skills, came up with a seemingly seamless plan.
The pair would use the not-too-hard, not-too-soft spherical delicacies in their
backpacks to make a trail that would lead them back home. But alas, Goldie neglected to consider that a wild gefilte fish might eat all the loose matzoh balls,
leaving the kids lost in the woods far longer than the fifty-five-minute time slot
their mother had designated in their schedule as forest walking time . . .*

What do you mean, you've heard enough? I haven't even gotten to the part about the mandel bread house. Or how Howie and Goldie begged the witch to let them move in so they could escape their overscheduled existence!

Oh well, you probably think I'm giving extracurriculars a bad rap, but really, I'm not. In fact, I'll be the first to admit that extracurricular activities play a central role in our kids' social, emotional, and physical development and well-being. The trouble is that while healthy doses of extracurriculars offer our children all kinds of delicious perks, in excess (as we discussed in Chapter 1) they can lead to any number of unsavory results—from anxiety and depression to psychosomatic and physical complaints to being burnt out on life before bar or bat mitzvah age.

So how do we enable our children to enjoy all the yummy benefits of extracurriculars without becoming maxed out, stressed out, and wiped out in the process? By balancing their activities with ample doses of downtime. You know, *downtime*—the lost art of doing absolutely nothing!

I know, it just doesn't feel right to let our kids spend extended periods of time without a planned purpose or destination. It seems so acutely unconstructive. But the amazing thing about downtime is that it *is* constructive. In fact, experts believe downtime can be as, if not more, constructive than all of our children's extracurricular activities combined. After all, it's only during bona fide downtime that our kids have a chance to be absolutely, unequivocally *bored*.

Did I miss something? You may be wondering. Since when is being bored a productive use of my child's time?

Sure, it seems counterintuitive for staring into space to rival a yellow belt karate class in terms of constructiveness, but it's true! In fact psychologist Mihaly Csikszentmihalyi, author of the highly acclaimed *Creativity: Flow and the Psychology of Discovery and Invention*, found that some of the most ingenious ideas on the planet were generated during stretches of stark boredom, and that one of the main characteristics of profoundly creative people is that they spend oodles of time doing nothing.

Only by allowing our kids to reach the bedrock of boredom—without a parent, coach, remote control, video-game joystick, or computer mouse to bail them out—will we set the magic in motion. Only then will the light switch of creativity that's been superglued in the off position by back-to-back extracurriculars suddenly turn on inside their brains as they work to devise a boredom-busting plan—a resourceful plan like building a fort out of chairs and blankets; a creative plan like staging a skit complete with costumes and scenery; an inventive plan like constructing an entire city out of blocks—the kind of resourceful, creative, inventive plan that will one day catapult our children much farther in life than superb soccer skills, picture-perfect pirouettes, and killer karate kicks ever could.

This is not to say, of course, that we should go to the opposite extreme and ban extracurriculars altogether, but we do need to keep them in a beneficial and manageable realm. While there's clearly no magic number (extracurriculars vary greatly in terms of frequency and intensity), a general rule of thumb is no more than two activities per season. If Hebrew school, tutoring, or other after-school commitments are in play, reduce that number to one.

Helping Kids Make the Most of Downtime

Okay, so you let your kid get completely bored and he never got past the staring into space stage. Or the only plan he devised involved slugging his sibling. Don't worry, you're not alone. The reality is that many kids need a kick-start to make the most of their downtime. We can provide them with just that—without squelching their budding independence—by helping them create a "what to do during downtime" idea list. Here are some suggestions to bring to the table:

- Design a driveway mural with washable paint.
- Put on a skit, complete with costumes and scenery.
- Play paper football and make your own ball and field.
- Create a spooky haunted house in the basement.
- Organize a backyard picnic.
- Have a paper-airplane-flying competition.
- Decorate a tzedakah box for a particular cause.
- Write and illustrate an original story.
- Record a book on tape for a younger child to enjoy.
- Invent a new board game (or play an old one).
- Design your own stationery with stamps, markers, and stickers and use it to write a letter to someone special.

You might be wondering why well-meaning parents pour on the extracurriculars like horseradish sauce on gefilte fish. As I see it, there are two reasons. First are the Mommy 500 pressures that we discussed in detail in Chapter 1. A close second is a phenomenon I think of as the Diner Menu Effect.

The Diner Menu Effect

Born and raised south of the Mason-Dixon Line, I didn't step foot in a diner until I was in graduate school. I was floored, therefore, when the waitress handed me a menu offering three hundred–plus options.

Head spinning, I tried to make sense of the myriad of palatable possibilities. *Do I want spinach lasagna or stuffed grape leaves? Matzoh ball soup or bean burritos? Bagels and lox or baklava?* But to no avail. I ended up ordering way too much, and leaving the diner overstuffed and undersatisfied.

Similarly, when we are selecting extracurriculars for our kids, the sheer breadth of possibility can be overwhelming. Ballet or hip-hop? Baseball or soccer? Science club or cub scouts? Not wanting our children to miss out on anything, we sign them up for everything, only to end up with exhausted, stressed kids who are unable to truly appreciate any of their activities.

Yet if we can manage to take a deep breath and listen to our parental guts, the options don't seem nearly as daunting. We are suddenly capable of using our intuitive understanding of our children to make wise choices regarding their extracurriculars: "I would like my daughter to take twice-weekly private violin lessons, but she's such a social butterfly, perhaps she should start with group lessons" . . . "True, I was a softball star in college and was hoping to coach my child's Little League team one day, but the reality is he would rather be painting than pitching, so my dream will need to take a backseat to art lessons for the time being" . . . "I know all the other parents swear by that big prestigious soccer league, but it seems a little intense for my daughter, who tends to crack under pressure. Perhaps I should look for a more laid-back program where she can play soccer without all the stress" . . . "I was really hoping to sign my son up for an extracurricular this fall, but he seems so overwhelmed with homework and Hebrew school that I'm afraid another commitment will push him over the edge. Looks like a fall extracurricular siesta is in order."

In our parental gut we have the perspective and insight we need to ensure our kids have happy, healthy, fulfilling extracurricular experiences.

Free Samplin'

Okay, you may be thinking. I listened to my parental gut, but I'm still having trouble narrowing down the list of possibilities. Now what?

The truth is that even post heart-to-gut conversation, we can still be unclear on which activities would make the best matches for our child. Some kids are mega-versatile with tons of interests. Others don't seem interested in doing anything other than hanging out at home. In cases of hard-to-peg children, the extracurricular taste test is the way to go.

Check the local paper for weekend sports clinics for kids. Ask nearby karate, dance, or art studios if they offer trial classes. Explore weeklong specialty summer camp options. Inquire about short-term instrument rentals from a music center. Check with neighborhood arts and crafts stores to see if they offer one-time classes. Keep the samples coming until your child finds an activity that he wants to commit to for the season.

The Top Three Fab Reasons
Parents Enroll Kids in Extracurriculars:

1. To give them a fun and constructive alternative to watching TV and playing video games.
2. To provide them with social, emotional, and physical benefits.
3. To help them pursue their personal passions.

The Top Three Not-So-Fab Reasons
Parents Enroll Kids in Extracurriculars:

1. To keep up with the Jonesbergs.
2. To beef up their college résumés.
3. To help them pursue *our* personal passions.

The Hidden Costs of Extracurriculars

Caught up in the heat of sign-up day, we rarely consider the possibility of an extracurricular becoming a money pit apt to deplete our checking account, or a thirsty sponge waiting to sop up our family's every free minute—and especially not a danger zone that could compromise our child's safety and/or physical development. But depending on the type of extracurricular, the philosophy of the individual program, and our child's level of involvement, this is precisely what it can become.

Before jumping head first into an extracurricular, therefore, we should take a good, hard look at what may be lurking beyond the application.

Soccer

Financial: Average cost for recreational teams generally runs $100+ per fall or spring season, more for traveling teams. Uniforms (socks, shirts, and shorts) are usually included. Shin guards, cleats, and balls usually are not, so tack on another $30 or so.

Logistical: For children under eight, count on a one-hour to hour-and-a-half-long afternoon practice per week and one weekend game. Add one or two additional practices as kids get older and more competitive—possibly more than that if they join a select league.

Physical: Many experts tout soccer as the safest organized sport, which may be why it's also the most popular among parents. The American Youth Soccer Organization discourages "heading" (using the head to hit the ball) for younger players. Other soccer-related risks include tripping, getting hit in the face with a flying ball, and getting caught up in the net. Soccer also requires a lot of running back and forth, which can be tough in extreme heat or cold.

Hockey/Figure Skating

Financial: Hockey: $25 to be a member of USA Hockey; about $300 for equipment. As your child moves up, team fees may be $500 to $700 per fall/winter season. Skating: Ice time is about $9 per hour for practice. Coaching fees start at $20 per half hour; group lessons are about $75 for seven weeks. Skates are $50 to $400.

Logistical: Hockey: about two hours a week; more for traveling teams. Skating: an hour a week for beginners to four hours a day for advanced skaters. Keep in mind that hockey and skating have odd hours, from very early to very late.

Physical: Hockey injuries generally involve a thigh, wrist, or shoulder. Skating injuries are mostly bumps and bruises. Still, the ice can be unforgiving and poses an undeniable risk.

Gymnastics

Financial: $60–$70 per month at the recreational level (ages six to nine). Should you cross into the competitive realm expect $200–$300 dollars a month for lessons and coaching. Meets, USA or AAU membership, and coaches' appropriation fees will put you out several hundred more a year. Gymnastics team and competitive attire can cost a pretty penny too.

Logistical: An hour per week at the recreational level; between twelve and twenty hours a week at the compulsory and optional levels. (Yes, you read that right. In fact many serious gymnasts are home schooled for this reason.)

Physical: In addition to the obvious broken bone/concussion–type threats, female gymnasts may experience stunted growth and late-starting menstrual cycles.

Dance

Financial: Approximately $15–$20 per hour for a group lesson. Tack on dance shoes, leotards, tights, and recital costumes, and fees are almost certain to reach well into the hundreds of dollars.

Logistical: One hour a week at first, which builds to two, then three times a week by age nine, and eventually daily hourlong lessons.

Physical: Pointe ballet, when started too early, has been found to harm ankle and foot development and cause arthritis.

Swimming

Financial: Summer programs can cost $100 to $150; year-round (October–March) seasons run $400–$500 plus a team suit (about $35 for girls, $20 for boys). Swim cap and goggles are extra.

Logistical: Many teams practice one hour per day, two to five days a week with four-hour meets on weekends. Meets begin early in the morning, as do most summer practices.

Physical: Swimming comes through with high marks as the most injury-free of competitive sports. Coaches should be trained, of course, in CPR, first aid, and water-safety instruction.

Drama

Financial: From $150 to $550 for an eight-week workshop, depending on region of the country.

Logistical: Classes usually meet for one hour per week, sometimes twice a week. Count in extra time for rehearsing lines at home, dress rehearsals, and performances as well.

Physical: Other than falling scenery and some preperformance jitters, drama gets a thumbs up on the safety front.

Basketball

Financial: Around the $100 mark for eight- to ten-week leagues. Traveling and competitive leagues jack up the price. Basketball shirts are generally included; basketball shoes and balls are not.

Logistical: One hour of practice and one game per week for a typical league. Traveling or competitive leagues require a much heavier time commitment including longer daily practices and games at least once or twice a week.

Physical: Most basketball injuries are of the bump and bruise variety. Make sure kids' laces are tied to prevent unnecessary spills on a superhard wood floor.

Cheerleading

Financial: $15–$20 per basic group lessons and/or $50 for individual lessons. Count on upwards of $1,000 per year for uniforms, matching sweatshirts, shoes, socks, pom-poms, competitive or game day apparatus, and league and coaching fees. Meet, travel, and grooming fees can also add up.

Logistical: An hour a week at a basic level, upwards of six hours a week for more advanced cheerleaders. Meets can last all day or weekend, plus traveling time.

Physical: Broken bones, sprains, and concussions are the most frequent injuries. Of course things like back handsprings and kids throwing other kids up in the air pose more significant risks, by design.

Art

Financial: Cost depends on length of program, teacher qualifications, and whether materials are included, but expect around $100 for a six-week class in painting or drawing. Keep in mind that art supplies can be expensive and are needed to practice skills after the class is over.

Logistical: About an hour of class time per week plus any practice time. Some classes might have some homework.

Physical: Some art materials can be dangerous to kids if ingested or inhaled.

Baseball/Softball

Financial: League play is usually $100+ per season; generally includes a team T-shirt or jersey and cap—more for all-star or traveling leagues. Gloves, batting gloves, appropriately sized bats and cleats can get you for another 150 buckaroos.

Logistical: Count on practices anywhere from one to four nights a week. Seasons usually run 14 to 24 games (usually two to three games per week).

Physical: With hard balls and bats, plenty can happen. Players are required to wear batting helmets, catchers to wear protective gear. Older boys should wear cups. There is also a growing trend for players to wear chest guards.

Football

Financial: From $100 per season for league play. Other costs include cleats, helmet, and pads, so tack on another $100+.

Logistical: Lots of football programs offer summer training, which can consume up to ten hours a week. After school begins, expect at least three two-hour practice sessions and one game per week.

Physical: *Oy vey.* Tackle football has been found hands down to be the riskiest organized sport around. Not only does it push kids to their outer limits physically, it's entire premise is—my apologies to any hard-core football fans out there—positively barbaric. Bruises, sprains, fractures, and concussions are the most common football injuries at the grade-school level, but far worse can and does happen—even with protective equipment.

Music

Financial: About $20 per half hour for private lessons. Instruments can run into mega-bucks. Fortunately, most instruments (even pianos) can be rented until you know your child is going to stick with it for the long haul. Depending on the instrument, quarterly rental can run about $100, which can usually be applied to buying the instrument.

Logistical: Weekly lesson time plus daily practice time (experts recommend two 15-minute periods daily for younger children, and building to a 30-minute practice for older ones).

Physical: Safe as safe can be.

Quitsville

So you went to all lengths to pick an activity that matched your child's individual interests and needs. You made sure you understood the hidden costs, risks, and time constraints before signing on the dotted line. And your child is still begging to quit two weeks into the season! Now what?

A child's decision to bag an extracurricular midway through is as frustrating to parents as it is complex. We don't want our child to be miserable but we also don't want her to think she can bolt from anything remotely boring, unpleasant, or challenging. We want to teach our child the importance of living up to her commitments, but we hate to subject her to undue stress. We don't want our kid to waste her limited extracurricular time on something she doesn't enjoy, but we'd also like to see a bit of return on our hundred-fifty-dollar investment.

Further complicating the situation is that—as I mentioned before—all extracurriculars are not created equal. Some are short in duration but high in intensity. Others are moderate in intensity but go on indefinitely. Still others are both intense and never-ending.

The range of possible solutions runs the gamut as well. Sometimes we can easily ascertain the source of our child's discontent and simply address the issue (our daughter hates piano because she's been playing "Yankee Doodle" for the past three months, but it's nothing a little Kelly Clarkson sheet music can't take care of). Other times it's perfectly clear that an activity is not a good match for our child (our son would rather pull his toenails out with pliers than take another fencing lesson). Sometimes we deem the activity essential whether our kid likes it or not (learning to swim), other times the extracurricular seems simply frivolous (competitive video gaming).

In other words, while I wish I could tell you that the old "winners never quit and quitters never win" lecture will do the trick every time, I'd be lying if I did. Here are some important questions to consider when determining whether your child's extracurricular troubles truly warrant a midseason finish.

- Is my child the type to take the easy way out or is this uncharacteristic?
- How much longer is this activity going to last? Is it feasible for my child to see his commitment through?
- Does the trouble appear linked to the activity itself? To a teacher or coach? To some other factor?
- Are other kids on the team experiencing similar difficulties?
- Do I have a bad attitude about the coach or activity that may have rubbed off on my child?
- Has my child quit other extracurriculars before? Is a pattern developing?
- By my own assessment is the situation truly unbearable?
- Is my child overscheduled and desperate for a break?
- Is my child's participation in the extracurricular interfering with her emotional or academic well-being?
- What message am I sending my child in allowing him to quit? What message am I sending in not allowing him to quit?

When Hebrew School and Extracurriculars Conflict

Every parent must work to find a healthy balance between activities, downtime, and school; but many Jewish parents have an extra piece to work into the extracurricular puzzle—Hebrew school. Since Hebrew school can meet three or more times a week (depending on the synagogue and level of observance), running into a conflict with extracurriculars at one time or another is a virtual certainty.

While there's no one-size-fits-all answer for resolving the Hebrew school–extracurricular conflict, we can make our decision easier by using the split-screen strategy. You know, the split screen we used back in Chapter 4 during the Teacher from the Black Lagoon crisis? It was much easier to make a tough call regarding our child when we considered how it might play out in the future. Well, we can use exactly the same approach here. Take the following representative scenario:

Your son has been invited to play on an exclusive all-star traveling baseball team with mandatory practices Monday through Thursday from 5 to 7 P.M. You are kvelling, of course, and can't wait to start spreading the exciting news, but there's a glitch: Hebrew school is on Tuesday and Thursday nights from 5:30 to 7 and being on the team would mean ducking out of learning his *aleph bets* for the season.

That's when you should take a good hard look at the split screen. On one screen you see your child looking so cute in his baseball uniform with the words "All Star" glistening across his chest, and begging you to let him be on the traveling team. He already knows Hebrew he tells you, and besides, his bar mitzvah is three whole years away!

On the other screen there's your child as an adult. And at least for a moment you see the next Sandy Koufax (you know—the Jewish pitcher who refused to pitch in the World Series because it landed on Yom Kippur!). But then you get real. After all, while your kid may be a Little League all-star, chances are slim that he—or any of his teammates—will ever make it to the major leagues. Besides, even if he does make it to the major leagues, chances are even slimmer he'd make the same choice as Sandy Koufax if faced with a similar decision. After all, his Judaism has taken a back burner to his baseball since way back in Little League when he bailed out on an entire semester of Hebrew school to play on the all-star team.

Don't get me wrong here. I'm not suggesting that we should rule out all-star teams for Hebrew-school students across the board. But we should take the time to explore all of our options (i.e., signing up our little shortstop for a league that has fewer practices on nights that don't interfere with Hebrew school, or talking to the coach about reaching a compromise) and consider the long-term impact of our choices, before making a decision.

And a Cherry on Top . . .

My father, a psychologist and researcher at MARIAL, the Center for Myth and Ritual in American Life at Emory University, often jokes that when twenty-first-century kids grow up, their definition of comfort food—meals that spark fond memories of childhood—will be anything eaten out of a paper bag in the backseat of a mini-van. While this image makes us laugh, it also tears at our heartstrings, for we know it is true. In fact studies show one in three toys received by an American child is delivered via a drive-thru window.

Unfortunately, the prevalence of Happy Meals in modern kids' lives represents far more than an onslaught of cheap imported action figures. It represents the demise of the old-fashioned family dinner.

Just how close to brontosaurus status is the family dinner? So close that in 2001 the National Center on Addiction and Substance Abuse (CASA) and Coca-Cola teamed up to launch an annual "Family Day," designed to encourage families to sit down and eat dinner together on the fourth Monday in September. The government even provided a list of tips and suggestions for parents on facilitating this annual event, including the following: eat dinner together; during dinner, turn off the TV and talk and listen to each other; involve the entire family in planning and cooking the meal.

Family dinners are nice, you may be thinking. But government mandates, major corporate involvement, research centers devoted almost exclusively to studying them—isn't it all a tad extreme?

It certainly might appear that eating a plate of pasta with our kids is an insignificant event in the scheme of things, but a plethora of recent research suggests that simple family dinners may in fact be among our most powerful parenting tools. Studies show that kids whose families have regular meals together tend to have higher self-esteem, interact better with their peers, and show higher resilience in the face of adversity. CASA and other large-scale studies found family dinners to be the single most significant preventive predictor of smoking, drinking, illegal drug use, experimentation with sex, even fistfights in children. Still other studies show regular family mealtimes to be linked with kids who are more emotionally content, work harder and perform better in school, and have better social skills and healthier eating habits. (Amazingly, these results apply regardless of a child's gender, family structure, or socioeconomic level and hold true for as little as one family dinner a week.)

Perhaps the most salient rewards of the family meals, however, are those that can't be measured: the happy buzz of stories passing between parent and child; kids wrapped securely in the familiar comforts of home.

Luckily, our decision to limit our children's extracurriculars to a glorious few and give them the delectable gift of downtime comes with a big juicy cherry on top—newfound opportunity for enjoyable, resilience-building, *legitimate* self-esteem-building (see Chapter 2), social-skill-enhancing, nutritionally advantageous family dinners. And you've got to admit, they don't make cherries on top much juicier than that.

Jewish Parent 911

Making the Most of Your Time in the Car

Let's face it. Even after we scale down the extracurricular load, our kids are bound to spend a hefty chunk of their childhood in transit. But we needn't write off all those hours on the go as wasted time. In fact, with creativity and forethought we can turn boring old car time into something that's fun as well as meaningful and valuable. So unplug the DVD player, turn off the hand-held video games, and try out some of the following ideas.

Talk. Especially for children who are private, the car provides an ideal, unintimidating venue for catching up. So throw out a few casual questions that require an answer besides yes or no. What was the best part of your day at school today? What was the worst part? Has anything funny happened at school lately?

Pop in a book on tape. Unlike passively watching a DVD, books on tape require children to actively listen and create their own imagery to go along with the words. Tapes of books like the Harry Potter series promise to fill rush hour after rush hour with so much whimsy and excitement you and your children actually look forward to hanging out in the car. (Note: since books on tape can be very pricey, renting, borrowing from the library, or buying a secondhand copy is your best bet.)

Make a "popcorn" story. Tap into your kids' creative juices while enhancing family connections by creating a cooperative tale on the go. Have one person in the car begin a fictional story. "Once upon a time there was a green, furry goblin . . . " When the storyteller finds herself at a loss for where to go next, she says "Popcorn . . . Mom!" That's Mom's cue to pick up where the story left off. Keep going around like this until you arrive at your destination or your cooperative story reaches a logical conclusion.

Play around with the alphabet. Alphabetical games are always a hit on the road. Of course there's always the garden variety: "I'm going on a trip and I'm taking an apple," at which point the next player says, "I'm going on a trip and I'm taking a balloon." But once kids get older it's time to kick up the difficulty. "My name is Allison, I live in Alabama, and I like aardvarks," "My name is Brandon, I live in Belgium, and I like brownies."

It's in the bag. Keep a bag of fun, creativity-boosting materials in the car. Legos, pipe cleaners, "model magic" clay, and "wicky sticks" (wax-covered sticks that can be found in most craft stores) provide end-less inventive possibilities.

Create a traveling library. Unless your kids get carsick, keeping a collection of books on hand in the minivan is a great way to help kids productively pass the time in transit. Swap out your library collection periodically to keep it fresh and enticing.

CHAPTER 7

The Schoolyard
Social Jungle

If my years of working with Jewish parents has made one thing clear, it is that there is no place our primal maternal instincts are more pronounced than in the depths of the kiddie social jungle. No, I'm not referring to a scene from *The Lion King!* I'm talking about the treacherous terrain known as the grade-school playground.

If you are new to the elementary social scene, you are likely doubting my sanity right now. Treacherous terrain? Social jungle? Isn't that a bit extreme? My kids' preschool playground is a charming little place. How bad could a bunch of swings and a seesaw be?

Pretty darn bad. Let me give you a nutshell course in childhood social development in order to illuminate how a preschool and grade-school playground could look virtually identical, but be as diametrically opposed as Queen Esther and Haman.

Back when our kids were in preschool, the playground was all about, well, playing. It was a place where they could bubble over with imagination and be anyone they'd ever wanted to be—from Superman to Dora the Explorer to SpongeBob SquarePants. Developmentally egocentric (they really did think the world revolved around them!), our preschoolers summed up the other kids on the playground as really fun animated playthings plopped down between the slide and the sandbox for the sole purpose of their personal entertainment. This is why psychologist Stanley Greenspan refers to the preschool years as the "world is my oyster" period of childhood.

Somewhere around first grade, children undergo a metamorphosis in terms of their social development—a cognitive transition that will ultimately allow them to become independent, strong, socially competent adults, but not before causing them a substantial amount of social heartache.

Like Superman after he's changed back to Clark Kent, grade-school-age children shed their superhero "I can be anyone and anything I want to be" mentality for a more vulnerable outlook. Suddenly clued in to the fact that an entire life exists outside themselves, the grade-schooler is thrust into a dog-eat-dog world, defined by those formerly fun playthings parked between the slide and the sandbox—their peers. Greenspan calls this stage "The World Is Other Kids." It is this cognitive shift that leaves the elementary and—even more so—the middle-school playground far less about play than about social power.

At the top of the playground social ladder (which experts say is already in place by the time children are seven or eight) are the *alpha males*, an elite group of physically adept, socially powerful boys, and the *queen bees*—socially gifted, pretty girls who gather a court of supportive, less confident girls around them. The vast remainder of the playground's inhabitants devote themselves to gaining as much social power as possible in order to make their way up the ladder.

How does one go about getting this coveted grade-school social power? By being accepted by the group—an *exclusive* group. Girls form "clubs," boys form "teams," feeling their social power soar as someone else's plummets. No wonder recent studies reveal that 80 percent of school-age children have been teased, taunted, bullied, excluded from the crowd, or otherwise tormented socially—within the past month!

It's rocky ground indeed, especially since it brings to the surface all the playground anguish we'd long tucked away from our own grade-school days. The harsh reality is that even if we stand on the playground day in and day out, we can't shield our kids from feeling playground-induced pain. How do I know? I tried it.

When Brandon was in second grade, I was teaching the second-grade class next door. A few of the boys in my class were the self-proclaimed kings of the football field and wouldn't allow any of the other second-graders to be quarterback. Brandon had his heart set on just that.

The first day, I stood on recess duty hoping that my presence alone would encourage my students to let my son hike the ball. No dice. The next day, I strongly encouraged the kings of the football field to share the joy of playing the primo position. Still, no dice.

Becoming more emotionally involved than I felt professionally appropriate, I passed the ball to the school counselor. She posted a schedule at recess specifying a different quarterback each day. Sounds like a great idea! Right? Wrong. On the days that the kings of the football field were not designated as quarterback, they convinced the troops to play basketball instead.

Alright, you may be thinking, you're telling me there's not a darn thing I can do to shield my kids from feeling schoolyard-induced emotional hardship. Does that mean I'm supposed to sit back and watch from the sidelines as they take social hits?

I'm not saying that at all, because what we *can't* do is only half of the story. It is true that we can't *shield* our kids from *tzar gidul banim* (a Hebrew phrase that refers to the intrinsic emotional pain of childhood), but we can *protect* them from it.

You're probably thinking, Protect . . . shield . . . What's the difference? I don't have time to worry about semantics when my kid is being socially tortured on the monkey bars this very minute!

Okay, here's the bottom line. We parents may not have a chance of keeping our kids from ever feeling the wrath of the social jungle, but we can do everything in our power to prepare them for their journey. No, I'm not talking about bubble wrap! I'm talking about social resilience, the ability to roll with the playground punches.

When children are socially resilient, their inevitable playground social setbacks become bumps in the blacktop rather than all out roadblocks. The daily social hits they endure may make them cringe, but never crumble. We can go about instilling this vital trait of social resilience by embracing the following four fundamental parenting practices:

1. Focus on friendships rather than popularity
2. Display social equanimity
3. Foster *realistic* self-esteem
4. Incorporate family rituals into your daily life

If you incorporate these practices into your daily family life, I promise the inherently bumpy travels that lie ahead in the school-yard social jungle for both you and your kids will be that much smoother.

Social Resilience-Building Practice #1:
Focus on Friendships Rather than Popularity

Among the most detrimental myths floating around the modern maternal population is that kids can be socially content only if they collect friends like Pokémon cards. But you have to believe me when

I tell you that a sandboxful of research shows sky-high playground popularity to be neither a realistic nor a remotely appropriate aspiration for us to hold for our children.

Studies consistently find that on any given school playground at any given time, the following statistics are apt to apply: 15 percent of the children will be wildly popular, 10 percent will be socially rejected, and 75 percent will fall somewhere in the middle. In other words, it's a safe bet that our son or daughter will be neither the most popular kid in the crowd nor the least popular. And that's okay. Really! Because despite diehard societal belief to the contrary, the evidence does not suggest that the supercool popular kids are any happier than anyone else in the pile.

What the research *does* overwhelmingly suggest is that it is friendship (not a nice cozy spot at the top of the popularity food chain) that arms kids to weather the inevitable rejection, disappointments, and losses of playground social existence—that the freckle-faced kid who hangs out with your child at recess (that's right, the one with his finger permanently wedged up his nose) is your chief ally in fostering social resilience in your grade-schooler.

Unfortunately, in modern-day America forming old-fashioned social-resilience-building friendships is no easy task. I mean, who has time for bonding with buddies when you are being shuttled from school to Little League practice to piano lessons to Hebrew school? And how are kids supposed to learn to negotiate the rules of the game with other kids when they always have a referee an arm's distance away? But there's still plenty we can do to ensure that our kids receive the skills, concepts, and opportunity they need to build healthy friendships.

Teach the Art of Friendship Through TV, Movies, and Books

We would never doubt that children require direct instruction to learn to read and write, so why would we assume they can figure out the art of friendship on their own? Sure, some kids are born socially gifted with a knack for making friends. But many kids need specific direction and guidance to maximize their chances of building meaningful peer relationships.

This is not to say that we should start throwing friendship workbooks at kids or have long, boring conversations about the true meaning of trust and dependability. We're better off sneaking in the back door with characters in our children's favorite TV shows, movies, and books who demonstrate the art of making and keeping friends.

TV and Movie Characters
Television may feel like the bane of our parental existence, but c'mon, the invention that brought us *Desperate Housewives* can't be all bad! The truth is that TV offers ideal opportunities to teach our kids about friendship. If your daughter is watching the Rugrats, for example, point out how Tommy is a loyal and caring buddy because he shared his last cookie with Chuckie. And how nobody wants to be with Angelica because she is so darn bossy! Make a bowl of popcorn and plop down with your son to watch a Harry Potter flick, as Hogwarts offers numerous lessons in friendship for muggles and non-muggles alike.

Books
The library is one of our richest resources for finding models for friendship. Almost every children's book includes a friendship in some form. The point here is to read the book *with* your child so you can stop and discuss ideas along the way. Ask open-ended questions

as you go: How do the characters treat one another? What kinds of things do they do together? How do they resolve conflicts? How could they have avoided conflict in the first place? (What you don't want to do is tell your kid to go read a chapter of *Charlotte's Web* in her room while you do the dishes and then give her a pop quiz when she returns on the progression of Wilbur the pig and Charlotte the spider's relationship.)

Don't assume older children are above sitting and reading a book with you either. Most middle-schoolers thrill to the chance to read and discuss a book with a parent (as long as there are no other middle-schoolers around to see!). If your child is having a particular friendship issue—maybe her best friend is moving away, or she is especially shy—ask the librarian to suggest a story dealing with that particular topic.

Here are some of my favorite books for teaching the art of friendship to kids:

Books That Model Friendship:

Ages 5–8

The Popcorn Dragon by Jane Thayer

Ice Bear and Little Fox by Jonathan London

Hot Day on Abbott Avenue by Karen English

Tacky in Trouble by William Lester

George and Martha: The Complete Story of Two Best Friends by James Marshall

Frog and Toad Are Friends by Arnold Lobel

Stella Luna by Janell Cannon

Sitting Ducks by Michael Beddard
You're Not My Best Friend Anymore by Charlotte Pomerantz

Ages 9–13
There's a Boy in the Girl's Bathroom by Louis Sachar
How to Be Cool in the Third Grade by Betsey Duffy
Skinnybones by Barbara Park
Class Clown by Johanna Hurwitz
The BFG by Roald Dahl
Harriet the Spy by Louise Fitzhugh
Maniac McGee by Jerry Spinelli
From the Mixed-Up Files of Mrs. Basil E. Frankweiler by E. L. Konigsburg
The Secret Garden by F. H. Burnett
Bridge to Terabithia by Katherine Paterson
Freak the Mighty by Rodbin Philbrick

Jewish Books on Friendship
Molly's Pilgrim by Barbara Cohen (ages 5–8)
Ike and Mama and the Once-a-Year Suit by Carol Snyder (ages 5–8)
Number the Stars by Lois Lowry (grades 9–12)
Once I Was a Plum Tree by Johanna Hurwitz (ages 9–12)
About the B'nai Bagels by E. L. Konigsburg (ages 9–12)
The Chosen by Chaim Potok (ages 11 and up)
Running on Eggs by Anna Levine (ages 9–12)

Find Models in Other Kids

We need to be careful with this strategy as we don't want our kids to feel that we are sizing them up against other kids. Nevertheless, I've found in my teaching experience that no one can drive a point home to a child like another child. This is why ten minutes of observing other kids play can teach our budding socialites volumes about how to make and be friends.

You'll want to select a neutral venue. Go to a park where your child won't know anyone. Or ask the school if you can sit at recess with your kid when another grade is outside playing. Tell your son or daughter that you are being private investigators and you want to find out which children are well liked by the other kids and which ones don't seem to have friends. What behaviors might they want to emulate themselves on the playground? What behaviors should they try to avoid? You'll be amazed how meaningful an activity this will be to both you and your kids.

Role-Play Important Friend-Making Skills

Let me start this one off by saying that role-playing is virtually guaranteed to make both you and your kids feel like total goobers. Nevertheless, this valuable activity takes some of the mystique of the social jungle away for kids by offering direction and practice opportunities, so you may as well go for it! Your best bet is to make role-playing feel like a game—somewhere in the neighborhood of charades. Here are some key skills to cover in your role-playing endeavors:

Entering a Group

Make sure your kids understand that smiling and establishing eye contact is a natural first step in breaking into a playground pack. They also should know that it's important to take the time to listen and find out what the other kids are talking about before jumping into a conversation. When giving children direction in group entry skills, it's important to get into the schoolyard mind-set (in other words, don't have kids role-play formal introductions and hand-shaking techniques). The lingo you want to convey is more to this effect: "Hi, I'm Alex. Do you guys need another player on the team?" or "This looks fun—is it okay if I play, too?"

Initiating a Conversation

Asking other kids about themselves is always a strategic conversation starter. Together with your child make a list of high-interest, "mainstream" questions he can ask to engage his peers. "Did you see the new *Scooby-Doo and the Invaders* movie?" "Do you collect Webkinz?" "Do you like Abercrombie Kids or Limited Too better?" "What is your favorite show on Nickelodeon?" "Do you like the Red Sox or the Braves better?" Keep rehearsing and feeling like goobers until your kids are comfortable with this crucial social skill.

Compromising

Kids want what they want when they want it. But as children move up through the elementary grades the ability to negotiate and find middle ground becomes increasingly essential in maintaining friendships. Write down different situations where compromising is an option and put them in a hat; have your child pick one and role-play a solution that reflects the needs and desires of both parties (i.e. "How about you get to play with the yo-yo for five minutes and then I get to play with it for five minutes?" or "Since you and Emily both want me to sit with you at lunch, why don't we all sit together?").

Giving Compliments

Buttering up buddies (with sincerity) is a sure way to deepen friendships. Encourage your child to practice by complimenting family members. ("I really like this chicken pot pie, Mom!" or "You did an amazing job pitching tonight, Bro.") Reinforce this behavior by placing a star on a chart each time your child offers up a worthy accolade.

Provide Opportunities for Kids to Foster Friendships Outside of School

Considering that a) school systems all across the country are eliminating recess to make time for an increasingly demanding academic curriculum and b) hanging out after school with the neighborhood kids is largely ancient history, we modern parents are essentially left with three options for ensuring that our kids have ample opportunity to forge resilience-building friendships: scheduling playdates, signing them up for group extracurriculars, and sending them to camp (day and/or overnight).

Playdates
So they've been known to require more elaborate planning than a summit meeting at Camp David, but playdates are still a primary way to solidify critical friendships for our children! Don't worry. I won't leave you hanging on the ins and outs of this complex topic. In fact, I've devoted the entire next chapter—"Grade-School Playdate Protocol"—to exploring this modern social phenomenon.

Group Extracurriculars
Group sports and other group activities provide excellent opportunities for kids to connect with other children who share their interests. Just keep in mind that—as we established in Chapter 6, "Extra, Extra, Extracurriculars"—our children are far more likely to form

lasting friendships with kids who share their passions when their extracurricular activities reflect *their* interests—not *ours*.

Summer Camp

Camp is a place where kids can let down their guard, kick up their feet, and leave the familiar social hierarchy of their school playground behind. It is also an intense social experience. For all of these reasons, summer camp provides fertile ground for forging lasting friendships. Even if your child doesn't live in the same city—or even the same state—as her camp buddies, simply having the security of these summer relationships can help her more gracefully hop social hurdles year round.

Do's and Don'ts for Helping Shy Kids Make Friends

Do accept that some kids are wired to be more tentative about jumping into the group.

Don't label your child as shy. Comments like "Sorry, Josh never answers adults, he is so-o-o shy!" leave kids believing that their shyness is a set-in-stone personality trait rather than a changeable behavior.

Do involve yourself in your child's activities. By being the Brownie troop leader or the soccer team mom, you have the perfect excuse to hang around and boost your kid's comfort level.

Don't follow the suggestion above if it results in your kid sticking to you like Super Glue. Instead, tell her you will stay for the first ten minutes of the Brownie meeting and then you're out of there.

Do let your child struggle a bit. If you're at a restaurant and the

---

waiter asks your daughter whether she wants chicken fingers or a hot dog, don't answer for her. Even if it feels awkward, let there be a dead silence. The only way shy kids can overcome their fears is to see that they can survive doing things that may feel uncomfortable.

Don't compare your shy child to more outgoing kids (especially siblings) by saying things like "Look how Jacob is playing with all the other kids on the playground. Why can't you do that too?"

Do arrive at birthday parties a few minutes early so your child can get acclimated before all the other guests arrive. (You may want to fill in the host mom on your plans so she's not wearing a bathrobe and a towel on her head when you show up on her doorstep.)

Don't impose unreasonable expectations. Just because you gave your child an extra thirty minutes to get acclimated doesn't mean he's going to be the life of the party. It's appropriate to expect him to go sit with the other kids and play pin the tail on the donkey, but don't push him to raise his hand and volunteer to be the magician's assistant.

Do form a partnership with the teacher by talking to her early in the year and requesting her help behind the scenes. She can subtly push friendships along through proactive moves like assigning your shy child an outgoing recess "buddy."

Don't consider being shy a problem. Shyness should only be of concern when it interferes with a child's ability to form and maintain friendships or causes undue anxiety—for the kid, that is, not the parent.

Do follow your gut if you think your child's social fears warrant professional intervention. While most kids eventually outgrow their shyness (though they are unlikely to grow into social butterflies), some children are stymied by their anxiety. If you sense this to be the case with your child, contact the school counselor or your pediatrician for a referral.

Social Resilience-Building Practice #2:
Display Social Equanimity

I define social equanimity as the ability to maintain a rational mommy mind-set over our kids' every playground plight. By working to achieve balance, we will spare ourselves unnecessary ulcers and foster critical social resilience in our children.

Do you remember when our kids were toddlers and they'd fall down and scrape their knees? The very first thing they did was look at us to see our reaction. If we began screaming something like "Oh, my poor *bubbeleh!* Quick, someone get the Neosporin!" our kid would predictably follow suit. If, on the other hand, we smiled reassuringly and told our tots they were perfectly fine, they'd brush themselves off and get back to business.

Not much has changed since then. When our daughter returns from school complaining of being excluded from the latest social club, or our son gripes that he was last kickball draft pick at recess, each is watching ever so carefully to see how we handle the news. If we well up in tears or start bad-mouthing other kids, we confirm and exacerbate the severity of the problem in our children's minds.

Making matters worse is a counterproductive habit that never fails to deliver a hefty dose of after-school stress to us and our kids. It is what psychologist Wendy Mogel calls "interviewing for pain," and it runs through the Jewish maternal population like matzoh ball soup on Seder nights.

The Daily Social Misery Survey

Your kid comes home from school, you give her a snack, and then you casually begin the interview process. "Was recess any better today?" "Did you get teased anymore about your braces?" "Did you have enough friends to sit with at lunch?"

Of course, we "interview for pain" only with the best of intentions; but taking a daily social misery survey after school only adds fuel to the fire. Consider the following incident between a former student of mine named Molly and her mother, Michelle:

What happened at school: During recess, nine-year-old Molly and her two best friends, Lauren and Sophie, decide to play a round of freeze tag. When Lauren announces Molly is "it" Sophie concurs. Molly spends exactly fourteen seconds feeling distraught over being singled out as "it," then proceeds to have a blast running and freezing with Lauren and Sophie for the remainder of her fifteen-minute break from academia.

What happened at home: When Molly returns from school, Michelle hands her some string cheese and a juice box and begins interviewing for pain:

Michelle: *Was recess any better today than it was yesterday?*
Molly: *No, it was a hundred times worse!*
Michelle: *What happened?!!!*
Molly: *Lauren and Sophie ganged up on me at recess.*
Michelle: *What did they do to you? I knew that Lauren was trouble!*

Partially due to the fact that she's successfully hooked her mom enough to divert her attention away from Molly's little brother Max, and partially due to the fact that her mom's excessive reaction confirms the severity of the problem, Molly proceeds to offer her mother an embellished play-by-play of her dreadful fourteen-second experience (neglecting to mention the remaining fourteen minutes and forty-six seconds she spent happily freeze-tagging, or the other perfectly fine five hours and forty-five minutes of the school day). Later that evening, Molly's mom calls Lauren's mom, who in turn calls Sophie's mom. Molly stays home from school the next day complaining of a stomachache.

Had Michelle skipped the interview and asked Molly about all the fun things she'd done at recess, social equanimity would have remained intact. But because Mommy Michelle opted to interview for social hardship, her maternal blood pressure skyrocketed, Molly's stomach twisted, and Lauren and Sophie's mothers got pulled into the mix.

Molly and her mother demonstrated an all too typical parent–child dance. The more a parent reacts to a situation, the more upset the child gets, the more upset the child gets, the more the parent reacts. We can stop this social equanimity–disrupting cycle from reeling out of control in our homes by controlling our reactions to our kids' social ups and downs.

We shouldn't dismiss our children's playground troubles as meaningless, but we do need to put these normal childhood hardships in perspective—for ourselves and our children—and be careful not to make an already difficult situation worse. If we maintain a composed approach, we boost our kids' social resilience by teaching them to gracefully hop everyday schoolyard hurdles.

The Equanimity-Restoring Power of Multigenerational Commiseration

One of the most effective ways we can restore social equanimity for both ourselves and our kids is to share stories of our own childhood playground plights. Such familial tales of schoolyard success, failure, hardship, and triumph—when told with the right tone—empower kids to overcome social stumbling blocks and give them a perspective on life.

My friend Adele, for example, often shares stories with her kids about the times she was teased about her hair as a child. Throughout the majority of her school career, Adele answered to "Brillo Pad" and "Poodle Head" as readily as she did her own name. Somewhere in her eighteenth year, Adele discovered the power of the straightening iron and things went progressively uphill from there.

When Adele's three children look at their mommy today, they see a strong, funny, happy person. By sharing stories of her childhood social struggles—even in the context of hopelessly frizzy hair—Adele fosters social resilience in her kids (and herself) by showing them that people can overcome schoolyard adversity and go on to live happy, productive lives.

Jewish Parent 911

Achieving Familial Social Equanimity

Turn lemons into lemonade. If your daughter is crushed because she failed to receive an invitation to a highly exclusive slumber party, seize the opportunity for a girls' night out on the town. Leave any siblings with your husband or a babysitter and share a mother/daughter dinner and movie. Don't forget to throw in an ample helping of multigenerational commiseration while you're at it!

Get two for the price of one. If your child comes home from school each day reporting a plethora of anxiety-provoking playground pitfalls, reclaim social equanimity for all involved by striking a deal and agreeing that for every problem he shares with you, he needs to tell you two positive things that happened that day.

Change the subject. We modern parents have been programmed to "validate" our kids' feelings by talking out their every problem. But the reality is that sometimes we serve them better by changing the subject. If our child brings up the issue again, we'll know it deserves more attention.

Arrange an objective observation. Sometimes children misperceive situations or embellish their severity in order to get a rise out of parents. This is the reason that anytime our kids consistently report a playground problem, we need to get a third party (i.e., a teacher or school counselor) to spend some time checking out what's really going on during recess. That said, schoolyard instigators can be underhanded in making social jabs and occasionally a legitimate problem will be missed by an adult onlooker, but more often than not, an objective observation will offer keen insight into whether or not a problem warrants our worry.

Know when to tap into outside resources. Experts have found that helping kids deal with social anguish is the area in which parents feel the most helpless (and nothing gets our equanimity out of whack like feeling helpless!). If your parental sixth sense is telling you this is not a passing concern and your child is being chronically bullied or excluded, or additional factors are at play like learning disabilities, attentional or anxiety disorders, or childhood depression (all of which can impact social functioning), a call to the school guidance counselor or other professional is likely in order.

Social Resilience-Building Practice #3:
Foster Realistic *Self-Esteem*

Since I've had at least one preschooler living in my house for the past thirteen years, I've gotten to know a certain musically challenged purple tyrannosaurus rex exceptionally well. In fact, I'm proud to report that—although we've never formally met—Barney loves me *very, very* much, and thinks I am *very, very* special. Why does Barney deem me so lovable and special, you ask? Why do you think? Just because I'm me!

Do you notice something slightly amiss about dancing purple dinosaurs convincing our children the world should love and adore them simply because they exist? Do you think our kids might be a tad disappointed when they realize that in real life—with the exception of Barney and their immediate relatives—nobody else feels compelled to shower them with devotion? (Especially not the inhabitants of the grade-school social jungle.) But it wouldn't be fair to blame the whole thing on Barney. He's just the dissonant byproduct of the self-esteem movement gone awry.

Okay, you're probably thinking, but what's your beef with self-esteem?!

You couldn't have already forgotten about Hannah, the bright, precious, spunky student you met in Chapter 1 whose mother had managed to convince her—in the name of boosting her self-esteem—that she was a gifted artist (despite the fact that she couldn't draw a stick figure to save her life). Do you recall how Hannah had assured her partners on an in-school project that she would draw an impeccable reproduction of a toucan while they were in the library doing rain forest research? Do you remember what happened when Hannah's group returned from the library and saw the rainbow-beaked blob she'd smeared across their poster submission? They were horrified, Hannah was heartbroken, and the self-esteem that Hannah's mother had worked so hard to build was history.

The same premise applies to our kids in the social arena. By building children up with a daily deluge of unearned praise, we are setting them up to come toppling down in the schoolyard social jungle.

This is not to say that a sturdy self-concept isn't an absolute must for our kids as they navigate their way through the disappointments and losses of grade-school playground existence. Healthy self-esteem is a fundamental building block in our kids' social resilience! But as Hannah's story demonstrates, self-esteem is only healthy when it is based in reality.

How can we make sure we are fostering the healthy social-resilience-building kind of self-esteem, rather than the counterproductive parentally fabricated variety? We can begin by getting past preconceived societally driven notions of who and what our kids should be, and zeroing in on what they really have to offer.

Remember when we used the palm tree as a parental role model back in Chapter 2? Well our old fronded friend is about to help us out again. The following section of the Midrash refers to the role of the date palm tree in the lives of the Jewish people:

No part of the date palm is wasted:
The fruit is eaten,
the embryonic branches are used for the Four Species of Sukkot,
the mature fronds can cover a sukkah,
the fibers between the branches can make strong ropes,
the leaves can be woven into mats and baskets,
the trunks can be used for rafters. (Numbers Rabba 3:1)

Back in biblical times, long before the evolution of the self-esteem movement, the Israelites neither expected nor wanted every inch of their beloved date palm tree to serve exactly the same purpose. So the leaves didn't perform too well in the roping department, but they made killer baskets. The dates were not stellar sukkah coverers, but they sure tasted good after a long tiring day in the desert heat.

Similarly, each of our children has a unique set of gifts to share. Maybe they're not the kinds of gifts that will make them playground alpha males or queen bees. It doesn't matter, because planting the seeds of social resilience in our children doesn't mean driving them toward a playground-imposed standard of perfection, and then watering them daily with unsubstantiated praise. It means being flexible enough in our estimation of our children's strengths to arm them with realistic self-esteem based on their true gifts and abilities (even if they go unappreciated in the schoolyard).

By showing our kids that we rejoice in their uniqueness and encouraging them to do the same—at a time in their lives when it feels as though the only choice is to be like everyone else—we boost their social resilience in a very real way. Maybe our daughter is shy with other kids but is a devoted friend to those who know her. Maybe our son is perpetually picked last for the recess basketball team, but he makes up for his lack of dribbling finesse in sportsmanship. By being infinitely flexible in our definitions of success and taking the time to point out to our children what they really have to offer the world and the inhabitants of the playground social jungle, we help ensure that they are prepared for the tumultuous journey that lies ahead.

Jewish Parent 911

Boosting Social Resilience with Realistic Self-Esteem

Don't underestimate kids' ability to accurately appraise themselves. You can walk onto any playground in America and ask the students to point out the best kickball players, the prettiest girls, the alpha males and queen bees, and they'll be able to do so with amazing accuracy. In other words, trying to boost self-esteem by convincing kids they are something or someone they are not, is pointless.

Give them a sense of perspective. Explain to kids that even though being a wonderful creative writer may be far less appreciated by their peers on the playground than being able to do a cartwheel, the former will ultimately take them farther in life.

Praise specifics rather than generalities. Generalized comments like "Daniel, you are such a fast runner" set kids up for disappointment upon losing a playground fifty-yard dash. Instead, say, "I like the way you put forward so much effort when you run."

Help kids overcome their weaknesses—if they so desire. Your son may not be the fastest runner, but that doesn't mean he should give up on winning a schoolyard race. If something is important to our children, we owe it to them to practice with them at home or offer them lessons to help improve their skills.

Give them venues to bask in their strengths. Once you tap into your children's strengths, arrange for them to have opportunities to shine. If your daughter feels empowered because she makes beautiful pottery in her after-school ceramics class, for example, those inevitable schoolyard social stings won't hurt nearly as badly.

Social Resilience-Building Practice #4:
Incorporate Family Rituals into Your Daily Life

Family rituals? you may be thinking. I thought we were talking about helping kids survive the schoolyard social jungle!

We are indeed. Because no matter how well prepared a jungle dweller may be when he sets out on his excursion each morning, he needs a safe safari retreat at the end of the day—a warm, predictable haven where he can refuel, recharge, and refocus.

How exactly do we go about turning our home into a safari retreat, you ask? In addition to fostering loving, mutually respectful family relationships within its walls, we anchor it in ritual and tradition.

To illustrate the power of family ritual, I'm going to take you on a quick trip back in time to my family dining room, Erev Rosh Hashanah, 5767 . . .

The change is subtle but undeniable. A slightly deeper shade of brown; carrots cut lengthwise rather than sliced; some scattered sprigs of rosemary. Any other day of the year, such a discreet rift in recipe might go unnoticed. But this is not any other day of the year—this is Rosh Hashanah.

"What's up with the brisket, Grandma?" asks my preteen son, echoing my suspicions that Bubbe's famous brisket—the eternal pillar of my family's High Holiday feasts—has undergone an unprecedented facelift.

"I thought I'd try something a little different this year," answers my mother (who has recently become obsessed with Rachael Ray of the Food Network).

"But I like the old brisket," says my younger son.

"Me, too!" agrees my daughter.

"Oh, no. Not the brisket!" adds the eldest of my grumbling foursome.

I know what you're thinking—that my kids were acting like spoiled, unappreciative brats. But I promise that—while they've admittedly had their moments—such was not the case here. You see it didn't matter whether Rachael Ray herself had prepared that brisket, because it wasn't about taste at all.

In the predictable presence of Bubbe's brisket on our Rosh Hashanah table, my children had found solid ground; a sturdy link between their past, present, and future, and the safety net of knowing where they have been and where they are going. Its abrupt replacement with a swankier roast represented a break in tradition—a glaring rift in their predictable path.

No, I'm not being melodramatic. In fact, oodles of experts believe that it is in the simple rituals and repetitions of life—not the grand black-tie affairs—that kids find the stability they need to thrive in a complex, inconsistent world. By filling our children's daily lives with ritual and tradition, we give them a soft place to land after a long hard day in the ever-unpredictable schoolyard social jungle.

Sure, you may be thinking. But we're not the Waltonbergs here. How am I supposed to incorporate consistent family rituals when every night of the week has us going in a different direction?!

But that is the magic of family rituals! They can easily and effectively be integrated into even the craziest of home lives (although if your home life seems *too* crazy you may want to take another look at Chapter 1, "The Mommy 500"). Research suggests that even seemingly mundane traditions can significantly boost emotional well-being and resilience in our kids.

One family I know has a chocolate-chip pancake breakfast every Sunday morning. Another has a weekly Scrabble showdown. My friend Jodi plays a game of "High-Low" every night at bedtime, when her children share the best and worst parts of their days, while my friend Abbie's children wake up every morning to the "tickle mon-ster." Even something as minor as making the same corny statement every time your kid walks out the door, like "I love you to the moon and back!" offers the predictability and stability kids need to feel stable and secure on the emotionally hazardous school playground.

Simple Family Rituals

A ritual is any predictably repeated, shared activity that is meaning-ful and rewarding to family members. Here are some easy-to-incorporate suggestions:

Recognition night. Celebrate children's achievements in the class-room or extracurriculars, like getting a one hundred on a spelling test or scoring a soccer goal, by serving an "honoree dinner" on a spe-cial plate reserved for that occasion. Let the guest of honor pick the menu that night.

Family night. Designate one night each week (even if it changes sea-sonally with activity schedules) to put all other commitments aside. Bake cookies, play board games, watch a movie or a favorite family television show. The point isn't what you are doing, it's that you are all there doing it.

Tzedakah day. Every six weeks or so, do a family mitzvah project. Play cards with nursing home residents, bring old towels down to an an-imal shelter, or pick up trash in a local park.

Around the world night. Once a month introduce your family to other cultures and cuisines. Try Israeli, Thai, Chinese, Ethiopian, Ital-ian, and Mexican foods. Get out the atlas and show your kids a map of the country. Use an encyclopedia or the Internet to learn more about the culture.

Family reading time. Set aside fifteen or twenty minutes a couple of times a week for everyone in the family to sit together and read—*silently.* (Little ones can flip through picture books.) You'll be wanting to do this ritual seven nights a week.

Bedtime routines. Say the Shema, read books aloud, sing the same songs; regular bedtime routines serve as security blankets for kids big and small.

The Weekly Shabbat Dinner: The Whole Social-Resilience-Building Enchilada

If there's ever been a time when we Jewish moms and dads have had an unfair advantage, this has got to be it. In addition to the aforementioned homegrown variety of family ritual, we just happen to have a zillion meaningful, tried-and-true traditions ripe for the picking in our rich religion—from brisket on *yontif* to dreidels at Hanukkah to Passover Seders that last late into the night.

I'll go into a holiday-by-holiday guide for incorporating meaningful Jewish ritual into our homes in Chapter 11, "Here Comes Santa Claus," but I want to zero in now on one of our traditions that I believe to hold special significance in helping kids weather the inevitably rocky terrain of the schoolyard social jungle. Here's why I've tapped the weekly Shabbat dinner as the whole (kosher) enchilada of social-resilience-building family rituals:

It's a weekly family dinner. No, I'm not questioning your intelligence! But as you may recall from Chapter 6, traditional family dinners—which are chock-full of essential emotional, social, and nutritional vitamins and minerals for kids—are fast going the way of the eight-track tape in modern-day America. As if our ancestors could see eons into the future when they devised it, the age-old Shabbat dinner ritual forces modern families to sit down together and savor a warm, hearty, renewing bowl of chicken soup at least once a week.

It fosters family bonding. What better gift to give our kids after a week of schlepping all over town than a family Shabbat dinner—where the only place they need to be is home with the people they love?

It promotes a sense of closeness with God. Taking part in the Shabbat rituals brings children spiritually closer to God and fosters a sense of safety and resilience throughout their social ups and downs.

It builds Jewish identity. For grade-school-age kids, being part of a group is the ultimate power booster. When our children take part in our Jewish traditions, they are empowered by knowing exactly who they are and where they belong.

Its roles are clearly spelled out. In stark contrast to the schoolyard social hierarchy, where the whole playground is fighting for the primo positions, everyone knows their place during Shabbat. In my house, for example, the girls and women say the blessing over the candles, the men over the wine, and the children uncover the challah and say the *Motzi*. Period.

It's rich with ritual opportunities. From using special Friday-night dishes to eating Grandma's famous chicken, the Shabbat table provides a perfect palette for creating unique family rituals. One of my kids' favorites is sharing the highlights of their week following the traditional blessings over the children. Here are some other easily implemented suggestions:

- Serve challah French toast on Friday morning, to remind children that Shabbat is coming.
- Let kids make their own special Shabbat place mats. Get them laminated and use them every week.
- Set up a "Shabbat *Naches* Board" on Friday nights where children can post aced spelling tests, art projects, creative writing, and other sources of pride from the previous week.
- Bless the children using the traditional blessings ("May God make you like Ephraim and Menashe" for boys and "May God make you like Sarah, Rebecca, Rachel, and Leah" for girls) or make up your own.
- Light an additional candle for each child in the family, suggests Rabbi Joseph Telushkin, author of *And You Shall Be Holy*. Then tell them something they did during the past week to bring light into your life.

Like Bubbe's famous brisket, the weekly Shabbat dinner fills our children's bellies and souls with familiar, secure, beautifully predictable rituals and traditions that can weave their lives together week in and week out. And that, my fellow Jewish parents, is what social security is all about.

CHAPTER 8

Grade-School Playdate Protocol

When I first started teaching, I couldn't begin to fathom what would possess an otherwise with-it mom to morph into a neurotic disaster at the sheer mention of her child's social life. I mean, I could have just wrapped up a thirty-minute conference with Mrs. Xberg about Justin's math and reading woes without so much as a sniffle, only to watch her well up with tears and start fishing around in her purse for the tissues the moment we broached the issue of playdates.

What's the big deal? I used to think to myself. Can't Mrs. Xberg just tell Justin to go play with the kid down the street? But when my own son hit grade school and I began agonizing over his social calendar, I alas understood. For I—the cool-as-a-cucumber teacher—had inexplicably morphed into a maternal tossed salad.

At an especially low point, following a momentary glimpse of my shy first-grader hanging solo in the schoolyard, I managed to convince myself that if I didn't get on the ball with playdates soon, my son would grow into an antisocial recluse living in a cabin in the woods whose only friends were raccoons.

Determined to spare my six-year-old this solitary fate, I willed myself to become the playdate hostess with the mostest and began stocking up on all available literature on the topic—a counterproductive strategy, I might add, at least from an anxiety standpoint.

One article, for example, entitled "Plan the Perfect Playdate," suggested I orchestrate a caterpillar cookie recipe that would have daunted Wolfgang Puck. And do people really have potato sack races anymore? Or stitch the participants' initials on burlap sacks before the big hop-off?

And then there were the unwritten rules about playdating that I was petrified of breaking. Like the one that says if someone invites our child for a playdate, we must reciprocate within a reasonable period of time; and if, perchance, the other mother invites our child back prior to reasonable reciprocation, we must profusely apologize and promise to have her kid over two times in a row next time. Or the one that says we must act like a cruise director and orchestrate ongoing activities for the playing pair from bubble blowing to Batman figure time.

With our children's social well-being and our parental reputations riding on these contemporary kiddie rendezvous, it's no wonder that at last count two zillion of the five zillion unanswered questions I discussed in the preface revolved around the topic of playdates. Fortunately, four kids and four trillion magazine articles have rendered me a bona fide expert in the field of playdates; and I will now attempt to answer as many of those two zillion questions as logistically possible.

Playdate Question #49,403,500: If my daughter only wants me to schedule playdates with one particular child, should I invite other kids over anyway to help her make more friends?

You haven't already forgotten about our conversation in the last chapter, have you? You know, the one about serving our kids much better by focusing our parental energies on building their friendships, not their popularity. Well, the same quality-over-quantity logic applies with playdates. It is far more important for our children to have a few close friends they can count on to sit with at lunchtime than to have numerous superficial relationships. Our goal in playdating, therefore, is not to ensure that our kid has a one-on-one social interaction with every child in the class by Hanukkah, but to plan repeat performances with the old standbys.

Playdate Question #39,344,590: How often should I plan playdates for my child?

Back in preschool, when our kids had lunchtime dismissal, it was easy to schedule playdates during the week. Such early-afternoon gatherings offered the fringe benefit of ensuring our kids were tuckered out enough to crash right after dinner and bathtime. When kids are in elementary school, they don't need anyone to tire them out. They are already tired enough just going through their daily drill.

The vast majority of Jewish grade-schoolers go from working in class to working on homework to working in Hebrew school. They then spend the rest of the afternoon and evening practicing soccer strategies, violin techniques, and karate moves. Trying to fit a weekday playdate into the mix, in my experience, just adds one more organized activity into our kids' already hectic agenda, not to mention that such late-afternoon rendezvous often set friends up to have a lousy time, as they are inevitably too tired, whiny, and grumpy to enjoy their playdate.

Besides, kids need to learn that it can be both acceptable and fun to be all by themselves. One playdate a week—during the weekend or on a school holiday—is more than enough to fill an elementary school child's social quota.

Playdate Question #602,499: When my son was in pre-school he used to play so well with my best friend's son Daniel. Now he says he doesn't want to get together with Daniel. My friend's feelings are hurt. What do I do?

Once our kids take the leap from preschool to grade school, we parents have to do a mental turnaround regarding playdates. Back in the early days our kids' friends were for the most part our friends' kids. We met up at the park and dished with our girlfriends while the kids ate sand in the sandbox. Sure a baby fight broke out every now and then over who had first dibs on the Elmo shovel, but as long as there was no blood or skin-breaking teeth marks, there were generally no ill feelings among any involved parties.

Around the time our kids enter kindergarten, things change. Our children begin forging their own friendships—separate from ours—based on mutual interests and compatible personalities. They develop definite playdate preferences that may or may not mesh with our own. Think about it this way: would you want to spend a huge block of your free time with someone just because your mother is friends with her mother? Would you want her to hang out in your room and play with your favorite things? Like your new Kate Spade purse? I think not.

Forcing grade-schoolers to spend time with kids just because we moms happen to be friends often dooms the playdate from the get-go. In fact, things are liable to get so bad we'll be wishing for blood and skin-breaking teeth marks.

But we don't have to throw in the towel on getting together with our friends and their kids. It's critical for our children to learn to deal with people who are not their best friends and be respectful and *menschlich* to them regardless of whether or not they are prime play-date material. We can help maximize the chances of a peaceful playdate between mismatched kids by selecting high-interest activities that require minimal interaction. Here are some suggestions:

Good Ideas for Playdates with Our Girlfriends (and Our Incompatible Kids)

- Go to a mutually agreeable movie
- Go out to eat and seat kids as far away from one another as possible
- Go to a children's museum
- Go to a very loud, distracting place with games, tokens, and the like
- Go swimming and throw diving toys in opposite directions

Bad Ideas for Playdates with Our Girlfriends (and Our Incompatible Kids)

- Moms chat in the kitchen while kids "play" in the basement
- Anything that involves a winner and a loser
- A weeklong beach vacation

Playdate Question #702,498: Now that my child is in kindergarten, is it appropriate to drop him off for playdates?

Perhaps the number one law of preschool playdate etiquette was that except in extreme cases—or a very brief run to the grocery store—both parents were expected to hang out for the duration of the gathering. This was due to the fact that 1) it's not fair to dump two barely potty-trained preschoolers on one mom and 2) preschool moms are so starved for adult conversation that they jump at the chance to have a semicoherent discussion with someone who doesn't regularly pick her nose and eat it.

The big kid playdate is a different animal. Not only is the other parent not expected to hang around, chances are the hosting mom doesn't even want her to do so (no matter how clean her hands may be). Having our kids occupied for a few hours frees us up to actually do a full load of laundry! Since elementary school kids are old enough to entertain themselves (theoretically) and take care of their own needs pottywise, we can drop them off for a playdate with a clear conscience.

Playdate Question #842,907,593: Is it okay to drop my child off for a playdate if I don't know the family?

Back in the preschool days, we naturally got to know the other moms through casual chitchat in the carpool line, at birthday parties, and the like. But in elementary school, such casual chitchat opportunities are few and far between. Kids ride buses to school; and birthday parties—like playdates—have evolved to drop-off status. Consequently, most of us grade-school parents will find ourselves, at one time or another, leaving our child off at the home of a parent we couldn't pick out of a police lineup.

I am not a big fan of making mountains out of molehills, but you are dropping your most precious cargo off at the home of a complete stranger, for heaven's sake! And just because the family lives in your neighborhood or the mother is president of the synagogue sisterhood doesn't mean their home is a safe place for your kid! Therefore, you have a bit of homework to do before you get to enjoy the adrenalin rush associated with having a temporarily empty backseat and the staff at Bloomingdale's eagerly awaiting your arrival.

If you prefer not to come off as completely nosy and neurotic, you can diffuse the upcoming inquisition process by starting out with a comment like "I hope you don't mind if I ask you a couple of questions. I know I'm being a pain, but what can I do? I'm a neurotic Jewish mother!" and then proceed.

The big drop-off playdate question, of course, is whether the family has a gun in the home. If they answer affirmatively to this question, you can either put your child back in the car and suggest the playdate take place at your house, or ask whether the gun has a safety latch, if the ammunition is stored separately, and if it is kept locked up and out of children's reach.

Once you are past the ultimate inquiry, trust me, it's time to move gracefully into an inquiry like "Will you be at home for the duration of the playdate or will the kids be under the watchful eye of a nanny or babysitter?" If the answer to the latter is yes, who is this person and how well does the parent know him or her?

This is also the time to fill in the host on food or insect-bite allergies, or any other quirks your kids may have. (It would have been helpful, for example, if Brandon's friend Sam's mother had clued me in to the fact that her son had a habit of hiding in closets and keeping mum before I frantically called his name for forty-five minutes and notified the police.)

A fringe benefit of the parental inquisition is that you get to spend a few minutes checking out the way the house flows. If the other parent doesn't invite you in, blame it on your kid by saying, "Alex always likes me to hang around for the first couple of minutes of his playdates. I hope you don't mind."

Chances are that this other mother is a perfect person and her house is a positive playdate site. Nevertheless, it is our parental duty to get through that front door for a quick grounds check before we leave our child. Take a cursory glance around for rottweilers and rats. Turn on your parent radar for any inexplicable gut feelings that tell you to take your child and run. If all checks out, leave your list of telephone numbers and a secondary emergency contact, make sure your cell phone is on and not on silent mode, and be on your way.

Playdate Question #943,382,992: I have a wonderful nanny. Is it appropriate to schedule a playdate that will take place under her supervision?

The answer to this question lies not so much in our own comfort level with the babysitter, but in that of the other parent. Fortunately, by the time grade-school rolls around, most moms and dads are perfectly at ease leaving their kids under the care of another child's trusted caregiver. Still, it's important that we adhere to the following protocol when scheduling a sitter-supervised playdate:

Step 1: Lay the cards out on the table. "Hi, Mrs. Schwartz, Max would love to have Gabe come over for a playdate on President's Day. I just want to let you know that I'll be working, and my nanny, Dorothy, will be watching the boys."

Step 2: Build confidence. "Don't worry, Dorothy is one of the most responsible people I know and she's been with our family for years. I'll be checking in with her throughout the day, and please feel free to do the same. Oh, I almost forgot. I never let babysitters drive my children's friends around, so there's no need to worry about Gabe riding in a car with her."

Step 3: Seal the deal with vital stats. "Does Gabe have any allergies that the babysitter should be made aware of? Where can you be reached if she needs you? Is there anything else you'd like her to know? If you think of anything else, don't hesitate to tell her when you drop Gabe off."

Finally, should you find that—despite your efforts at reassurance—the other parent still seems tentative, offer up an alternate plan. "You know, on second thought maybe we should schedule the boys' playdate for this weekend. That works out just as well for us and Gabe could join us for a family picnic at the park."

Playdate Question #590,008,858: How involved should my child be in planning the playdate?

Let your child be as involved as possible on the front end. Once children are in second or third grade, they are ready to start doing much of the legwork of booking and planning their get-togethers. Give your child a school directory, show her how to look up a friend's number, and have her make the call herself to set the time and date (pending adult approval). As the scheduled gathering approaches, have your child call her soon-to-be playdate and plan some highlights for the big day.

In encouraging our kids to take an active role in scheduling and planning their own playdates, we are not being slacker moms. We are promoting independence while ensuring that our children have as much interest in making the gathering flow smoothly as we do.

Playdate Question #579,348,483: What if I'm not thrilled with my child's playdate choice?

Sometimes our child's idea of playdate material does not mesh particularly well with our own. Perhaps the last time this kid came to your house he convinced your son to sneak out the back door and run up to the Starbuck's for an Oreo Frappuccino. Perhaps you overheard this girl telling your daughter that she would only be her friend on odd-numbered days. Or you have recurring nightmares about this kid ten years down the road convincing your son to forgo college and follow Phish. Whatever the reason, when your mommy gut tells you to watch out, you are wise to listen.

If your child is insistent, do a bit of investigation by calling or e-mailing the teacher with the following question. "I was wondering what girls in the class might make a nice friend for Emma. Can you share a few names with me?"

What you don't want to do is to make a comment like "Mrs. Goldstein, don't you think Arielle is evil?!" It would be neither appropriate nor comfortable for a teacher to answer such a pointed question. If this child's name is noticeably absent from the teacher's list of "nice friend material," you can bet that your gut feeling is right.

At the least, you can agree to have the child over one time and do plenty of hovering and spying (not usually a recommended playdate hostess activity, but I'll make an exception on this one). Most of the time, it's not that the other child is blatantly offensive, it's that he or she is not a healthy mix with your son or daughter. Here's a list of red flags that a playdate pairing does not warrant a repeat performance:

- The children butt heads over just about everything.
- Their arguments escalate to put-downs and insults.
- They end up in separate rooms with the doors locked (by choice).
- The other child is especially cruel to your younger children and/or encourages your kid to act the same.
- The other child is inordinately bossy and controlling.
- (Okay, this is a selfish one.) The other child walks into the kitchen every five minutes to tell you he is bored and hungry.

Playdate Question #39,344,590: How strict should I be when a child comes to play at my house?

A playdate is a special occasion and children should have some leeway as a result; however, this doesn't mean we should allow them to behave like banshees. This is why any playdate that takes place on our turf must kick off with a pow-wow about house rules. It may sound a bit harsh to start out with restrictions and boundaries, but trust me, it's now or never!

Here are some key concepts to cover during your house rules discussion:

- Activities that involve balls, running, or loud voices should take place outside.
- Siblings should not be excluded or teased (although I strongly suggest you help this cause along by planning simultaneous playdates for brothers and sisters. In my house the policy is eight heads are better than five. If you don't have four Rugrats at home like me, adjust your math accordingly).
- Outdoor play should take place within parentally designated parameters.
- Hard baseballs, metal baseball bats, and tackle football are out of the question.
- Rollerblades, scooters, and bikes may be used only with helmets.

Playdate Question #7,888,489,439: How much adult supervision is appropriate for older children during playdates?

One of the most widely accepted unwritten playdate rules is that the host parent should stick to the playing pair like superglue, supplying them with a long-range walkie-talkie in the event she should have to run inside to check on dinner. Such intense supervision is not in our grade-schoolers' best interest.

Sadly, it's true that awful, unthinkable things can happen to kids when they are out of a parent's sight and earshot (and the media makes sure we don't forget it!). But there is a fine line—especially as our children get older—between being cautious and being smothering. Our kids are growing up in a nervous world as it is. Our refusal to leave their side when they are old enough for us to do so sends a message that we genuinely believe our absence will jeopardize their safety—an unsettling message for children just getting their feet wet in the waters of independence.

This doesn't mean we shouldn't be prudent and check in on our kids at regular fifteen-minute intervals. It does mean that we should never lose sight of the fact that (as we've established throughout this book) our objective in parenting is to raise children who fly not because we tell them when, where, and how to do so, but because they can figure out how to soar on their own. And what better time to flex their wings than during a playdate with one of their best buddies?

Playdate Question #9,344,590: How involved should I be in entertaining my grade-schooler and his friend?

In the old days, if we and our friend got tired of hopping on our pogo sticks, one of us would say something profound like "This is boring, let's do something else," and we'd move on to a new activity like climbing a tree or watching *The Flintstones*. During the modern playdate it is a widely accepted notion that the host parent is the designated boredom buster. Unfortunately, such micromanagerial adult involvement ultimately backfires on both parents and kids.

Part of the childhood socialization process is thinking up things to do together. Many of the ideas kids consider fun would not even cross the adult mind. Still, if your kids are like mine and give you that pitiful blank stare whenever you tell them to figure out something to do on their own, there's nothing wrong with making a few ever-so-subtle suggestions. By tossing the following low-maintenance, high-interest ideas out to your kids, you will help maximize their chances of independently entertaining themselves during a playdate.

High-Interest, Low-Maintenance, Independence-Fostering Playdate Ideas

Imaginative kids:

- Build a fort with chairs and blankets
- Make a movie or television show using a camcorder
- Invent something new and useful
- Put on a puppet show (no puppets? use dolls and stuffed animals)

Artsy kids:

- Make a collage using magazines
- Cover a table with cellophane, spread shaving cream around, and "fingerpaint"
- Make a mural on the driveway with sidewalk chalk
- Bead necklaces (no beads? use pasta)

Stylish kids:

- Put on a fashion show
- Open a beauty shop complete with manicures, pedicures, and hair braiding
- Sketch out new fashion designs
- Give pals tattoos with nontoxic paint

Sporty kids:

- Make an obstacle course in the backyard
- Play driveway hockey (with or without skates; use brooms if you don't have hockey sticks)
- Organize a neighborhood Olympics
- Play the basketball game "Horse" using kids' names instead

Nature-loving kids:

- Collect leaves of all shapes, colors, and sizes
- Catch bugs and make a habitat for them in a jar
- Plant flowers
- Pick up litter

Hungry kids:

- Turn pretzel sticks, marshmallows, and licorice into edible K'nex
- Decorate slice-and-bake cookies
- Make bugs-on-logs by spreading peanut butter on celery sticks and sprinkling raisins on top
- Make ice-cream sundaes

Helpful kids:

- Organize bookshelves into categories or alphabetical order
- Wash the dog
- Clean windows
- Vacuum, mop, sweep, or rake

Enterprising kids:

- Earn the big bucks washing parents' and neighbors' cars
- Toss a bunch of pennies in the backyard, hunt for them, and pocket the findings

- Roll coins and keep a percentage
- Collect old knickknacks and hold a five-and-dime sale in the garage for neighborhood kids

Menschlich kids:

- Combine the above knickknacks with other gently used games and toys and arrange for them to be picked up by a charity
- Be mother's helper to an overwhelmed new mom
- Open a lemonade stand and donate your proceeds to tzedakah
- Take a neighbor's dog for a walk

Playdate Question #3,998,004,479: If my child is misbehaving, is it okay to punish him in front of his friend?

If your child requires a verbal kick in the pants during the course of his playdate, it is important that you try not to embarrass him in front of his pal. You can accomplish this by adding a simple cautionary clause to the beginning of your statements like "Jake, I know you are excited having Jordan over to play, but it's still not okay to feed Pop-Tarts to the hamster." If his unruliness continues, take him in another room and talk to him privately. Or, if need be, leave him there for a time-out while you distract his friend with a snack in the kitchen.

Playdate Question #3,998,004,480: What if the other kid is the one misbehaving?

We may be masters of "the look" with our own lot, but when it's someone else's child stirring up trouble, things get stickier. The key to disciplining a kid who does not belong to us is to avoid sounding judgmental and confrontational. We can masterfully accomplish this by personally owning the rules.

If we notice our son's playdate drinking a grape-juice box on our new white sofa, for example, we should not respond with an emotional "What on earth are you thinking, Jordan?! Get that slurpable permanent stain maker off my couch this second!" Instead we should matter-of-factly state, "Jordan, in our house we drink juice boxes in the kitchen."

If your child's playdate continues to act in an adversarial, disrespectful manner despite your honest attempts to steer him in the right direction, it is time to make a call to the other parent. (Running to your room and screaming into your pillow prior to dialing is optional.) Granted, it may feel uncomfortable to ask the other mother to pick up her misbehaving young one, but it's bound to be better than watching him swing from your crystal chandelier for the next three hours. Besides, you can be certain that the next time this child pays a visit to your house (if you're brave enough to allow a next time) the only swinging he will be doing is on the jungle gym in the backyard.

Playdate Question #8,709: My daughter and her playdate are at each other's throats. What should I do?

Sparks can fly even among the closest of friends. Fortunately, we can usually keep these heated encounters from becoming wildfires.

- *Give them a chance to work it out independently.* When emotions start to run high between buddies, we as parents should let kids have a go at settling the issue themselves. Children are more capable of arriving at a resolution on their own than we adults give them credit for.
- *Feed them.* Hungry tummies and grumpy kids go hand in hand. If your charges are at each other's throats, it's worth a try to shove something in their mouths.
- *Try a 180-degree change in activity.* Whatever activity the kids are

engaged in when they start going at it, subtly shift them to its polar opposite. If kids start butting heads over Chinese checkers (indoor, competitive, couch-potatoish), for example, get them outside to fly kites (outdoor, noncompetitive, physical). If one player is vehemently insisting he had "Horse," and his chum is certain he only had "Hors," squelch that basketball marathon (outdoor, competitive, physical) and suggest they move inside to water paint (indoor, independent, sedentary).

- *Get outta there.* If peace continues to elude your playing pair, round them up and take a walk to a nearby park. Even a dash around the block can do the trick.
- *Pop in a DVD.* Normally, I would say TV is a playdate no-no. (What's the point of a playdate when there is no social interaction?). But in cases of mounting incompatibility, an exception is in order. So slip in a movie and let the kids blow off steam with a bowl of popcorn.
- *Call it quits.* Even the old standby is not foolproof. I once tried the DVD strategy when my son Jake and his friend Jonah were at odds during a playdate, only to watch them argue for another fifteen minutes over whether to watch *Air Bud World Pup* or *Air Bud Spikes Back*. Fortunately, Jonah's mom was understanding when I called her to say it was time to call it quits. (By the way, when a playdate escalates to this level, it's a good idea to sit down with your son or daughter afterward to discuss what went wrong and how the problem may be avoided or remediated in the future.)

Playdate Question #107,962,443: Should I allow my kids to play video games during a playdate?

I believe kids should spend the vast majority of their get-togethers engaged in nonelectronic play. However, I don't think there is anything criminal about allowing older children to play video games for a limited period of time during a playdate. I know from my experience spending eight hours a day with grade-school-age students that video games are part of the modern-day culture of childhood, and part of the fun of a playdate is getting to play a round or two of Mario Tennis together. As long as video games are not the primary focus of the playdate and they are age appropriate, don't feel guilty about letting your kids and their friends have a little nibble.

Popular E-Rated* Video Game Series for Playdating Six- to Twelve-Year-Olds

- Mario
- Lego
- Backyard Sports
- Madden
- Bratz
- Donkey Kong
- Ty the Tasmanian Tiger
- Dance, Dance Revolution

*E = "for everyone" (some games are rated E10+). Most of these games come in Game Cube, PlayStation 2, XBox, and PC versions.

Playdate Question #2,181,937,002: My son and his friend are always begging to go on the Internet during their playdates. Should I let them?

The thought of our kids hanging out in cyberspace during a playdate may give us a touch of the *shpilkes*, but just because computers were the size of Rhode Island when we were young, that doesn't mean they shouldn't be a part of our children's lives—or their playdates. In fact, the Internet offers our kids and their friends a world of excitement and exploration at their fingertips.

True, frightening entities lurk online—cyberpredators, cyberbullies, and pornographic websites, to name a few. But most worthwhile things come with a degree of inherent risk; every time we get in a car, we risk a multicar pileup. Just as we use seat belts to minimize the intrinsic danger of being on the road, we can take precautions to ensure that our children's cyberjourneys are safe.

While I promise to get into the details of online safety measures in Chapter 13, "Parenting the Net Generation," I will tell you now that the two most effective parental steps toward ensuring kids stay on the sunny side of cyberspace are 1) absolutely NEVER—no matter how much begging and complaining goes on—put an Internet-connected computer in a child's bedroom, and 2) remind them that they should NEVER communicate online with anyone they don't personally know.

If you heed these measures (as well as the cardinal rule of everything in moderation) you can confidently allow a portion of your grade-schooler's playdates to take place in cyberspace.

Playdate-Friendly Websites

Sporty websites:
- www.playfootball.com—The official NFL site for kids is a haven for pint-sized football fans.
- www.sikids.com—The Sports Illustrated for Kids website has it all (except, of course, the swimsuit models).

Wild animal websites:
- http://kidsgowild.com–This fun location offers up oodles of animal facts and exciting arcade games.
- www.switcheroozoo.com/zoo.htm–Playdates will have a wild time mixing up animals' heads, tails, bodies, and feet to create their own zany animals.

Interplanetary websites:
- www.Artyastro.com–Space lovers can zip around the solar system with Arty the Astronaut.
- http://spaceplace.jpl.nasa.gov/en/kids–At NASA's Space Place, children can enjoy out-of-this-world adventures.

Girly websites:
- www.gogirlsonly.org–No boys are allowed at this feminine cyberstop from the Girl Scouts.
- http://barbie.everythinggirl.com–Playdates are sure to enjoy visiting Barbie at her home on the World Wide Web.

Websites with character:
- www.pbskids.org/arthur–Arthur and the gang provide worthwhile games galore to playdating pals.
- www.berenstainbears.com–The virtual Berenstain Bears offer kids entertaining games that sneak in valuable lessons.

Book-happy websites:
- www.seussville.com–A site as fun and clever as Dr. Seuss himself.
- www.jkrowling.com–Harry Potter fans will love muggling about this truly one-of-a-kind site.

Brainy websites:

- www.funbrain.com–Add a painless academic twist to any play-date with this teacher favorite.
- www.factmonster.com–Trivia-hungry pals can get the scoop on everything from sports to science to SpongeBob here.
- www.funology.com–Friends can get down and dirty with kid-friendly science experiments at this website.
- www.brainpop.com–So entertaining, kids barely notice they're learning.

Note: You know the saying "There's no such thing as a free lunch"? Well, that goes double for cyberspace. While I've tried to suggest kid-friendly websites that don't go completely overboard with the commercial plugs, it's wise to provide children a lesson or two in advertising and persuasive intent before letting them play on these—or any other—cost-free kid-friendly sites.

Playdate Question #7,997,687: How do I know if my child is ready for a sleepover?

There is no rule about when a kid is ready to be tucked into an unfamiliar bed by someone other than Mom or Dad. Some little ones can successfully manage a sleepover when they're in preschool, while others refuse to sleep out until they enter college. Here are some signs that your child is ready for an all-night playdate:

- He feels comfortable playing at a friend's house for several hours without you.
- She's independent with her bedtime routines.
- He wants to do the sleepover and seems confident it will go well.

Here are some telltale signs that your kid is *not* ready yet:

- She has an elaborate bedtime routine that includes specific books, songs, and a thirty-minute back rub.
- He wakes up every night demanding a glass of water—with crushed ice—in his favorite Buzz Lightyear mug.
- She is a sleepwalker or has frequent nightmares.
- The sleepover is *your* idea rather than your child's.

If you determine that your kid is not ready for prime-time sleepovers, let him cut his teeth on some middle ground. Spending the night with relatives or going pajama-clad to his buddy's house for a few hours of nighttime fun and getting picked up at 9 P.M. will help prepare him for the real McCoy.

On the other hand, if your child seems ready for a night away and he's eager to try it, you can up his chances of successfully slumbering out by packing a comfort item like a blanket or stuffed animal and a familiar toothbrush and pajamas. Remind him that he can call you if he needs you (although preferably not at 3 A.M.). When you drop him off, don't belabor the point by asking repeatedly if he is sure he is ready for this. Just kiss him and be on your way . . . with your cell phone handy.

Playdate Question #38,404,916: My daughter always comes home from sleepovers cranky. Am I awful not to let her spend the night out?

More often than not, when we drop our kid off for an overnight, we pick up the Tazmanian Devil the next morning. But consider the benefits of an all-night playdate. From the kids' standpoint, there's something magical about spending a whole, entire night—and morning, too—hanging with a good buddy. (So magical, in fact, that my older boys consider themselves shortchanged if they are forced to leave a friend's house before 10 A.M. the next morning.)

These overnight getaways help foster independence in our children while preparing them for longer stays at overnight camp or weeks at Grandma's. Since a lot of bonding goes on when you are giggling in the dark pillow to pillow, they deepen peer relationships. Sleepovers help our kids learn to be flexible, as they have to adapt their behaviors to blend in with another family's flow.

From a parental perspective, sleepovers give at least one set of parents a much-needed break for the night. Some parents I know with only one child consider a sleepover invitation an excuse for an evening on the town. But even if you've got a houseful of children like I do, you have to admit that having one less kid bopping around for the night feels vaguely honeymoonish . . .

Playdating: The Big Picture

You didn't really expect me to answer all two zillion questions, did you? What's the point of even trying, because next week you're certain to have two zillion more! The truth is you already know the answers. You just have to track them down.

Do you remember back in the preface when we talked about finding the answers you need in the big picture of what you really want for your children? The trick is to use your ultimate goal of raising resilient, empowered, *menschlich*, happy children as a lens to focus in on the answers you need. Why don't we run through a few practice rounds?

Playdate Question #434,320: Do I really need to buy forty dollars' worth of art supplies before my seven-year-old's playdate?

Big-picture-based response: Is making a fuchsia and lavender tie-dye shirt embellished with coordinating ribbons going to make my daughter more resilient? No. More *menschlich*? No. Empowered? Maybe, if she was the one who came up with the idea and does all the legwork to make it happen. How about happy? Probably. Can we accomplish these very same goals for free? Definitely.

Playdate Question #5,843,498,997: If my child is invited for a playdate with a shy child in his class who doesn't have many friends and he does not want to go, should I make him go anyway?
Big-picture-based response: This one is a bit trickier since we're getting some hard-core resistance, but let's give it a try anyway . . . Will going to play with a lonely child who is not on his "A list" of friends make our kid more resilient? Yes, he will learn he can survive doing things he doesn't really want to do. *Menschlich?* Absolutely—he is showing compassion for someone other than himself. Empowered? Yes, by going on this playdate, he will see that he is capable of doing things that may not be fun, but are right. What about happy? Probably not immediately, but in the long run being a resilient, empowered *mensch* is bound to make him smile.

Playdate Question #80,492,683,903: What if the other mother thinks I'm a lousy playdate hostess?
Big-picture-based response: Will impressing the parent of another kid make my child more resilient? No. More *menschlich*? No. More empowered? No. More happy? No. Should we care what the other mother thinks if we know our children are safe, happy, adequately supervised, and well nourished? Not even for a millisecond.

CHAPTER 9

Birthday Party
Blowouts

It was the wedding invitation that convinced me—we modern moms and dads had officially lost our gumballs regarding our children's birthday parties. "Master Jacob Estroff" read the ivory parchment envelope. It took a moment to register that the addressee was in fact Jakey, my five-year-old, and the bride-to-be, "Miss Sophia Rosenthal," [not her real name] was Sophie, his toothless classmate.

The party lived up to its invitation. There were bridesmaids, groomsmen, and of course a mini-groom, a wedding cake taller than the bride herself—even a mini-chuppah! The mother sitting beside me in the linen-covered guest chairs whispered to me wide-eyed, "I can't wait to see the bat mitzvah."

In all fairness, we Jewish parents come by it honestly. I mean, we've barely cleared labor and delivery before we're expected to be on the phone with the caterer ordering bagels and lox for two hundred for our newborn's bris or baby naming.

It seems only a natural progression to plan a three-ring circus in the cul-de-sac when that little bundle of joy turns six. It's just that somewhere between the petting zoo, the pony rides, and the moonwalk, we end up with an empty wallet, a giant headache, and a kid who is so overwhelmed by the hoopla he can barely enjoy his big day.

Sure, you may be thinking, that's easy for you to say, but if I plan a birthday party where the main event is pin the tail on the donkey, I may as well have the kids play pin the tail on the maternal pariah!

I'm not suggesting that we put zilcho time, energy, and effort into planning our kids' parties. Our children's birthdays are much-awaited events in their lives and are fully deserving of special recognition. But going to the opposite extreme is not the answer either.

Fortunately, it's perfectly possible to plan a kid-friendly birthday bash without compromising our values, sanity, and pocketbook. All it takes is a little panning for gold. You know—when you put a big clump of mud in a pan and swoosh it around until a few glistening specks of gold are all that remain. Well, we are going to do exactly the same thing here. Only instead of mud, we're going to swoosh a big, mushy mess of modern birthday party madness.

Are you swooshing yet? Do you see those overpriced invitations and F.A.O. Schwartz goody bags spilling over the sides of the pan into a bucket by your feet? Great, keep swooshing. But don't go peeking at those golden nuggets just yet. Not until we've spent some time looking at the slush in the bucket—at the maternal myths that have contributed to our current state of birthday affairs.

Myth #1:
Our kid's birthday party is a direct reflection of our parental prowess

We accomplish lots of amazing feats as parents. Getting our kids out the door and into school on time every morning; keeping them safe, healthy, and happy; giving them big sloppy kisses at bedtime—even when they beg us not to. Your child's birthday party is but one little parenting accomplishment in a year of millions; it's hardly a major manifestation of your parental savvy. And in case there is anyone out there who thinks our parental worth is wrapped up in a birthday party goody bag, well, we don't really care what they think anyway—do we?

Myth #2:
The only place they serve grocery store birthday cakes is in the maternal hall of shame

How many times have you bought a magazine based on the teaser "foolproof birthday party ideas" only to realize a page and a half in who is indeed the fool for buying the magazine in the first place? I mean, not only is making tulip-shaped cupcakes not foolproof, it takes a degree from the World Culinary Institute! Besides, our kids couldn't care less if their cupcakes are shaped like tulips or toilets as long as they're yummy, icing-smothered, and flanked with just the right number of candles.

Myth #3:
Good parents plan one-of-a-kind parties for their children

You know that sinking feeling we get when we learn another kid is having a birthday gala at the same secret site we've booked for our own child's party—only a week earlier? The nerve, we think to ourselves. I've had that inflatable jumpy place booked for a year and that parent just swooped in and stole the idea right out from under me. And she's even copied my menu—cheese pizza! *Oy gevalt!* But the reality is our kids love playing on inflatable jumpy stuff and eating greasy pizza. They would do it day in and day out if we'd let them. Just because we parents get bored with the same old same old—and get a migraine just thinking about spending another Sunday afternoon at the inflatable jumpy place—doesn't mean our kids do. Think about it like this: would you turn your nose up at an opportunity to go to a spa and eat trays full of Godiva-dipped strawberries just because you did the same thing last weekend? I think not.

Myth #4:
It is supposed to go off without a hitch

For my niece's sixth birthday, my sister-in-law booked the highly acclaimed Marvin the Magnificent Magician, months—if not years—in advance. You could taste the excitement as every child in the room—magic hat on head and magic wand in hand—counted down the seconds until Marvin made his grand entrance. And then they counted some more. And some more. Until it became painfully evident that Marvin the Magnificent Magician had taken his vanishing act to the next level. By then my sister-in-law was all but catatonic staring helplessly at a roomful of antsy six-year-olds—and worse yet their parents. That's when the kids decided to build Oreo towers. They went through package after package of double stuffs, until they'd constructed a bona fide Eiffel made out of chocolate cookie bricks and creamy white mortar. And then it was time to go home. "Thanks, that was fun," the guests said as my still-shaking sister-in-law handed them their personalized goody "bags of tricks." Lesson learned? Despite a catastrophic birthday party disaster, my niece turned six, the guests were entertained, and we had a family memory that would last years.

Myth #5:
Paying through the nose for our children's birthday parties is our financial obligation (like paying for college or health insurance)

Although we've been programmed to believe that we haven't done our child justice unless we spend megabucks on his birthday party, it's simply not true. In fact, one of my boys' all-time favorite parties was the time we went to the park and played baseball. I brought a cake, some Gatorade, plastic bases and sunblock, and they were happy as hamantashen for the duration.

Myth #6:
We are supposed to throw a big bash for our child's birthday every year until he is married (or at least until his bar mitzvah)

A close cousin to Myth #5 is the modern parental assumption that it is our responsibility to facilitate a gargantuan blowout party every time our kid rounds the calendar. Clearly, our child's birthday is cause for celebration. It is the day God gave us life's most precious gift! But does that mean we must rent out a skating rink and invite a hundred of our child's closest friends in honor of the occasion? No. In fact, as our kids move up through the elementary grades into the double-digit ages they rarely desire such sizable celebrations. While I'll elaborate further on this point in the "Making *Menschlich* Guest Lists" section, for now let it suffice to say that our love for our child is not defined by birthday party size and extravagance. We know that. Our child knows that. That's all that matters.

Okay, then. I think we're finally ready to peek at the golden nuggets. At those few precious, glimmering, *real* reasons we plan birthday parties for our children. They look something like this:

· A celebration of their existence.
· A fun, memorable day spent with family and friends.
· A means of making them feel happy, proud, and loved.
· A reinforcement of our family's values.

Planning a Party with a Conscience

Okay, you may be thinking. I'm with you on the first three golden nuggets, but what's up with the last one? It's a birthday party, for heaven's sake. How many values can you reinforce with a tub of ice cream and some party favors?

I see your point but bear with me here. Psychologists have found that certain events in our lives—also known as "flashbulb memories"—are etched in our minds for the duration. Birthday celebrations and other milestone events are among these enduring memories. In other words, birthday parties are not just fleeting (albeit overpriced) moments in our children's lives, they are destined to be among the memories that ultimately define their childhood—

fertile ground for making (or breaking) our big-picture parenting goals.

Don't get me wrong here. I'm not implying that we should replace our child's dream party at the Braves game with an afternoon working at a soup kitchen (although the latter is certainly a worthy activity for another weekend). The objective is to plan a birthday celebration that's festive but not frivolous; whimsical but not wasteful; indulgent but interwoven with a sense of gratitude, tzedakah, and compassion for others. Here are some practical suggestions for doing just that:

Make a special party favor. If your child's party activity involves a craft—say a Build-a-Bear Workshop—have her make an extra one to donate to a pediatric hospital.

Tie tzedakah into the party theme. If you'll be partying at the zoo, ask guests to bring old towels or pet food for your local animal shelter. If the big bash will be a sleepover, ask them to bring gently used blankets and pillows for a homeless shelter.

The gift is in the goody bag. Rather than cramming the goody bags with the standard overpriced yet worthless candy and junk, slip in a packet of seeds or a tree seedling. That way you celebrate your child's growth with a bit of *tikkun olam*.

Make a tzedakah station. If your guests will be rotating through several activities during the course of the party, make one of them a card-decorating station where they can make cheerful messages for nursing home residents. Take your child to personally drop them off for postal delivery the following day.

Be a charitable example. We can't very well expect our kids to be altruistic on their birthdays if we don't do the same. By making a donation to tzedakah to mark our latest rounding of the calendar (at least it will give us something to celebrate) we help ensure that our kids keep up this worthy tradition for years to come.

Let them give upon receiving. After your child unwraps his birthday haul have him "make room" for his new loot by selecting a few of his gently used toys to donate to tzedakah.

Making *Menschlich* Guest Lists

During my years as an elementary teacher I saw the same scene play out time and time again. First thing in the morning, a large group of girls would huddle together in the back of the classroom clutching tiny white envelopes in their hands. They'd whisper and giggle conspicuously until they caught the attention of the only two non-envelope-toting gals in the room. On cue, the curious pair would scurry over and inquire about what the huddlers were holding. "NOTHING!" the group would inevitably respond in unison.

Hearing this familiar choral proclamation, I'd quickly scoop the envelopes out of my students' eager little hands and put in a call to the parents of the birthday girl reminding them that invitations could not be distributed at school unless every child in the class was invited. But by then the damage had already been done. (And truth be told, even if the invitations had arrived via mail truck rather than backpack, the invitees would have still been huddled in the back of the classroom giggling and whispering all too obviously about "nothing.")

It's not that my students were inherently cruel and hurtful children. It's just that they were in a developmental place where—as you may recall from Chapter 7—being accepted by a group is right up there with oxygen on their list of life essentials. Sealed inside each of those tiny white envelopes was not just a fluorescent pink card etched with the date, time, and location for Carly's ninth birthday party, but a declaration of their acceptance by the inhabitants of the schoolyard social jungle—a declaration made that much more potent by the fact that some children had not received it.

Don't get me wrong here. I'm not suggesting we throw massively expensive, preposterously populous birthday parties for our children year after year in the name of never excluding a single child. Or that we discount our kids' guest preferences altogether and invite whomever we want to their birthday parties. But I do believe it is our responsibility as Jewish parents to ensure our children show basic *derech eretz*, or respect, concern, and decency toward others (see Chapter 2), regarding their birthday celebrations. We can help maximize *menschlichkeit* and minimize hurt feelings by adhering to one of the following types of party guest lists:

The Whole-Class Guest List
In the spirit of the old days when our kids' birthday guest lists and their class rosters were essentially one and the same, this strategy eliminates the potential for hurt feelings by simply including every child in the class. If you decide to take on a whole-class megaparty, consider selecting a vast sprawling venue without a per-head charge (like a park, playground, beach, or swimming pool) or a reasonably priced gender-neutral activity like bowling or skating.

The Only the Boys or Only the Girls Guest List

While there is certainly something to be said for keeping up those early boy–girl friendships forged before the onset of the opposite-sex cooties, splitting an elementary class list down gender lines allows for immediate volume reduction while opening up the possibility for stereotypically girl or boy party activities (i.e., tea parties or laser tag), as well as slumber parties. A key point to keep in mind, however, is that inviting *only* the boys or girls in a class entails inviting *all* the boys or girls in the class.

The Closest Buddies Guest List

I know what you're thinking. What happens when my daughter throws herself on the ground and refuses to attend her own birthday party if she has to invite girl classmate X. It is at this moment that we turn to Option C—the very bestest friends party. The objective here is to keep the kids in the class who were *not* invited to the party in the majority. While some children may still feel left out, they won't experience the same kind of devastating, singled-out exclusion I described during the huddle scene. Of course we may need to spend some time discussing how many closest buddies one can reasonably have—three to six as a general rule of thumb—and the qualifications for the title (someone with whom you enjoy socializing both in and out of school) before expecting your child to nail down a final list.

Truth be told, however, even if our child doesn't throw herself on the ground, *menschlich* option C is a fab choice for the school-age set as it sets up a win–win–win situation. Our child wins because she gets to invite only guests she truly cares about and enjoys spending time with. Her classmates win because nobody feels like odd man— or woman—out. We win because our costs stay down and the crowd remains gloriously manageable.

Scheduling *Shpilkes*

Ideally, we want to schedule our child's party as close to his or her real birthday as chronologically possible. There are other factors, however, that we must consider before indelibly etching a date and time on the invitation.

The School Calendar

Unless you'll be partying during the lazy hazy days of summer, taking a glimpse at the school calendar is a preplanning prerequisite. This proactive move prevents us from making such scheduling slipups as inadvertently slating our child's party for ski week and having all our guests run for the hills. It may also enlighten us about an opportunely placed teachers' professional day on which to schedule the celebration (just be sure to send out the invitations well in advance so parents who work and have grandparents and babysitters on call have ample time to make their logistical arrangements).

The Jewish Calendar

If our child made his or her worldly debut during the High Holiday or Passover seasons, checking the Jewish calendar before setting a date and time for his birthday party is an absolute must. I mean, we don't want to risk planning our child's big day smack dab in the middle of Passover (when the cupcakes could double as hockey pucks) or on the morning of Erev Rosh Hashanah (when everyone is scrambling with last-minute holiday preparations). The Jewish calendar is also ripe with opportunities to incorporate Judaism into our child's birthday celebration. If your child's big day coincides with Purim, for example, why not throw a masquerade ball in her honor? Or if it falls close to Lag b'Omer, have a traditional festive picnic, with a ballgame and mock bow-and-arrow competition.

On Scheduling Parties on Shabbat . . .

To a Jewish parent, Sundays can be absolute mayhem. From the second the alarm clock goes off in the morning until we hit the pillow at night, we are liable to be rushing from Sunday school to baseball and soccer games at the JCC to other kids' birthday parties. Logic might tell you, therefore, that for a non-Shabbat-observant Jewish family a Friday-night or Saturday birthday party makes perfect sense. Yet in this case, the logical answer may not be the best answer.

Choosing whether or not to take part in activities on Shabbat is a personal choice. If we have other Jewish children on our guest list we may be putting them in an uncomfortable position as their families—while not particularly religious—may truly value Shabbat. Furthermore, planning a party on Friday night or Saturday to avoid the Sunday hustle sends a message to our children that missing a soccer game presents a bigger problem than missing a Shabbat family dinner or synagogue services.

Ruling out Shabbat, however, doesn't mean we absolutely must schedule our child's party on Sunday. Saturday-evening pizza and bowling gigs, Saturday-night sleepover parties, and the previously mentioned school holidays and teacher professional days are all prime opportunities to celebrate our children's birthday while leaving Shabbat free to celebrate their being Jewish.

Other Kids with Nearby Birthdays

It's never a happy situation when we send out our child's birthday invitation only to find out after the fact that the party conflicts with that of a classmate. We can head off such a quandary by putting in a prescheduling courtesy call to parents of kids born within a few weeks of our child. The conversation should go something like this: "Hi, Mrs. Rubenstein, this is Alex's mom. Isn't it hard to believe the boys are turning nine already? I know that Danny's birthday is around the same time as Alex's and I just wanted to let you know I was hoping to hold his party on [X date]. Does that conflict with your plans? Great! Look out for Danny's invitation."

Of course, not every parent is quite so agreeable. Then we can opt for several different approaches.

- The Happy-to-Accommodate Approach: "Oh, I didn't realize that Danny's brother's bar mitzvah is that weekend. It really makes no difference on my end. I'll just hold Alex's party the weekend after his birthday instead of the weekend before."
- The More-the-Merrier Approach: "Since both the boys' birthdays are on Sunday the 10th and I've already got the skating rink booked, why don't they just have the party together?"
- The Let's-Make-a-Deal Approach: "If Alex can have his party on October 1 this year, I promise you can have the pick of the calendar next year."
- The Desperation Approach: "True, there is only one weekend in October that's not a Jewish holiday, so how about I do Alex's party in the morning and you do Danny's in the afternoon."

Masterminding the Main Event

When our children were in preschool, they didn't give a flip what they did at their birthday parties as long as they had a birthday party. They were just as happy eating pizza with giant dancing rodents as they were watching a magician pull an emaciated rabbit out of a hat or jumping on a moonwalk in the backyard. Now that our kids are in grade school it's a whole different ball of birthday-candle wax. They have their own interests, agendas, and stringent definitions of what qualifies as a hopping birthday bash, leaving us with the task of planning a soiree that meets their approval—and ours.

Broadly speaking, we can take our grade-schooler's birthday party in one of four different directions: The At-Home Palooza; The Outsourced Palooza; The Full-Service Birthday Salon; and The All-Night Parent Torture Fest. All have their perks and pitfalls. Let's take a peek at each.

The At-Home Palooza

There are lots of good reasons to throw birthday parties for our grade-schoolers at home: They feel less generic and provide a great outlet for untapped parental creativity. They eliminate the possibility of forgetting the birthday cake and other party essentials at home, while feeling *hamish* and comfortable.

There are also good reasons not to throw birthday parties for our grade-schoolers at home: We have to get our house ready beforehand and are virtually guaranteed that it will be a disaster zone afterward. Guests are more likely to linger far beyond their welcome and the host or hostess can be put under megapressure.

If—after weighing out the pros and cons—you opt to hold a birthday party at home, the following survival tips will come in handy:

Arm yourself with adults. It is a foregone conclusion that—unless otherwise specified—grade-school birthday parties are strictly drop-off. Since it's impossible to orchestrate a party while peeling an eight-year-old on a sugar high off the ceiling fan, we are wise to surround ourselves with other members of the legal adult population. (Hint: This can be accomplished by inviting every empty-nester relative and neighbor we know to join in on the fun—and ensuring they stick around for the long haul with platters of food and coolers of drinks, or by hiring a babysitter to help out for a couple of hours.) Dole out responsibilities to your support staff: drink refills, camera duty, or keeping a vigilant eye on an especially rambunctious guest.

Overplan. It's truly amazing how a party game that took hours to pull together can be over in a matter of milliseconds. Rather than projecting that a three-legged relay race will occupy our guests' attention for half an hour, therefore, we must assume that it will keep them amused for minutes (at best) and plan accordingly. If you don't get to all the games, simply stash them away for next year.

Keep it together. Nothing can ruin a perfectly good home party like wandering guests. Keep your celebration cohesive and intact by giving your guests definite boundaries (i.e., the backyard, the basement, the playroom).

Be cool and safe. When planning a swimming bash in a backyard or neighborhood pool we should always hire additional lifeguards. (One for every ten kids is a good rule of thumb—and don't forget to factor in siblings.)

Have a rain plan ready. When it comes to birthday parties, Murphy's Law rules: If you plan an outdoor event with zillions of kids, it *will* rain. This is why having a backup indoor activity is an absolute necessity. It doesn't need to be fancy. A kid-friendly movie and some packages of jiffy pops or beads, lanyards, and slice-and-bake cookies will make sure your bases are covered in case the skies open up.

Check the Internet. Whether you're planning a superhero soiree, a baseball bash, or a princess ball, you can find everything you need—from games and goody bags to decorations and invitations—and way, way, way more with the click of a mouse. Here are some party-hearty cyberspots worth visiting:

www.birthdaypartyideas.com—The self-proclaimed "World's Largest Collection of Birthday Party Ideas" leaves not a celebratory stone unturned.

www.amazingmoms.com—Amazing moms give amazing ideas for amazing parties.

www.coolest-kid-birthday-parties.com—The name speaks volumes.

Two Easy (Really, I Mean It) Reality-TV-Inspired Big Kid Home Party Ideas

Sure, basing our child's party theme on a reality TV show may not be the most PC of parental moves, but the truth is grade-schoolers are fascinated with television. By giving regular old home party activities a small screen twist we can kick up their interest and excitement to a big kid level.

The *American Idol* Party

[Must-know background info: *American Idol* is an insanely popular program in which contestants belt out songs week after week in hopes of being voted the next great pop star and receiving a recording contract.] The mainstay of this party is a karaoke machine, so if you don't have one, you may want to rent or borrow one. Go to the fabric store and purchase a red remnant to roll out when the guests arrive. As the stars enter, give them a contestant number and march them over to the makeover area, where they can spend a good chunk of time adorning themselves with kid-safe makeup and glitter hairspray, and dolling up with fun accessories like feather boas, hats, sunglasses, and gaudy jewelry. (Hint: buy divawear in bulk from Oriental Trading—www.orientaltrading.com—and let it double as a goody bag.) When everyone is ready (or seems to be losing interest) dim the lights and get the show on the road. Record the performances so you can buy yourself some more time at the end by letting the guests watch and giggle over their *American Idol* debuts. Add a final twist by handing out notepads and letting the stars swap autographs. Snap and hand out Polaroids of the children as each one exits on the red carpet, and send them on their way.

Survivor Party

[Must-know background info: At the beginning of each *Survivor* season, a vastly diverse group of contestants is dropped off in a remote location. They are divided into two competing tribes who go at it via *Survivor* "challenges."] Before the party, divide your guest list into two tribes. Go to the sewing store and purchase a yard each of two different colorful fabrics (one for each tribe) and cut them into survivor "buffs" (bandannas). When the guests arrive give them their designated tribal buffs. Let the teams start out by building shelters (give them Lincoln Logs or Legos) and hunting for food (hide canned goods in the backyard). Next up is fishing (fill a bucket with water and plastic fish—or real ones if you dare—and let blindfolded guests try to scoop them up with a cup). Keep the party going with a very simple obstacle course, relays, and puzzle challenges. Cap off the challenge with a reward of cake and ice cream. Tell them they all won immunity and send them back to civilization happy as coconuts.

The Outsourced Palooza

Let's be honest here, we all have our strengths and weaknesses, and for some of us planning and executing a socially appropriate at-home-palooza falls under the latter umbrella. But the fact that we have a bagel's chance at a Passover Seder of successfully entertaining twenty-five seven-year-olds for an hour and a half doesn't mean we must bail on any hope of hostessing a home party for our child. This is the purpose of outsourcing, or—sparing the euphemism—paying an outside individual to bring in the fun to our kid's birthday bash.

Since Tickles the Clown and Barney clones are unlikely to fly with the grade-school set, we need to look beyond the standard party hires. Here are some big-kid-friendly outsourcing options.

Dance instructors. If your daughter has the hippest hip-hop teacher around, ask her if she might be willing to pay a house call and teach your guests a fun dance routine. Prior to her arrival let the kids get all jazzed up with cool hair accessories and child-safe makeup. An even more budget-conscious option is hiring a couple of teenage drill team members to teach the crowd some cool moves.

"Mad scientists." This popular "edu-fun" party concept—where guests stir up slime, blow person-sized bubbles, make bouncy balls, and the like—is always a hit with kids, but it can also cost beakers full of bucks. Accomplish the same effect for a whole lot less, by calling the chemistry department at your local college and asking if any grad students would be willing to do some fun, kid-safe experiments at your child's party. Scope the grads out first to make sure they have the right attitude (cool) and safety awareness (high).

Artists in residence. If your child is a budding Michelangelo but you can't draw a straight line to save your life, don't despair. Ask his art teacher if she might be interested in making a few extra dollars over the weekend by orchestrating an art project in your garage. The best part is that the finished product can double as the goody bag.

Amateur athletes. From a kids' perspective, there's nothing cooler than shooting hoops with a real college (or even high school) basketball star. Ditto for a backyard soccer clinic with a collegiate Mia Hamm.

Hairdressers and manicurists. Okay, maybe it seems a bit superficial, but big girls love getting hair wraps and decorating their fingers and toes. Ask your favorite hairdresser if she might be game, or call kid-friendly hair salons or beauty schools for names and numbers of outsourcing possibilities.

A Jewish Perspective on Gratitude

It's no coincidence that the Modeh Ani—a proclamation of gratitude—is the very first prayer a Jewish child learns and the very first prayer we say every morning. Our religion considers gratitude to be a fundamental virtue, and one of our prime responsibilities as Jewish parents to be guiding our children toward being grateful for their blessings and the kindness of others.

Rabbi Joseph Telushkin points out that "gratitude is not just pleasant for the recipient, it also makes us feel good about ourselves." In fact, he says, the ability to be grateful is a bona fide prerequisite for happiness!

In other words, how could we possibly consider letting the five Hefty bags full of birthday loot our child raked in at her birthday party become clutter on the playroom floor before we've put them to good use as the building blocks of gratitude?! By interspersing the unwrapping frenzy with comments like "Wow, Hannah is such a good friend to know that you've been wanting a brand new Bratz doll" or "Look how Noah made a card for you, it looks like he really took a lot of time on it," we infuse our children with *hakarat hatov*, the Hebrew term for recognition of the good [another has done you]. By helping them write thank-you notes—even if a couple of misspelled words and a drawing is all they can muster—we teach them to show it.

The Full-Service Birthday Salon

The most obvious advantage of paying an institution to organize and implement our child's birthday party is just that—someone besides us organizes and implements our child's birthday party. And they do it somewhere—anywhere—other than our house! Also on the plus side is that many party venues (i.e., stadiums, whirly ball) offer a breed of excitement that can't be achieved in a home environment. Last and most important, passing the birthday party baton frees us up to focus on our child, rather than nitpicky details.

Using a party factory also has its downside. Depending on the nature of the venue and activity the cost can be exorbitant. There is also that little problem of being forced to relinquish all control. Many of the more popular birthday sites host a revolving door of parties throughout the weekend. They've got their systems down to a perfect science and are in no mood to accommodate our special requests (especially when they've already run our credit card), or to let us dillydally around a millisecond past our official stop time (regardless of whether or not our kid has had a chance to blow out his candles). Finally, we can't help but cringe at the cautionary tales that manage to leave us second-guessing our choice of full-service party venue until the fat lady sings:

"Are you sure you want to have Zach's party at the Puppet Playhouse? I heard the puppeteer is on the sex offenders' registry."

"I'm sure it's fine to have Maddy's party at the water park—their E. coli scare was a whole entire summer ago!"

"I hope you're not planning on serving pizza at Danny's party at the bowling alley. You know, they have rats in the kitchen."

"Sorry, Eli has to RSVP no to Aaron's birthday invitation. Last time he went to a laser tag party he got so freaked out by the darkness and guns he hid in a fetal position in the corner for an hour and a half."

Despite disturbing suburban legends, throwing our child's party at a full-service birthday salon is not so much an "if" as it is a "when." The reality is that as our children grow up, the old water-balloon toss in the backyard no longer makes the cool party cut. (Besides—truth be told—we big-kid parents aren't quite as gung ho as we used to be about orchestrating backyard water-balloon tosses, either.)

Beyond Chuck E. Cheese: Full-Service Birthday Salons from A to Z

Aquariums

Bowling alleys

Ceramics (paint-your-own)

Dance studios

Equestrian centers

Fun factories (aka excruciatingly loud places where kids shoot foam balls at each other)

Gymnastics facilities

Hobby stores

Ice-skating rinks

Jumping places

Kiddie museums

Local fire stations

Movie theaters

Nature centers

Orchards

Putt-putt golf

Q-zar (laser tag)

Roller rinks

Stadiums

Tae kwon do and karate studios

U-make-it stuffed animals or crafts

Vegetable and fruit farms

Whirly ball

Yoga studios

Zoos

The All-Night Parent Torture Fest

The first question we must tackle is: "Why?" Why in a million trillion years would we—otherwise sane human beings—voluntarily invite a bunch of overly excited kids into our homes and keep them there for eighteen hours straight? Because from our child's perspective, nothing comes closer to birthday nirvana than being swaddled in a SpongeBob sleeping bag and surrounded by good buddies when the clock strikes midnight. And so we plug ahead.

Being perfectly honest here, there is no way in H-E-double-birthday-candles that we can turn our child's slumber party into a pleasurable personal experience. Rather we need to focus on damage control. To that end, here are some sanity-saving slumber party survival tips:

- Don't take the plunge too soon. To avoid unnecessary tears, over-tired meltdowns, and middle-of-the-night departures, it's generally best to hold off on an official slumber party until a child hits second or third grade. If your under-eight is dead set on an overnight celebration, try the mock sleepover mentioned in Chapter 8, where pajama-clad guests show up with pillows, blankets, and sleeping bags, participate in standard slumber party fare . . . and go home by 9 P.M.

- Keep it small. It's a proven fact that slumber party chaos increases exponentially with the number of guests. Consequently, it's always better to err on the side of too few kids, rather than too many. What's that magic number? Probably somewhere between four and eight including the birthday boy or girl, depending on your child's age and personality. (We're also wise to shoot for an even number of guests to help circumvent the odd-man-out dynamic.)

- Maintain guest list veto power. I know that what I'm about to say is not very nice, but I'm going to say it anyway . . . If your mommy gut whispers to you that one particular member of your child's guest list is likely to turn into a werewolf during the wee hours, listen to it.

- Set a late drop-off and early pickup. I once brought home five prepubescent boys after a half day of school to celebrate Brandon's twelfth birthday. They didn't go home until noon the next day. It was—without exception—the longest twenty-four hours of my life. To spare yourself a similar fate, schedule a dinnertime drop-off (unless your party will involve an off-campus field trip like a movie or a ballgame) and a breakfast pickup.

- Foresee their forgetfulness. To prevent unnecessary bouts of homesickness, have extra sleeping bags, pillows, and toothbrushes ready to go. A stock of clean towels and washcloths is also helpful should your guests be hit with a hygienic urge.

- Have a pre-party pow-wow. Remember back in Chapter 8 when we discussed the importance of laying down the law at the beginning of a playdate? Well it's the same situation here—only the stakes are higher. Within minutes of your all-night guests' arrival it's absolutely imperative that you gather them together and establish boundaries—both physical and social. Using a friendly yet firm tone, clearly outline to your charges which parts of the house are off limits, which are fair game, and how far they may venture outside. Explain that there will be no teasing, ganging up, or exclusion, and that yelling and running are strictly outside sports. Finally, state that although you are certain it won't be necessary, noncompliant guests may need to be sent home early.

- Don't go overboard on the sugar and caffeine. A slumber party is a mighty special occasion and—in my personal opinion—a perfectly appropriate time to indulge a bit in empty calories. However, unless you plan on having your guests running amok at 2 A.M. to let out their extra energy, it's best to serve caffeine-free drinks and put a cap on the cookie jar by 9 P.M. If tummies start rumbling for a midnight snack, popcorn is a fun and filling choice.

- Strike a happy balance. While we don't want to jam our child's sleepover with back-to-back activities (half the fun of a slumber party is enjoying a touch of abandon), we also don't want it to be a free-for-all. Give kids room to create their own fun, but be ready and willing to jump in with new activities if—or should I say *when*—the natives get restless.

- Wind your partyers down with a video. When they get ready to settle down (or you reach your wit's end, whichever comes first), have them all crawl into their sleeping bags, turn off the lights, and pop in a video. If you choose your movie wisely (nothing too scary or peppy) and luck is on your side, the whole crowd will be crashed by the closing credits.

- Designate a separate sleeping area for early-to-bedders. Some kids need more beauty rest than others, so set up a room away from the action where guests who want to hit the hay early can retreat for some shut-eye.

When Your Child Is the Guest

As of publication time, my four children have cumulatively attended 437 birthday parties and delivered seven thousand dollars' worth of presents. How could I even consider closing out a chapter on birthday parties without addressing the other side of the celebration equation—when our child is the guest?

To Drop Off or Not to Drop Off

We can't help but feel a bubble of guilty excitement over the prospect of leaving our child in a safe, fun environment while we steal away for an hour or two. But before we start hightailing our way to the mall, we need to ask ourselves a few key questions.

Do I feel comfortable leaving my child alone in this environment? (Okay, technically we aren't leaving our child *completely* alone, but the reality is that no matter how vigilant the birthday kid's parents may be, they are a tad preoccupied—and besides, nobody watches our child like we do.) This is not to say that we should never leave our child at a party without us, just that we take a moment to sniff out the territory before ducking out. Some birthday party venues are bright and happy, others are dark and creepy. Some feel small and secure and others are miles wide with dozens of exits. As a general rule of thumb, if we drop off our child at a birthday party site and we start getting a funky feeling about the prospect of her going into the bathroom alone—or have serious doubts that the host will lay eyes on our child until she shows up in the party room for cake and ice cream—we need to stick around for the duration.

Is my child self-disciplined enough to stay here without me? Let's be honest, we all know our child. We know if he's the type to wander away from the slime-making table at the science museum and head for the elevator. We know if he gets overly stimulated at inflatable jumpy places and is liable to belly slam the other jumpers. If we believe there's a distinct possibility that our child may be headed for trouble as soon as we head out the door, we owe it to the host family—and to our child—to stick around.

Does my child feel comfortable with being left? While most school-age kids feel comfortable being dropped at a birthday party, some—especially those who have a hard time acclimating to new situations—beg their parents to stay. This scenario is tricky, as heeding our child's wishes only reinforces the behavior, while leaving her high and dry can cause her anxiety to go into overdrive. Rather than going to extremes, therefore, we are better off telling our child in advance that we will be hanging around for the first ten minutes and will then be making our exit. If she starts working up the crocodile tears as we head for the door, we plainly state that she has a choice—either stay at the party with her friends or leave with us right now.

It's in the (Gift) Bag
It's tricky enough buying a birthday gift for our own child, let alone someone else's. Here are some suggestions for big-kid presents that promise to please without blowing your budget (although some like to spend a bit more on gifts for bestest friends):

- Collectible cards. Whether it be baseball, football, or Yu-Gi-Oh!, the success of this gift is in the cards.
- A disposable camera. Give this gift to the birthday kid at the start of the celebration so she can document her special day. If your budget permits, throw in a cute album.
- A basketful of dollar-store stuff. Hey, sometimes you've just got to pick quantity over quality. Keep the surprises coming by wrapping each gift separately.
- Vortex balls. This line of sporting goods is fave with my boys and their friends as they are soft, easy to throw, make cool noises, and travel fast and far.
- Gel pens and fun stationery. I'm not sure what it is about gel pens that makes kids go ga-ga, but they do—especially over the neon ones.
- World record books. Doesn't everyone want to know the farthest nasal spaghetti ejection (7.5 inches)?
- A box of cookie mix, sprinkles, and cookie cutters. This yummy gift is sure to hit the sweet spot.
- A gardening kit. A couple of small colorful pots filled with potting soil, some seeds, and a plastic watering can make a super spring or summer gift.
- iPod gift cards. If the birthday child has iPod headphones growing out of his ears, he's sure to enjoy adding a few more tunes to his collection.
- Beads. Jewelry lovers can have hours of fun designing their own bracelets, necklaces, anklets, and keychains. Look for beads with alphabet letters or those that reflect the child's interests.
- Legos and K'nex. Kids who love to build can never have enough interlocking plastic pieces.

While I'm at it, here are some birthday presents that are best left on the store shelves if you want your child to be invited back next year.

- Super Soakers, foam dart launchers, and other jet propulsion gadgets. It's common knowledge that cowboy guns are birthday present no-no's, but many parents are uncomfortable with any toy that may fall under the umbrella of "gunlike."
- Makeup kits. While lipstick, eye shadow, and face glitter seem like a sweet present for a budding princess, some moms and dads have strong views and rules regarding when and if they will let their daughter go glam.
- Anything with tons of tiny accessories. Some parents are really not bothered by toys that come with a zillion accessories (microscopic traffic cones, minuscule shoes, miniature evening gowns), others really are.

Getting Real About Accepting Invitations

Of course we want our children to be able to celebrate their friends' birthdays with them. And of course we want our children's friends to be there when they celebrate their own. But if I have learned one lesson over the course of those 437 birthday parties, it is this: *Do not sacrifice your family's sanity in the name of a birthday invitation.*

No, I'm not implying that we should send those invitations to the shredder the second they show up in our mailbox. But we do need to get into the mind-set that while birthday parties are fun and special, they are not as fun and special as spending quality time as a family.

By asking yourself the following key questions before calling in your next RSVP, you will help ensure that birthday party invitations represent special outings rather than stressful obligations:

What is the nature of the party? Not all birthday celebrations are created equal. An all-day water park affair will take a bigger bite out of your family's day than a ninety-minute Chuck E. Cheese lunch break.

How will siblings be impacted? Are you dealing with a drop-off party that is miles away and will leave you and your other children stranded in the car for the day? Will you need to find someone to watch the sibs in order to take your child to this party?

Does the party venue hold family entertainment potential? Some birthday party sites—like movie theaters, putt-putt golf courses, bowling alleys, or roller rinks—can double as fun weekend outings for your whole brood. Just be sure you pay for your additional kids at the door.

Are you already dreading the party lineup? If it's a month out and you're feeling overwhelmed by the prospect of a particular party or a pending party marathon, there's only one way for your anxiety level to go—up.

Is the birthday boy or girl a special friend of your child's? As we discussed in Chapters 7 and 8, lasting friendships are critical to our children's overall well-being. Parties of close friends, therefore, should likely be given priority status over other invitations and plans.

Now that we've wrapped up our discussion of basic birthday party blowouts (I know they don't *seem* basic, but in light of what's to come, trust me, they are), you should be in just the right frame of mind to tackle the next chapter . . .

CHAPTER 10

Having Our Bar/Bat Mitzvah Cake and Eating It Too

I was struggling to secure a tiny *kippah* to the scalp of my eight-day-old son when it hit me like a ton of Pampers. One day (assuming we both survived the main event at the bris), this precious little baby would be standing on the bar mitzvah bimah!

Determined not to let this postpartum hormonal surge take away from my enjoyment of Brandon's Judaic debut, I snapped myself back to the task at hand, tacked on the teeny beanie with some double-sided tape, and comforted myself with the notion that thirteen was still a jillion years away.

Then one day when Brandon was in fourth grade a letter arrived in the mailbox from my synagogue assigning him a bar mitzvah date. Surely they jest, I thought. But they didn't. In fact by the time I'd made my way back to the house the phone was already ringing off the hook.

"We just got our date, did you get yours?" panted a voice I scarcely recognized as that of my friend Barrie. "You know that Contagious is booking three years out, so you have to call them right away!"

"Contagious?" I replied, dazed.

"Tell me you're kidding," she said. "Contagious is only the best band with the most motivating motivational dancers in the entire city of Atlanta."

And just like that, I was thrown head first into the maelstrom of bar mitzvah planning.

Focusing on the Mitzvah Instead of the Bar (Food, Salad, and Otherwise)

As Brandon's bar mitzvah day inched closer, I began to see the world in a whole different light—a disco ball light, to be exact. For as my child grew, so did his friends, officially putting us both on the "bar mitzvah circuit."

And what a hopping circuit it was. There were casino getups that could rival Caesar's Palace; midriff-baring Britney Spears clones beckoning guests to the dance floor; video presentations that would give MTV a run for its money. And—while I hate to admit it—a yellow-taloned Freddy the Falcon mascot swooping down upon my own son's bar mitzvah party, leading the crowd in a round of the Macarena.

How did this happen? my fellow bar mitzvah circuiteers and I would wonder. How did the guests who came to witness our child taking part in an age-old Jewish tradition end up playing limbo draped in glow necklaces and feather boas? How did our resolve to remain focused on what really mattered evolve into a safari-themed ballroom and five cases of leopard-skin-print "free-pahs" (my boys' term for giveaway *kippahs*)?

The answer is not difficult to find. We got lost. Lost in intense societal pressure to follow up our kid's Judaic rite of passage with a killer party. Lost in a sea of products at the local bar mitzvah expo with no apparent link to the Jewish religion. Lost in our child's insistence that she's "only been looking forward to having a candy-themed bat mitzvah for her whole entire life!"

But my daughter really *has* been looking forward to having a candy-themed bat mitzvah for her whole entire life, you may be thinking. We've got it all planned out—Samantha's Candy Shoppe. Every table is going to have a centerpiece made out of a different type of candy and . . .

I know, I know—and the favors are going to be Hershey bars with all her vital bat mitzvah stats etched on the label in hot pink. The trouble is that following up a meaningful religious milestone with a party that focuses exclusively on Kit Kats and Jelly Bellies tends to undermine the point of our child having a bar or bat mitzvah in the first place. "The way we choose to celebrate sends a message to our child," says Rabbi Jeffrey Salkin, author of *Putting God on the Guest List: How to Reclaim the Spiritual Meaning of Your Child's Bar or Bat Mitzvah.* "It's not fair to leave our values at the front door."

How can we ensure the spiritual core of our child's big day doesn't melt away faster than a Hershey's Kiss ice sculpture? By weaving threads of tzedakah and *tikkun olam* (repairing the world) throughout our child's bar or bat mitzvah celebration. Here are some practical ways we can do just that:

Plant the seeds with the invitation. Even if we are extremely craft-oriented and have an affinity for calligraphy, there's a good chance our child's bar or bat mitzvah invitations will cost us a pretty penny. As long as we're spending the money *anyway,* why not let it go to a worthy cause? The Jewish National Fund (www.jnf.org) offers beautiful watercolor bar or bat mitzvah invitations—and they plant a tree in Israel in the name of each guest, to boot! The Jewish Foundation for the Righteous (www.jfr.org) sells invitations through the Checkerboard Company (available at most upscale paper stores) that recognize and help support elderly and needy Righteous Gentiles who risked their lives to save Jews during the Holocaust. Keshet (www.keshet.org), a nonprofit organization that sponsors programs for children and young adults with special needs, prints colorful invitations that are accompanied by a statement that a donation has been made to their organization in honor of your child's bar or bat mitzvah.

Spread the joy. It's always heartwarming to watch a Jewish child become a bar mitzvah—even if you've never laid eyes on the kid before in your life! Contact a local nursing or retirement home and invite several residents to attend the service and share in the kiddush.

Put tzedakah center stage. Rather than spending hundreds of dollars on throwaway centerpieces and bimah arrangements, why not build your celebration's focal points from donatable items such as stuffed animals and toys, children's books and DVDs, colorful scarves, gloves, and mittens, or cans of food? Be sure to tack on a card stating where the donations will be sent. (BTW—in case you're like me and don't have an artistic bone in your body, a party store or party planner should be able to point you toward people who can help you assemble festive and meaningful centerpieces.)

Do a favor with the favors. Rather than giving out your standard "I had a cool time at Andrew's bar mitzvah" coozies or "I danced my pants off at Leah's bat mitzvah" boxers as favors, opt for a keepsake that makes a statement and difference. Following the 2004 tsunami in Thailand, a former student of mine handed out bracelets she'd created using ribbon and metal washers inscribed in her hand with "Tsunami Life Preserver." Items that support particular causes—such as pink ribbon bears benefiting breast cancer research (www.avon.com), JNF (www.jnf.org) or Livestrong (www.livestrong.org) bracelets, or plants and flowers for *tikkun olam*—also make meaningful parting gifts.

Leftover with love. Arrange to have the uneaten food from your kiddush or reception taken to a soup kitchen that feeds the hungry. If your caterer refuses because he or she is afraid of being sued, says Danny Siegel, founder of the Ziv Tzedakah fund and author of *"Who Me? Yes You!"* tell them about the federal Bill Emerson Good Samaritan Food Donation Act, which states no one can be held liable for any illness resulting from the donation of food. (Relevant passages from the law can be found on Siegel's website, www.ziv.org.)

Tzedakah Spin-offs of Popular Party Themes

So you're still thinking about that candy theme, are you? You're afraid your daughter is going to be crushed if Samantha's Candy Shoppe doesn't come to fruition. But I never said that there's *no* place for secular themes in our children's b'nai mitzvah celebrations. To the contrary, while it's clearly not what the Talmudic rabbis had in mind, I think it's sweet that the bar/bat mitzvah has evolved into a celebration of the whole child. The trick, as we've already established, is to maintain a consistent balance between the spiritual and the secular—between Jewish values and kid-defined rules of party cool. This can be seamlessly accomplished by spinning a tzedakah project off our party theme.

My son Brandon, for example—whose bar mitzvah party revolved around the inspiring theme of football—added meaning to his Super Bowl XIII celebration by collecting sporting goods for Camp Twin Lakes (www.camptwinlakes.org), an overnight camp for children with life-threatening diseases. We constructed his table decorations out of donatable sports equipment and set up a decidedly athletic collection station where guests dropped off their personal contributions (Brandon had written them in advance requesting their assistance in supporting his cause). My son's party theme didn't suffer an iota, and Camp Twin Lakes received nothing short of a U-Haul full of brand-new sports equipment.

To help you infuse the mitzvah into your child's dream party, here are some of the most popular themes on the bar/bat mitzvah circuit today and potential recipients for tzedakah spin-offs:

Theme: Animals/safari

Tzedakah spin-offs: Local zoos, humane societies, and animal rescue organizations; Wildlife Conservation Society (www.wcs.org); Animal Welfare Institute (www.awionline.org); Guide Dog Foundation for the Blind (www.guidedog.org).

Theme: Wilderness/extreme sports

Tzedakah spin-offs: Local parks and playgrounds; local nature centers; Outward Bound (www.outwardbound.org); Foundation for Jewish Camping (www.jewishcamping.org); Sierra Club (www.sierra club.com).

Theme: Books (Harry Potter, Nancy Drew, etc.)

Tzedakah spin-offs: National Jewish Coalition for Literacy (www .njcl.net); Reading Is Fundamental (RIF; www.rif.org); Jewish Braille Institute of America (www.jewishbraille.org).

Theme: Sports

Tzedakah spin-offs: Special Olympics International (www.special olympics.org); U.S. Paralympic Team (www.usoc.org/paralympics); The Jewish National Fund's Project Baseball (www.jnf.org/baseball).

Theme: Board games (Monopoly, etc.)

Tzedakah spin-offs: Donate board games to local Jewish family and children's services agencies; Boys and Girls Clubs of America (www.bgca.org); Marine Toys for Tots (www.toysfortots.org); Big Brothers/Big Sisters of America (www.bbbsa.org).

Theme: Bikes/motorcycles

Tzedakah spin-offs: Tour de Cure for Diabetes (http://tour .diabetes.org); Muscle Mountain Mania for ALS (www.alsride.org); Lance Armstrong Foundation (www.livestrong.org). And who could forget . . .

Theme: Candy

Tzedakah spin-offs: Mazon: A Jewish Response to Hunger (www .mazon.org); Make-A-Wish Foundation of America (www.wish .org); Jack and Jill Late Stage Cancer Foundation (www.jajf.org); local children's hospitals.

The Pre–Bar Mitzvah Family Mitzvah

A child's bar or bat mitzvah is a monumental occasion for the whole *mishpacha!* We can make the experience even more meaningful by heading off the big weekend with a familial act of *gemilut chasadim*, or loving kindness. Here are some *menschlich* suggestions for your bar/bat mitzvah–bound crew:

- Show off your crew's musical, magical, and/or other talents at a facility for people with developmental disabilities.
- Spruce up the garden at your child's school with some colorful flowers.
- Make cheerful get-well cards and bring them to your local hospital for distribution to patients.
- Pick up litter in your local park.
- Go around to grocery stores and bakeries and ask if they'd like to donate their day-old bread to a soup kitchen.
- Collect old towels and blankets for your local humane society and spend a morning playing with the pups and kittens. (Caution: This particular act of *gemilut chasadim* landed me a high-maintenance—albeit very cute—lab/something mix three days before my son's bar mitzvah.)
- Find a specific volunteer opportunity in your community at www.pointsoflight.org.

Raising the Bar on Bar Mitzvah Behavior

By focusing on the spiritual aspect of our child's bar/bat mitzvah, we twenty-first-century Jewish parents are well on our way to returning the meaning and spirituality to the modern American bar/bat mitzvah. Unfortunately, we can't call it a day just yet—not until we've addressed another significant threat to the sanctity of our kids' b'nai mitzvah celebrations: our kids themselves.

Our sages taught that a parent is responsible for the actions of a child until that child reaches the age of thirteen years and one day, at which time he's ripe and ready to assume full responsibility for all of his deeds. Perhaps our sages should have specified that "all deeds" include stuffing up synagogue toilets with rolls of toilet paper, text messaging buddies during the rabbi's sermon, having elevator races in upscale hotels, and (gasp!) engaging in sexually precocious behavior in bathrooms with other newly pubescent Jewish "adults."

Don't get me wrong here. I'm not suggesting that all Jewish kids run around like wild banshees during their friends' b'nai mitzvot. Many of them are respectful and gracious guests. But the reality is that kids of this age group are not known for their stellar judgment calls, or for their ability to fend off peer pressure. This, in combination with the sheer nature of the twenty-first-century bar mitzvah celebration (i.e., tons of teens; distracted adults; free-flowing alcohol; loud music; exciting venues), can leave even typically well-behaved kids engaged in less than pious activity.

Unfortunately, these young guests' misbehavior has a wide impact. It affects synagogue congregants who are disturbed during prayer and rabbis who are forced to add policing to their list of Shabbat duties. It hurts parents and grandparents who see the day they've been awaiting since the bris or baby naming irreversibly tarnished. It forces the bar mitzvah child himself—watching his friends fool around from the bimah—to make hard decisions as he balances his entry into Jewish adulthood with middle-school rules of cool.

Perhaps the most unsettling repercussions of tween/teen misconduct at b'nai mitzvot, however, are those that reach past the scope of our personal celebrations: The shock felt by gentile guests who witness Jewish children audaciously misbehaving at supposedly sacred events. The emerging hesitation by hotels and catering halls to reach out to the bar mitzvah "industry" for fear of risking property damage and disturbing their guests. And—saddest of all—a generation of jaded kids who perceive their own Judaic traditions and prayers as unworthy of their reverence and respect.

So where do we go from here? We begin by facing up to the reality that a) while thirteen and one day might have been plenty old to take on full responsibility for one's deeds back in the days of our sages, in the days of Beyoncé and Eminem, thirteen-year-olds need ongoing direction and guidance in that department, and b) it is our responsibility as true adults to be sure they receive it. The following tips will assist in our efforts:

At your own child's bar/bat mitzvah:
- Arrange for ushers to be present at services and prepared to manage any behavioral problems.
- Ask a party planner or good friend to stand lookout at the evening celebration.
- Don't hesitate to hold a pre-party pow-wow with your young guests regarding behavioral expectations and consequences of misconduct (i.e., calling parents for early pickup).
- Reduce the likelihood of kids acting out due to boredom or being tempted by alcohol by planning a separate kids' party.

At other kids' bar/bat mitzvah:
- Accompany your child to services and model appropriate behavior.
- Nix sexually suggestive and other improper or clothing choices.
- Organize meetings with parents of your child's religious school or day school classmates to brainstorm ideas and join forces.
- Remember that responsibility for our children's behavior at a friend's b'nai mitzvah doesn't belong to day school principals, religious school directors, rabbis, or other parents. It belongs to us.
- Embrace the hidden gifts of the bar or bat mitzvah that we'll discuss in the next section.

The Hidden Gifts of the Bar and Bat Mitzvah

When we think of bar and bat mitzvah gifts many things come to mind: fountain pens, cuff links, picture frames, checks. But the true gifts of this religious rite of passage extend far beyond the envelopes and boxes piled up at the party door. Here are a few of the intangible yet invaluable presents the bar or bat mitzvah ritual bestows upon our families.

What the Bar/Bat Mitzvah Process Gives to Our Child

Confidence. If we look into the eyes of the bar mitzvah boy during the first moments of his service we will see one thing and one thing only—pure, unadulterated panic. But as the service progresses, he stands up straighter and walks taller, until he's officially playing the crowd by *Adon Olam*. At the kiddush—as the mazel tovs pile on like lox on bagels—we look again at the bar mitzvah boy, and we see that he is beaming with pure, unadulterated confidence (the kind of confidence that grows into *genuine*, deserved self-esteem, which will help him to make strong, independent decisions at a time in his life when peer pressure is at its pinnacle).

Resilience. Researchers have tapped resilience—the fundamental ability to roll with the punches of life—as among the most powerful predictors of children's future success and happiness. The bar/bat mitzvah experience is an exercise in resilience. For not only must our children study their Torah portions for months on end—they must stumble over them for months on end as they struggle to recite them (ask anyone who has ever tried to read trope!). Not only do they write and rewrite their *d'var Torahs*, they must conquer their nerves and deliver them to hundreds of congregants. The bar/bat mitzvah process is a series of hurdles and jumps. A long, hard course with a brightly wrapped gift of steadfast resilience waiting at the end.

L'dor v'dor. A beautiful and increasingly popular tradition is to open the ark and pass the Torah from grandparents to parents to the bar/bat mitzvah child. This passing of the holy scroll is the embodiment of *l'dor v'dor*—from generation to generation. Adolescence is by definition a time of transition—a steady stream of physical, emotional, and social changes. Yet when our child receives the Torah—passed hand to hand to him—on the morning of his bar mitzvah, he feels the stability, consistency, and safety that comes from being embedded in generations of tradition.

Sharing the Spotlight

One of the most generous, heartfelt acts on the part of a bar or bat mitzvah is "twinning," or symbolically sharing his or her big day with another deserving individual. Not only does this humanitarian deed infuse additional meaning into the ceremony, it makes the abstract concept of social responsibility tangible for our child. Here are some bar/bat mitzvah twinning programs and opportunities adapted from *Mitzvah Chic* by Gail Anthony Greenberg:

Twinning with an Israeli AMIT Child
For $250, your child can be twinned with a less fortunate Israeli child in an AMIT school. Your gift pays for an Oneg Shabbat for the Israeli bar/bat mitzvah and a bronze State of Israel medal and personalized

certificate for your child. Twins are encouraged to keep up their relationship as pen pals. (www.amitchildren.org)

Twinning with an Israeli Child through Emunah of America
This organization provides a broad range of social services in Israel including housing, care and education of neglected and abused children, and settlement of immigrant families. They sell "Simcha Share" certificates in multiples of $36; a contribution of $360 or more earns a medallion. (http://www.emunah.org/bar-bat-mitzvah.php)

Twinning with a Russian Child
The Bay Area Council for Jewish Rescue and Renewal matches American children with children in the former Soviet Union. The twins communicate with one another and form a bond that only grows stronger when the American child spiritually includes his or her twin in the ceremony. (www.bacjrr.org)

Twinning with an Ethiopian Child
The North American Conference on Ethiopian Jewry (NACOEJ) matches children worldwide with Ethiopian Jewish children living in Israel. In addition to the personal benefit from the friendships that often develop between twins, your financial gift helps to improve quality of life for all the Ethiopian Jewish children in the community. (www.nacoej.org)

Twinning with a Rescuer
This program of the Jewish Foundation for the Righteous allows a child to help the Jewish community repay a collective debt of gratitude. The child selects a particular rescuer to be twinned with and

makes a donation to the JFR. The suggested minimum gift is $180. The bar mitzvah or bat mitzvah receives a Twinning Certificate and a presentation can be made from the bimah if your rabbi approves. (www.jfr.org)

Holocaust Twinning

Remember Us: The Holocaust Bnai Mitzvah Project is a simple, yet meaningful program. It provides a bar/bat mitzvah student with the name of a child lost in the Holocaust, information about him or her, and suggestions on how to incorporate this child's memory into your child's *simcha*. Remember Us also provides teacher and parent guides. The program is free. (www.remember-us.org)

What Our Child's Bar/Bat Mitzvah Ceremony Gives Us

An opportunity to express our love for our child. Caught up in the rocketing pace of twenty-first-century life, we scarcely have a moment to tell our children how we feel about them. Sure we kiss them goodnight and tell them we love them (if they are nice enough to still let us do so), but rarely—if ever—do we express it in the emotional, heartfelt way we do on the day they become a bar or bat mitzvah.

Reaffirmation of our purpose. All modesty aside here, bringing our son or daughter to the bar or bat mitzvah bimah is a mega-accomplishment! It means we've put valuable time and resources into ensuring our child receives a Jewish education and is armed with a Jewish identity, and have fulfilled our obligation to God, to ourselves, to our children, and to our people.

A rite of passage of our very own. The bar or bat mitzvah is a rite of passage for our children—a marker of their transition from one stage of life to another. But it is also a rite of passage for us. For as our children transform into teenagers, we must transform as parents. In our child's bar or bat mitzvah we have a stepping-stone to help us find our way to the next stage in our parental journey.

A wonderful, happy family memory. Do you remember the concept of flashbulb memories from Chapter 9—memories that stick around in our minds for the long haul? Well, our child's bar or bat mitzvah is a surefire flashbulb memory—a festive, jubilant, meaningful family memory that will nourish our souls for years to come.

Life in perspective. It's all too easy to get caught up in the everyday hassles of parenting. But every now and then something comes along and puts it all in perspective, enabling us to savor the moment and stop—at least temporarily—and smell the roses. Our child's bar or bat mitzvah is one of those rare and glorious times in our lives when all the universe lines up—when we feel God's divine presence, know exactly what matters and what does not, and understand precisely why we're here.

CHAPTER 11

Here Comes
Santa Claus

One of the certainties of Jewish parenthood is that at some time or another we'll find ourselves caught between an ornament-draped evergreen and a stocking-strung fireplace.

We're inevitably at the mall—in the midst of a (clearly desperate) Hanukkah shopping trip—when our child asks, "Please, can I get a picture with Santa Claus?" Upon hearing this plea, our shopping-bag-clad arms instantly tense—not due to the two-mile-long line of kids currently standing between our child and jolly old Saint Nick, but because we have no idea whatsoever whether to a) plop down our packages and heed this request, b) eliminate Santa's appeal by revealing that he's merely the mall custodian in yuletide drag, or c) pretend we didn't hear the question, grab our kid, and hightail it out of there.

Sure, we've all attempted to placate our kids' Santa fascination with the tried-and-true "eight nights is better than one night" argument. But this technique rarely does the trick, as Hanukkah is neither intended to nor can it stand in for Christmas. Besides, even a fully decked Hanukkah bush doesn't change the fact that at the brownie troop holiday party there were nineteen red and green cupcakes and a single blue-and-white one.

So what *is* the best way to approach our seasonal Santa stickler? As I see it the answer is an anthropological one.

You know—as in Anthropology 101, the scientific, comparative study of human cultures, customs, and beliefs. (Okay, I agree it seems a solution straight out of left field, but bear with me as I get to the point.)

When anthropologists set foot on foreign turf, they don't feel threatened by the unfamiliar customs, or tempted to ignore them altogether. They don't worry that in allowing themselves to experience someone else's traditions, they'll be turning their back on their own. Instead they release themselves to the moment. Tasting it. Savoring it. Fueling themselves with insight into a rich culture that does not belong to them.

It's the same situation with Christmas. The entire experience is captivating. The music, the lights, the cheesy television specials—it is a holiday overflowing in contagious excitement. But that doesn't mean we must shield our children from the yuletide festivities, as if allowing them to breathe in the Christmas spirit will somehow reduce their Jewishness. To the contrary, it will only confirm who they are.

By approaching Santa and the rest of it as a vehicle for enlightening—rather than alienating—our kids, we let go of the sleighful of Jewish parental guilt that traditionally accompanies the Christmas season. We afford our children the basic foundation and cultural literacy they need to effectively integrate into our predominantly Christian society. But most important, in lowering our guard and letting our children experience that which is not theirs, we help them recognize and appreciate all that is.

What Would a Jewish Anthropologist Do?

(Disclaimer: The following tips are drawn from my personal experiences and beliefs as a Conservative Jewish parent. They are not meant to replace the philosophy or level of observance of another parent. In intermarried families, especially, the boundaries may differ significantly.)

- A Jewish anthropologist *would* celebrate the beautiful, meaningful holiday of Hanukkah with her family.
- A Jewish anthropologist *would not* try to make Hanukkah a replacement for Christmas by using yuletide knockoffs like Hanukkah bushes or blue-and-white stockings.
- A Jewish anthropologist *would* allow her family to attend Christmas celebrations in the homes of gentile friends.
- A Jewish anthropologist *would not* bring Christmas into her own home.
- A Jewish anthropologist *would* allow her children to give Christmas gifts to non-Jewish teachers, friends, neighbors, and other special people.
- A Jewish anthropologist *would not* worry if her kids felt a little left out of the Christmas fun, knowing it's all part of building a strong Jewish identity.
- A Jewish anthropologist *would* add Hanukkah fun to her child's class holiday party (i.e., sending in dreidels—complete with game rules—and Hanukkah books for the teacher to share with the class or popping by school with a box full of jelly doughnuts).
- A Jewish anthropologist *would not* remain silent if her child's public school seemed to be going blatantly overboard in the Christmas festivities department. (For a full rundown of what is and is not constitutionally acceptable in the classroom—and your protocol for recourse—check the Anti-Defamation League website at www.adl.org.)
- A Jewish anthropologist *would* have faith that in making Judaism an ever-present defining force in her family's daily lives, she is

ensuring that—picture with Santa or no picture with Santa—her children's Jewish souls remain filled to the rim from Christmas to Christmas, from Rosh Hashanah to Rosh Hashanah.

Nourishing Our Children's Jewish Souls

One of the most glorious side effects of opening our kids' eyes to that which is not theirs is helping them embrace that which is. After all, our most powerful antidote to the December dilemma (and many of the parenting hurdles we face the other eleven months of the year, for that matter) is making Judaism an ever-present, defining force in our children's daily lives. The following guide will help you make the Jewish holidays extra meaningful for your kids.

Shabbat

Thanks to the predictability and frequency of Shabbat, this wonderful Jewish holiday—often considered the heart of Jewish life—is among our most powerful means of building a strong Jewish identity in our kids. Refer back to Chapter 7 for lots of kid-friendly Shabbat suggestions.

Rosh Hashanah

What better way to start off the year than by showing the true apples of your eye just how much you love them? Here are some sweet, Jewish-identity-fostering suggestions for Rosh Hashanah:

- Take your kids to a paint-it-yourself ceramic shop and decorate kiddush cups, apple plates, or honey bowls together.
- Leave Hershey's Kisses on their pillows on Erev Rosh Hashanah along with a note wishing them a sweet New Year.

- Celebrate the birthday of the world by planting a tree together.
- Have a honey-cake-baking party.
- Let your children design the Rosh Hashanah table cloth and challah cover using fabric crayons or markers.
- Take a family excursion to an apple-picking orchard.
- Log on to www.torahtots.com and www.babaganewz.com, where little "techies" can find fun Rosh Hashanah games and activities.
- Turn an apple on its side and cut it in half to reveal a star in the middle. Dip the fruit in washable paint and let your little stars stamp away.
- Steal some time to read a High Holiday picture book together (even if they complain that they're *way* too old to listen to a story!). Some noteworthy choices are *Gershon's Monster: A Tale for the Jewish New Year* by Eric Kimmel; *The World's Birthday* by Barbara Diamond Goldin; *Sophie and the Shofar* by Fran Manushkin; and *How the Rosh Hashanah Challah Became Round* by Sylvia Epstein.

Missing School for the Holidays

As a Jewish day school teacher it often seemed as if—barring the odd year when things shook out so the holidays fell on the weekends—I didn't see my students for the majority of September and October. The school calendar would then compensate (much to my students' dismay) by shortening the Thanksgiving and winter breaks.

For children who attend public, secular private, or non-Jewish parochial schools, however, class goes on, Jewish holy day or no Jewish holy day (unless you live in a region of the country with such a large Jewish population that they close for major Jewish holidays). As our children move up through elementary and middle school this can result in their missing a significant amount of academic material. Here are some suggestions to minimize academic stress in the wake of the holidays:

- Don't compromise your family's Jewish values over a few missed school days. Classwork can always be made up in the future, but a message you send your child that Judaism is less important than a stellar attendance record, cannot be taken back.
- Touch base with the teacher first thing in the school year, telling her that your child will be missing class for the Jewish holidays and letting her know which dates he or she will be absent. As the holidays approach, send a reminder note asking for any work your child can do in advance. Upon your child's return to school, send another note asking about work to be made up.
- While most schools are understanding and accommodating to Jewish students, it's important to be aware of your legal rights. Federal law states that no child should be penalized for missing school for a religious holiday. This becomes more significant as our kids move toward middle school and begin taking exams. If a teacher or school will not allow your child to make up a test administered on a Jewish holiday, don't hesitate to contact the principal, the school board, or the Anti-Defamation League.

Yom Kippur

Yom Kippur, the day of repentance, holds many important lessons for our children. It teaches them to be conscious of their actions, and own up to their mistakes. It helps them comprehend that while it's natural to slip up now and then, God expects us to learn from our transgressions and aspire to avoid repeating them in the future. It helps them recognize and embrace their ability to grow both morally and spiritually. Here are suggestions to ensure your children learn the invaluable lessons of the holiest day of the Jewish year:

- Gather the family together in an "I'm Sorry" circle. Have family members take turns apologizing to one another for hurtful things they've done in the past year, and say how they plan to avoid these transgressions in the future (i.e., "I'm sorry that I hit Emma when she took my football. Next time I will ask her nicely to give it to me . . . and if that doesn't work I will ask my mom for help").
- Have a Tashlich ceremony by a lake or river so kids can cast their sins away in the form of bread crumbs and start out the year with a fresh, clean slate.
- On the day before Yom Kippur, suggests Rabbi Yosef I. Abramowitz, author of *Jewish Family and Life: Traditions, Holidays, and Values for Today's Parents and Children*, have everyone in the family write a letter to themselves stating what they would like to do better in the coming year. Stash the letters away until the holidays roll around the following year, then put them in the mail. Kids will love receiving these annual letters and they can be used as a gauge of how they did in fulfilling their resolutions.
- Since the beginning of Yizkor on Yom Kippur is generally preceded by a mass exodus of the younger generation to junior congregation or the playground, this emotional service is something of a mystery to kids. To help children understand the meaning of the Yizkor service, Abramowitz suggests taking some time prior to the holiday to look at pictures of family members who have died, tell stories, and talk about the positive personality traits and values of these individuals.

Passover

For parents of restless kids, a Passover Seder can seem longer than
the forty years our ancestors spent wandering through the desert.
Taking into account that every family has different comfort levels,
objectives, and degrees of observance, here are some tips toward
creating a fun and meaningful Passover Seder for all kinds of kids—
wise, wicked, simple, and just plain unable to ask:

That's the ticket. Prior to the big night, make "matzoh tickets" out
of index cards. Award the tickets to children throughout the Seder
for reciting the Mah Nishtanah, answering tricky Passover trivia
questions, helping little brothers and sisters make Hillel sand-
wiches, and exhibiting oodles of other desirable Seder behaviors. At
the end of the evening let ticket holders redeem their winnings for
Passover-related prizes (i.e., stickers, candies, plastic frogs).

Keep the karpas coming. Grumpy kids and hungry tummies go
hand in hand. A steady flow of *karpas* (a.k.a. carrots and celery) and
kosher-for-Passover salad dressing for double dipping will keep
your kids happily crunching away until it's time for the main
course.

Give out goody bags. Keep your junior Seder participants content
and occupied with special plague goody bags. While you can purchase already prepared "bags of plagues" at Judaica stores and online for around twelve dollars apiece, you can accomplish the same
thing at the dollar store for a fraction of the price. Try plastic sunglasses for darkness; plastic frogs, wild beasts, and insects; kosher-
for-Passover marshmallows for hail; red dot stickers for boils; and
Band-Aids for blood.

Don't Passover the books. Visit a library or bookstore and stock up on Passover-themed books. Scatter them around the table for children to peruse during the longest stretches of the Seder. A few sure-fire hits are *Shlemiel Crooks* by Anna Olswanger, *Wonders and Miracles* by Eric Kimmel, and *Uncle Eli's Passover Haggadah* by Eliezer Segal.

Have an afikomen search party. It's always the same story at my house: the big cousins find the afikomen and the little cousins get upset; the little cousins get a prize anyway and the big cousins get upset. By making the afikomen hunt a team effort rather than a competition, we can do away with such griping. Use Post-It notes to lead the search party from one destination to the next (i.e., "Go to the place where Elijah will enter" or "Pharaoh had frogs jumping in his bed, see if there are any jumping in yours"). The clues should ultimately lead the pack to the elusive dessert of honor. Be prepared with inexpensive "afikomen finder" rewards for the whole crew.

Take plague breaks. Help kids stay focused and fidget-free during long Seders by periodically letting them get their wiggles out. Should your children's attention start to stray from the task at hand, call for a "plague break" and instruct all antsy guests to jump like frogs or run in place like wild beasts.

Have a matzoh match. Before the Seder, write matched pairs of Passover words on index cards. For example, write *Hillel* on one card and *sandwich* on another, *ten* on one card and *plagues* on another. Keep going—*four/questions; matzoh/ball; Elijah's/cup*—until you have enough cards to secretly stash one under every guest's plate. Sometime before dinner, tell everyone to lift their plates, look at the card, and track down their matching half. (Hint: For children too young to read—or to understand the matching concept—cut cards in half making irregular puzzle cuts and write one word on each half. When kids find a card that "fits" theirs, they'll know they've found their match).

Put a spotlight on stories. The true purpose of the Seder is to pass down the Passover story from generation to generation, but why stop there? Ask a few of your senior guests to come prepared to share stories about Seders past. When kids get antsy, pass a play microphone to a family patriarch or matriarch and let the storytelling begin.

Keep an eye on the big picture. Sure, planning a kid-friendly Seder is liable to take more work than simply bribing our kids to behave with a pound of chocolate-covered macaroons or locking them in the playroom with a babysitter for the night. But we'll know our efforts have been well worth our while when our fidgety children one day do the same for our fidgety grandchildren.

Observing Yom Hashoah (Holocaust Remembrance Day) with Children

Yom Hashoah is observed on the 27th of Nissan. It is a day to remember the six million Jews killed in the Holocaust, and is one we must recognize with our school-age children. Only in so doing can we ensure that this atrocity is never forgotten. How do we even begin to broach the topic of the Holocaust with Jewish children? By introducing this overwhelming concept little by little, layer by layer. Here is a framework for age-appropriate Holocaust discussion, provided by Jewish family educator Janet Schatten:

Grade Level	History	Concepts	Suggested Books
Kindergarten	Jewish life before the Holocaust	Jewish identity	*It Could Always Be Worse* by Margot Zemach
First grade	European Jewish life before the Shoah	Jewish identity	*The Tattooed Torah* by Marvell Ginsburg; *Nine Spoons* by Nancy Stillerman
Second grade	European Jewish life before the Shoah; Nazi occupation	Anti-Jewish laws and restrictions; yellow stars; Righteous Gentiles	*The Yellow Star* by Carmen Agra Deedy; *The Never-Ending Greenness* by Neil Walman
Third grade	Ghettoes; hiding	Jews helping Jews; spiritual resistance; Righteous Gentiles	*Child of the Warsaw Ghetto* by David Adler; *Twenty and Ten* by Claire Hutchet Bishop

Fourth grade	Concentration camps; forced labor; rescue	Spiritual resistance; Righteous Gentiles	*Keeping the Promise* by Tammy Lehman-Wilzig; *When Hitler Stole Pink Rabbit* by Judith Kerr
Fifth grade	Death camps; life reborn	Armed and unarmed resistance	*Number the Stars* by Lois Lowry; *Snow Treasure* by Marie McSwigan
Middle school	Nazi Germany; Hitler's rise to power	Tolerance vs. intolerance; genocide	*The Upstairs Room* by Johanna Reiss; *The Diary of Anne Frank*; *Escape to the Forest* by Ruth Yaffe Radin; *Night* by Elie Wiesel

Hanukkah

Thanks to its opportune timing, Hanukkah—a once minor holiday—has become a defining Jewish event for American children. It's especially important, therefore, that we take this holiday beyond a materialistic level. We can shift the emphasis away from presents and onto what the Rugrats call the "true meany" of Hanukkah—not to mention affording our kids all the benefits of family rituals we

(231)

discussed in Chapter 7—by establishing theme nights. Here are eight nights of ideas to get you started:

Hanukkah memory night. Invite friends and relatives over for a night of *sufganiot* (jelly doughnuts) and Hanukkah memory swapping. Follow the storytelling with Hanukkah picture-frame making. Inexpensive plastic frames, holiday accessories (like dreidels and colorful candles), and a hot glue gun are all you'll need to preserve the memory of Hanukkah memory night forever.

Tzedakah night. Take your kids to the toy store, where they can use a portion of their tzedakah money to buy a gift for a needy child. Let them personally deliver it to a children's hospital, homeless shelter, or toy collection site.

Dreidel showdown night. Your family will have "loads" of fun stacking up the gelt in an annual family dreidel tournament.

Movie night. Follow up the Hanukkah candles with a bowl of popcorn and a family movie. (Try *A Rugrats Chanukah* or Adam Sandler's *Eight Crazy Nights.*)

Latke-making night. Whether it is peeling, washing, or frying, making latkes is almost as much fun for kids as eating them.

Book night. Reserve the gift giving on this night exclusively for great reads. Follow up by baking Hanukkah cookies together and reading books aloud. (Try Eric Kimmel's *Herschel and the Hanukkah Goblins* and *How Mindy Saved Hanukkah.*)

"Share the magic" night. Invite non-Jewish friends to share in a night of Hanukkah fun. Play traditional games and songs and, of course, serve up plenty of latkes.

Big present night. Okay, so it's materialistic. But when balanced with seven nights of meaning and ritual, it feels just right.

I know what you're thinking. Only one big present night? That's not even going to make a dent in my kids' Hanukkah wish lists! Dreidels instead of designer jeans? Latkes instead of Lindsay Lohan music? I'll never hear the end of it!

You bet you will—as long as you read the next chapter . . .

CHAPTER 12

Toys, Toys, Toys

The Magic of the Spend/Save/Tzedakah Plan

If it seems your child walks through life with a shopping bag in hand, you're not alone. After all, grade-schoolers and "the gimmes" go together like Jewish mothers and guilt. But we shouldn't write off our kids as greedy and fiscally clueless until we have a clear understanding of how they got there.

Relentless Marketing

Did you know that toy commercials are most effective when they feature child actors two years older than their target market? Well, the toy companies do, because they spend gadzillions of dollars a year figuring out how to get our kids to beg us to buy them everything from Scooby Doo Goo to neon Nerf footballs to Bratz beauty salons.

Human Socio-Emotional Development

As you may recall from Chapter 7, school-age children are in what psychologist Stanley Greenspan called the "world is other kids" stage. That means being accepted by the group consistently tops their daily to-do lists. How does a grade-schooler go about being accepted by the group? By having all the same (or better) stuff as everyone else. And when I say the same, I mean the *same*—in the grade-school world, coolness and uncoolness are clearly separated by a two-inch name-brand label.

Human Cognitive Development

The vast majority of grade-schoolers (up to age eleven) are what cognitive psychologists call concrete thinkers. That means they have a tough time conceptualizing anything they can't physically see or touch. Money—thanks to credit cards, checks, Internet PayPal accounts, and the like—is a hugely abstract concept. Through the eyes of a grade-school-age concrete thinker, the difference between three hundred dollars, thirty dollars, and three dollars is largely inconsequential. I know it seems hard to believe, but trust me, after a decade and a half as an elementary school teacher, I can tell you that, with rare exception, the only way a five- to ten-year-old is going to truly understand the quantitative distinction between these amounts is if she actually sees three hundred one-dollar bills piled next to thirty one-dollar bills piled next to three one-dollar bills.

Pushover Parents

Okay, I apologize in advance for this one, but hey, if we are going to reel in our kids' materialistic tendencies, we need to face the harsh reality that we've played a part in creating them. We love our children. We want them to have all the wonderful things life has to offer. But at what cost?

Fortunately, it's perfectly possible to give these forces a run for their money thanks to the Spend/Save/Tzedakah Plan: A super-concrete, easy-to-implement program that helps kids grasp the value of money, empowers them with financial smarts, encourages them to give back to their community, and turns pushover parents into purposeful financial role models, all in one fell swoop. Here's what you need to know to put this marvelous plan into action for your little spenders.

All About Allowances

First things first—we can't teach our grade-schoolers to manage their money wisely unless they actually have money of their own to manage. Sure they've got the usual Hanukkah and birthday booty; but for the Spend/Save/Tzedakah Plan to have maximal impact, kids need to see at least some funds arriving in predictable increments. This is the reason that—somewhere around age five or six—children should begin receiving a weekly allowance.

Experts are split on the best way to approach allowances. Some say they should be linked to chores and responsibilities, others believe they should be a separate entity altogether. There are convincing arguments in either camp, and the direction you take should reflect a careful, personal choice.

In my house I've chosen to intertwine chores and allowances as I feel that preparing my kids for real life entails helping them understand that it's not a free ride—that money is earned, not awarded, and that most of the time you get back what you put in. This is not to say, of course, that I go overboard on the chores, sipping mimosas while my kids scrub the house for their allowance. But I do feel that reasonable, age-appropriate chores—clearing the table, taking out the trash, walking the dog, picking up the playroom—are perfectly fitting.

Still, there can be a fine line between tying chores into allowances and raising kids who won't lift a finger unless they are being paid. To avoid this mind-set, we approach chores as part of our responsibility to our family. We hold democratic family meetings to determine what's fair and expected of each child in the household job department—and what the consequences will be should someone drop the ball.

This brings us to the next allowance issue—how much should we give our kids? There are lots of suggested formulas out there, but when it comes to the Spend/Save/Tzedakah Plan, utilizing the popular dollar-per-year-of-age formula (a seven-year-old would receive seven dollars weekly, a nine-year-old nine dollars weekly) is always a good bet.

That's a ton of money! you may be thinking. Eleven dollars a week for my eleven-year-old?! I'll be in the poorhouse while my kids are rolling in dough!

I know it seems a bit excessive, but just keep reading. I promise that even if you have twelve-year-old quadruplets, if you stick closely to the S/S/T Plan you'll end up saving money (not to mention your sanity) in the end. Besides, the dollar-per-year allowance approach allows for fair, indisputable differentiation among older and younger siblings and predictable annual increases.

Three Little Piggies

The basic premise of the S/S/T Plan is to have our kids regularly divide their money into three distinct sections—one for personal spending, one for saving for the future, and one for giving to others. Deciding how to allocate the money (in my house it's 60 percent spending, 30 percent savings, and 10 percent tzedakah is a personal family choice, but it's important to make sure your kids stick to their designated amounts every week. (It's also a personal family choice as to whether or not your kids split their birthday and Hanukkah gift gelt among the three categories or just stash it all in the spending pile.)

To avoid confusion and misplaced or lost money, it's best to have kids store their spending, saving, and tzedakah money separately. A favorite traditional piggy bank works well for the spending piece. You can use a second piggy to stash the saved money, or check with your local bank to see if it offers kiddie savings accounts with no minimum balance and no service charges (many do). Finally, a traditional tzedakah box is ideal for the giving category. (If you prefer one-stop shopping, you can look for innovative piggy banks that are already divided into three sections. My personal favorite is the Learning Cents Bank, which can be purchased at www.learning cents.com for $21.99.)

Spending. For the S/S/T Plan to work its magic, children should be required to use their personal spending money for all nonessential purchases other than birthday and Hanukkah gifts. That means our kids pay for their own popcorn at the movies, Power Ranger Popsicles from the ice-cream man, and fruitless attempts on the "try-to-pick-up-a-stuffed-animal-with-a-metal-claw" machine. (See, I told you we'd end up saving money!) Still doubtful? Consider the following scenarios:

Shopping at Target <u>without</u> the Spend/Save/Tzedakah Plan:
Child: *Can I get that Hot Wheels car?*
Parent: *No.*
Child: *Please? It's only $1.29, and I've really been wanting that one.*
Parent: *I said NO.*
Child: *But, it's a Hummer Hot Wheels—with real monster truck wheels!*
Parent: *How many times do I have to tell you? No means no!*
Child: *Please? PLEASE? PLEEEEASE?!!!!*
Parent: *Okay, fine. Just put it in the cart and stop whining.*

(Epilogue: The same scene plays out the next day only this time the kid wants a pair of $70 Heelys roller sneakers.)

Shopping at Target <u>with</u> the Spend/Save/Tzedakah Plan:
Child: *Can I get that Hot Wheels car?*
Parent: *Sure. You can use your spending money any way you'd like.*
Child: *Well, I don't really need it. I'd rather save my money for those Heelys roller sneakers.*

One final point—when it comes to how our children use their spending money we parents largely need to keep our opinions to ourselves. In other words, even if it's crystal clear to us that our child is making a regrettable decision spending a week's worth of allowance on three cans of Silly String, we need to take a deep breath and let her make the purchase. After all, only by feeling the consequences of their unwise financial decisions—and realizing that, with extremely rare exceptions, their parents aren't going to bail them out—will our children come to understand the value of money and the importance of thinking before jumping into the checkout line.

I know what you're thinking. What happens when my son wants to cash in his spending money for a Mortal Kombat video game? Or my daughter returns from the mall with a microscopic miniskirt?

You can rest assured that implementing the S/S/T Plan doesn't entail turning over our parenting responsibilities to a pink piggy bank. Rather we should take this opportunity to communicate the thinking and values behind our edict: "I understand that it's your money to spend, but I'm not comfortable with the message that skirt sends. Why don't we go see if we can find one that's just as cute but not quite as mini?" "I know that lots of kids your age play Mortal Kombat, but I don't believe that blood, guts, and killing should ever be made into a game. Besides, it is rated T for Teen and you're only twelve; I wouldn't be doing my job if I let you buy that game."

While our children are unlikely to agree outwardly with our reasoning, such discussion will help them understand that values—not just affordability and availability—play a central role in our financial choices as well.

Keeping Up with the Trumpsteins

One thing we should understand about school-age children is that they are fairness fanatics. Whether we are talking about cookies or houses, they believe the goods should be distributed absolutely evenly—or they call foul. This is the reason that around the time our child enters second or third grade, we start hearing a whole heck of a lot about the Trumpsteins . . .

"Why don't you make as much money as Mr. Trumpstein?"

As our kids become increasingly aware of the inner workings of the working world, they recognize that the nice bank teller doesn't hand out dollar bills like lollipops, and that—unless we have a mega–trust fund—the amount of cash in our pocket is directly related to our occupation. The most important point to communicate to our child, say Eileen and Jon Gallo, authors of *The Financially Intelligent Parent*, is that salary size is not necessarily a scorecard of success, but often a reflection of life choices. We can drive home this crucial concept with comments like "There were lots of jobs that I could have chosen, and—yes—some probably would have given me a bigger paycheck. But I chose to teach at the university because I love working with students and doing important research. Plus it gives me more flexibility to be with the family."

> ### "Benjamin Trumpstein said his house cost \$3 million. How much did our house cost?"
>
> Although it is tempting to pretend we didn't hear the question when a curveball of this caliber is thrown our way, denial is hardly an appropriate response. After all, if our kid is old enough to think up the question, chances are that he's also old enough to grasp the answer to some degree. Rather, say the Gallos, it's okay for parents to reveal a dollar amount—as long as such information is followed up by a reality check to the effect of "It is true that the Trumpsteins' house cost more than ours, in fact there are lots of houses that cost more than ours; but there are also lots of houses that cost less than ours." On the tails of this comment must come a mushy, gushy, what's-really-important-in-life statement such as "But it doesn't matter how big a house is. What matters is what happens inside of it. If a family is loving and close, their house will be a nice, happy, warm place to be. Otherwise, it will be a lonely house, no matter how big it is—no matter how many plasma-screen TVs are on the walls."

Saving. Just to clarify. The kind of savings we're talking about here is the kind you put away for a long-term goal—like going to college or spending a high-school semester in Israel—not an exorbitantly pricey toy or an overpriced outfit. The key here is to help our children move beyond the instant gratification mentality toward understanding that some things cost so much money it takes years to save and pay for them.

Finally, it's important for kids to have a concrete representation of their savings progress. Have them place a sticker on a chart each time they pass a ten-dollar increment, or save the bank statements from their kiddie savings account in a notebook. We parents will be as excited as our kids to see how much money they are putting away for their future!

Tzedakah. Our children live largely within a vacuum. They have their families, their friends, their schools, their neighborhoods, and their material possessions. They don't often think about others who are less fortunate, not because they don't care but because they are not used to thinking outside their familiar worlds. The tzedakah component of the S/S/T Plan helps bridge this gap for our children and pave the way toward a *menschlich* philanthropic adulthood.

To make the concept of tzedakah more concrete for grade-schoolers, have them decide in advance on a particular cause to which they want to donate when they reach a target amount. They can decorate the tzedakah box to go along with the theme. A child who plans to donate his giving money to the Humane Society, for example, might adorn his box with magazine pictures of animals or photos of his own pets. A child who wants to donate to a hospital might use drawings of sunshine, hearts, and flowers. If possible, take your child to physically deliver the tzedakah box to the recipients.

By putting away a small portion of their allowance toward tzedakah each week, our children will begin to appreciate their responsibility as Jews and human beings to share their resources with the community. They'll come to recognize that many of life's most precious gifts come without a bar code.

Jewish Parent 911

Curbing Kiddie Materialism

You didn't think we parents could get off the hook that easily did you? After all, while implementing the Spend/Save/Tzedakah Plan is the cornerstone in our efforts to curb our kids' obsession with all things material, it doesn't stand alone. Here are other parental steps to ensure our children remain grounded, even in the midst of a spend-happy world.

Don't Be a Material Girl

We are our children's role models, the sculptors of their value systems, and they are constantly looking to us for direction. In other words, next time we are at the mall with our kids and we see a pair of strappy metallic sandals that make our heart skip a beat, we must fight the urge to lunge for our wallets, and instead say: "Wow, those shoes are really cute. But I already have plenty of sandals. I [deep cleansing breath] really don't need another pair."

Tune 'Em Out

As I mentioned earlier, media moguls spend billions of dollars a year trying to figure out when, where, and how to air television commercials that will prompt our child to bolt off the couch and plead with us to buy them particular products. We can loosen the media's hold on our children (and our pocketbooks) by limiting their overall TV viewing time. Enforcing a one-hour daily total screen time rule (television, Tivo, computers, and video games) works wonders in achieving this goal—as do choosing commercial-free TV, showing

DVDs or recording favorite shows, and fast-forwarding over the commercials.

Have Them Work Within a Budget
Even when our kids are shopping for something that falls outside their personal spending category—say, school clothes—we should have them work within monetary constraints. Rather than allowing our daughter to grab anything and everything off the rack during a back-to-school shopping spree, we should tell her she has X amount to spend and it's up to her (assuming she picks clothing we consider acceptable) to decide how to spend it. That way she'll think twice before blowing half her money on a $50 Juicy sweatshirt. (This is no guarantee, of course, that our fashion-conscious preteen will opt for the $9.99 Juicy knockoffs one rack over, but the experience will give her valuable hands-on experience making financial choices.)

Don't Go Overboard on Gifts
Just because our daughter *wants* three American Girl dolls for her birthday, and we happen to have received a nice bonus last week, doesn't mean we should *buy* our daughter three American Girl dolls for her birthday. Just the contrary, in fact, as such overindulgence promotes a sense of entitlement and frivolity that children are likely to carry with them throughout life.

Show Them How to Have Fun for Free
Modern kids often associate fun with expense—going to the movies, buying new video games, shopping for clothes, going on vacations. By planning special family experiences that just happen to be free—taking nature walks, swimming at a nearby lake or beach,

visiting the library, riding bikes, playing board games—we help our kids understand that entertainment exists beyond the wallet.

Help Them See What Is Truly Priceless
Most children have yet to gain the maturity and life experience to recognize that not everything of value comes with a price tag. We can help our kids understand intangible value by making comments like "This kiddush cup has been in our family for generations; it may be tarnished and old but I would never want to replace it." Or "There is nothing I'd rather be doing during winter vacation than spending time at home together as a family." While our children may not be fully prepared to grasp the meaning of such remarks, they are acquiring the foundation they need to ultimately learn the true meaning of the word "priceless."

Babes in Grown-up Toyland

If you really concentrate, you might remember the first time you bumped into the grown-up toy craze when you were an expectant parent registering for gifts at your local Baby Mega Warehouse store. You'd just used your funky portable gift registry scanner to inform anyone who was interested that you were positively dying for those cute teddy-bear crib sheets when you decided to take a casual stroll through the newborn toy section. But just as you began to ooh and ahh over a furry red dancing Elmo, you noticed something that looked suspiciously like a laptop computer. Upon closer inspection you realized that—by gosh—it *was* a laptop computer! Only the keys had cows and sheep on them instead of letters. Suddenly panicked that your unborn child was about to get behind the eight ball before he was even the size of an eight ball, you ended up registering not only for the My First Laptop toy but also for the Electronic Alphabet Ball and the I Can Learn French Before I Get My First Tooth Palm Pilot.

It's not that there's anything blatantly offensive about baby electronic toys. Well, I guess there is that rob-a-new-parent-blind pricing factor—and the possibility that overusing electronic toys in infancy could lead to future electronic game addictions and less opportunity for critical brain development. But the most troublesome aspect of baby electronic toys is that they replace good old-fashioned non-electronic, non-flashing, non-singing, non—instantly gratifying toys—like wooden blocks.

Proof positive of this premise is the recently launched Barbie prepaid cell phone, target market eight- to twelve-year-old girls. It wasn't too long ago that eight- to twelve-year-old girls cornered the market on Barbie dolls. But today, thanks to the grown-up toy craze, tweens are snubbing Barbie and setting their sights on cell phones bearing her likeness instead. The saddest part is that if these girls were honest with themselves and one another, they'd likely give their last free wireless minute for a chance to dress a real Barbie doll up for a hot date with Ken. Meanwhile, who's playing with Barbie and the gang? Preschoolers who can't decide whether to chew on Barbie's go-go boot or her patent leather pocketbook!

I must ask you this, my fellow twenty-first-century parents: Have you ever wondered why archaeologists find baby dolls wrapped up with ancient Egyptian mummies, toy-sized chariots that date back to the days of Julius Caesar, and cavern walls decorated with the prehistoric equivalent to crayons? It is because these are the timeless tools of childhood!

Wooden blocks, toy cars, and dolls are not just charming shelf warmers in the "retro" aisle of Toys "R" Us, they are essential springboards for learning about the way the world works. They are vehicles of exploration and experimentation, and props with which to practice being mommies, daddies, firefighters, and schoolteachers.

Childhood is a learning process by design, and traditional toys are a central part of the curriculum. As these core elements disappear from the scene like black squiggles on an Etch A Sketch board, experts worry about the long-term repercussions for twenty-first-century kids. Current research warns of stifled imaginations, poor interpersonal skills, and a digital divide down economic lines, but only time will tell the full impact.

In the meantime, we can do our part to ensure that childhood and high-tech toys coexist peacefully by employing the following suggestions for keeping imagination alive:

- *Make time for imagination.* When a child's day is booked solid with organized activities, creativity gets put on the back burner.
- *Have battery-free times.* Load up on good old-fashioned toys like blocks, dolls, puppets, and, of course, cardboard boxes, and set aside time for playing only with them.
- *Give gentle nudges.* While younger children are likely to dive into the world of imagination on their own, older children may need more encouragement. Props, dress-up clothes, and a subtle hint that they put together a special Shabbat skit should do the trick.
- *Have older kids "help" younger kids play.* By asking your ten-year-old to help his five-year-old brother build a rocket out of wooden blocks, you allow your big kid to save face while doing something he really enjoys but considers himself too old for.
- *It's all in the wording.* My kids balked at my suggestion to build a

city out of their trillions of Legos, but when I called it a "*Survivor* challenge," they couldn't wait to get started.

- *Accept the mess.* Creativity and imagination can be messy, so let your kids yuck it up!
- *Jump in.* If you stumble upon a couple of superheroes in the kitchen, join them in flight.
- *Pick worthwhile electronic toys and games.* Just because a toy requires an electrical current doesn't mean it's devoid of value, so search around for high-tech toys that offer opportunity for growth and imagination.

Should You Let Your Child Have a Cell Phone?

Parenting is easiest when the answers come in black and white. Can your daughter play with your butcher knife in her toy kitchen? The answer is no (black). Can she eat carrot sticks for dessert? The answer is yes (white). Can she have a cell phone for Hanukkah? The answer is . . . well, gray.

The truth is that there are both pros and cons to children owning cell phones. On the con side, the cost can be prohibitive. Many kids regularly rack up hundreds of dollars in text messaging and overage minutes each month. Not to mention that the cell phones children consider cool tend to cost a pretty penny, and are small enough to be easily lost. Also on the downside is that while many parents believe cell phones to simply be a traditional telephone without a wall jack, this could not be further from the case. Kids use cell phones to take pictures, surf the Web, IM and text message buddies, and download and listen to music. Technological advances will soon enable them to play state-of-the-art video games via their wireless phones. Children need adult supervision when engaged in any one of these activities, and the portable nature of the cell phone makes consistent parental monitoring impossible. There are also questions about the health risks of cell phones and radiation for children, in particular.

In all fairness, cell phones have a plus side. Many parents purchase cell phones for their kids as a means of staying in touch with them once the school day has ended. A cell phone is handy for children who participate in after-school activities. If the activity ends early or late or has been canceled, kids can call their parents to inform them about the changes. Additionally, children can call their parents to ask for permission should last-minute activities arise. Younger children in after-hours care may simply want to talk to their parents or ask them questions about homework and a cell phone allows them to do so. Some cell phones even have GPS tracking that can allow parents to ensure their children's safety by keeping up with their whereabouts at all times.

It's also not fair to completely write off the social angle. One of the joys and challenges of parenting is assessing situations in terms of today's world, not yesterday's. Peter N. Stearns, author of *Anxious Parents: A History of Modern Childrearing in America,* points out that "not too many decades ago, parents were having the same fuss about landlines. Children were coming home and spending hours on the phone talking to friends and dates."

If you do decide to let your grade-schooler have a cell phone of his own, steer clear of showy bells and whistles and look into purchasing one designed specifically for younger children, with parental controls and safety features already in place. Specifically, scout out cell phones that:

- limit who can call the phone
- limit who can be called with the phone
- don't have Internet access, instant messaging, or chat capabilities
- may have GPS tracking so that you literally know where your child (or at least his phone) is at all times
- has plans with prepaid minutes so your kids can't go over

Cell phones and/or plans that currently fit the bill on several or all counts include Disney Mobile, Firefly Phone, TicTalk, Chaperone Service through Verizon Wireless, Family Locator from Sprint, and Wherifone by Wherify Wireless.

Kid Meets Video Game

When it comes to the most popular electronic toys among kids, video games consistently top the charts. In fact research shows that modern children consider video games to be the most exciting form of entertainment on the entire planet—more fun than going to the movies, more fun than playing outside, and certainly more fun than reading.

In case your kids are just approaching the lower end of the video-game-obsessed bracket (around second or third grade, in most cases) here's a brief glossary of common gaming lingo. (If, on the other hand you're already far more familiar than you ever wanted to be with the ins and outs of video gaming, feel free to skip right to the "video game guilt" section.)

Console gaming system (Nintendo GameCube, Xbox, PlayStation 2 and 3): These are the big boys of video games. They plug into your

TV, come with shoebox-size consoles, and require handheld controllers. Exorbitantly priced cartridges are sold separately from the exorbitantly priced console gaming systems.

Handheld gaming system: If you like to game on the go, Nintendo GameBoy, PlayStation Portable (PSP), and Nintendo DS (for dual screen) will get you there. While all these systems and their associated game cartridges come with sky-high price tags, GameBoys are generally more affordable (relatively speaking).

PC gaming: You need not invest in a separate gaming system for these games, since they slip right into your personal computer. While there are certainly more educational and worthwhile choices in this category, there's plenty of not-worthwhile ones, too.

Multiplayer gaming: The evolution of the multiplayer gaming concept allows kids to play a handheld game against a friend across the room, or a video game against a stranger across the world. Note: the latter is not suggested for grade-schoolers as it involves an Internet predator risk.

Video Game Guilt

We parents can't help but feel pangs of guilt over letting our child enter a video-game-induced trance. Our trepidation may be attributed to the following inherent components of the video game/kid combination:

- The overstimulation factor. Studies indicate that kids who spend too much time on the Xbox Express may lose their ability to enjoy life's simpler, nonelectronic pleasures.

- The couch potato factor. Obesity in American children is at an all-time high, and having the bulk of the school-age set playing basketball with joysticks instead of their own two feet isn't helping.
- The antisocial factor. When kids play video games they play *near* each other, not *with* each other. In fact, if one kid were wearing his clothes inside out and his underwear on his head, his Game-Cubing pal would probably never notice.
- The cost factor. New video games cost thirty to fifty dollars—a hefty sum considering kids tire of them by the following week.
- The academic distraction factor. Who's got time to worry about long division when you've got important gaming strategies to consider?!
- The violence factor. Some of the video games most popular among kids have blood and guts practically flying out of the screen.
- The irresponsibility factor. On Planet Nintendo, homework and chores are distant stars, at best.
- The addiction factor. If we never tell our kids to turn off their video games, guess what? There's a good chance they never will.

So what's a genetically guilt-ridden parent to do with a houseful of video-game-obsessed kids? Cringe helplessly in the kitchen while they play SpongeBob SquarePants Revenge of the Flying Dutchman in the playroom? Sum up video games as intellectual and moral poison and ban them from our children's lives indefinitely?

After years of going back and forth myself on this issue, I've concluded that we should think of video games as chocolate rather than arsenic. It's fun to eat chocolate. Sometimes it's really fun to eat chocolate. But if we ate chocolate all day, every day, we would gain a hundred pounds, break out in a million zits, and feel horrible. Worst of all, we would never have an opportunity to enjoy all the other yummy foods the world has to offer.

Video games are no different. Occasional thirty-minute nibbles of Tetris or Mario Bros. are unlikely to doom our kids' chances of getting accepted to an Ivy League college. (Or steer them toward lives of violence, for that matter.) But just as we wouldn't let our kids eat platefuls of chocolate kisses for dinner, we need to impose boundaries and restrictions regarding video games to ensure they consume plenty of healthy non-couch-potato fare, and don't OD on empty calories.

Besides, while no match for the cons, video games do have a few redeeming qualities. They can boost eye–hand coordination and fine-motor skills and tweak problem-solving prowess. They provide entertainment during torrential weather and can keep siblings from strangling one another during extended car rides.

Some experts even say that video games can make our kids smarter. Studies at the University of Rochester and elsewhere show playing video games makes people more perceptive, trains their brains to analyze things faster, and prepares them for a fast-paced world. But most of all, and I may catch some flack on this one, I truly believe that a basic understanding of the video game world is part of the modern-day culture of childhood. As an elementary school teacher, I was privy to many a low-tech lunch conversation regarding Donkey Kong strategies.

It is my *personal* feeling (and please double-check with your parent gut before you listen to me on this) that by shielding our kids completely from the video game culture (and many other forms of kiddie pop culture, for that matter) we are doing them a disservice. In addition to its social disadvantages, banning video games completely for our children sets them up to get into trouble later. The reality is that video games are part of being a kid today, and there is not a darn thing we can do to change that. If your kids are going to dabble in video games and other forms of modern technology wouldn't you rather it be under your roof, under your supervision, using your guidelines? We need to teach our kids how to game responsibly at home so that they will know how to make responsible choices when they are not by our side.

Here are some tips on maintaining a happy, healthy video game environment:

- Set and enforce screen time limitations. The American Academy of Pediatrics recommends kids be allowed no more than one hour of daily screen time (television, computers, and video games combined). It's not a bad idea to nix these distractions during the school week altogether.
- Monitor attitudes, behaviors, and frustration levels. Studies show video games can impact children's real-life behavior. If you notice that your child has his playdate in a headlock over a game of Super Smash Brothers, for example, it's time to pull the plug.
- Responsibilities first—video games last. Require kids to finish all homework and chores before grabbing their GameCube controllers.
- Resist the electronic babysitter temptation. Video game time should never replace family time.
- Choose video games wisely. Check out the accompanying Jewish Parent 911 for everything you need to know about picking worthy games for your children.

Jewish Parent 911

Choosing Video Games Wisely

- *Pay attention to the cover.* If there are violence and sexual themes in the title and cover picture, it's a good bet they're also in the game.
- *Choose games that involve multiple players.* When video gaming involves a group effort it's a whole lot less isolating and a whole lot more fun.
- *Look for strategizing.* Choose games that require players to come up with thoughtful plans rather than just punch, jump, and run.
- *Try before you buy.* If possible rent the game and check it out "first-thumb" before you commit. Be sure to play it with your child (even if you'd rather pull your toenails out with pliers) and look out for objectionable content.
- *Pay attention to ESRB ratings.* The ESRB (Entertainment Software Rating Board) rating on the outside of the game gives you critical insight into the content of a video game. The following will allow you to decipher its meaning:

EC (Early childhood): Elmo and Dora the Explorer hang out in this category. It's basically a no-brainer in the appropriateness realm, but good luck finding a kid older than a kindergartner who's willing to play!

E (Everyone): These games are deemed appropriate for kids ages six and up. They can have minimal violence like punching and kicking, but no blood, guts, or guns. Parents are warned E games may have

some "comic mischief" and "mild language" (whatever that means).
Mario Bros., EA Sports, Barbie, Pokémon, and the vast majority of
Nintendo GameBoy games fall under this "family-friendly" rating.

E10+ (Everyone 10 and older): These games may be suitable for kids
ten and up. They may contain more cartoon, fantasy, or mild violence, mild language, and/or minimal suggestive themes. Ty the Tasmanian Tiger and Harry Potter gather in this huddle.

T (Teen): These games are apt to be violent and have mild to strong
language and suggestive content. While the ESRB has deemed T
games acceptable for anyone over thirteen, I wouldn't go rushing
out to buy one for your nephew's bar mitzvah present. The Sims,
Tony Hawk's Skateboarding, Dragon Ball Z and Star Wars gather in
this iffy genre.

M (Mature): Only ages seventeen and up should be playing these
games, says the ESRB, due to mature sexual themes, strong language, and really gory violence. Nevertheless M-rated Halo, Grand
Theft Auto, and Mortal Kombat are among the games most popular
with kids.

RP (Rating pending): These titles have been submitted and are
awaiting a final decision on where the joystick falls.

AO (Adults only): We're not even going there . . .

CHAPTER 13

Parenting the Net Generation

Warning: I'm giving you a heads up right now that this chapter may contain material unsuitable for viewing by parents still in the honeymoon period of parenting (a.k.a. the first decade with a first child, less than that with subsequent kids thanks to the educational power of older siblings). If, on the other hand, you have kids old enough to know the difference between a mouse pad and a keyboard, or an IM and an e-mail, it's absolutely imperative that you read this chapter as the issues discussed here are crucial to your family's well-being.

Getting Real

Before I start pointing out all the problems with the Internet/kid combination and detailing how we can help ensure our children have only happy and safe cybertravels, I want to make a few key points.

Key Point #1
The World Wide Web is not the devil.

There's no doubt that the Internet is currently stirring up plenty of trouble for modern-day kids and their parents, but that doesn't mean it's inherently evil. To the contrary, it's an incredibly cool invention. I mean, how awesome is it that you can shop at the Gap in the comfort of your own home? Or have a "cyberchat" with someone in Timbuktu for hours without spending a dime? How completely convenient is it that our children can access all the information they need for a research report on Golda Meir with the click of a mouse, and e-mail the finished product to their teacher in a matter of milliseconds? Lots of worthwhile things come with inherent risk, and the Internet is no different.

Key Point #2
The ostrich approach is not an option.

As you read this chapter, you'll be tempted to yank the Internet out of your home faster than a DSL connection, but the reality is that the Internet is now an integral part of the modern childhood experience. Rather than keeping our heads in the sand over the role of cyberspace in our kids' lives, we need to teach them safe Web-surfing skills and take measures to safeguard them against the Internet's dangers.

Key Point #3
It's high time we pulled out our mask and flippers.

Would you let your children go swimming at the beach without a lifeguard if you could barely dog-paddle yourself? Of course not! What if they got caught up in an undertow? How could you rescue them?

Similarly, how can we even consider dumping our kids into the stormy seas of the World Wide Web if we don't have the slightest clue how to swim in them ourselves? It is our responsibility as parents to spend ample time splashing around in cyberspace (even if it makes us feel like a fish out of water). Only in this way will we be able to make educated decisions about our children's Internet travels, by knowing when they are inching toward rough and dangerous waters, and how to rescue them if they get caught up in vicious undertow.

Key Point #4
You should make up your own mind about what is right for your kids regarding the Internet.

My objective in writing this chapter is to give helpful, balanced, current information on some of the most popular ways kids are using the Internet and on the associated dangers. The advice I give is based on opinions of cybersafety experts and on my own personal and professional experiences. That said, every child is different. Some are rule followers, some are rule breakers. Some are easily influenced by peer pressure, others march to their own drummers. Every family is different too, in terms of their morals, boundaries, and comfort zones. While it's important to be open-minded and willing to face up to unpleasant realities, in the end you should always listen to your parent gut before you listen to the recommendations in this book—or any other book, for that matter.

Key Point #5
Technology evolves at the speed of light—stay current.

Technological advances barrel in by the millisecond. What's hot and happening with kids one week may have sunk to has-been status by the next. While the topics I address in this chapter are up to the minute as of publication time, you can bet your bottom megabyte that there are new Internet threats to our children's safety just over the horizon. Modern kids hang out on the cutting edge of technology. It is our responsibility as modern parents to be right there beside them.

Now that we've gotten our parent-to-parent pow-wow out of the way, it's time to zip up those scuba suits and prepare to dive into the waters of the World Wide Web.

Keeping Kids on the Sunny Side of Cyberspace

Twenty-first-century kids take to cyberspace like matzoh balls to chicken soup. With a flick of the wrist and a click of the mouse, even the youngest of grade-schoolers can track down websites offering everything from late-breaking sports scores to the latest *American Idol* scoop to online homework tutorials. Unfortunately, not all websites are of the respectable sort, and chances are that at one time or another, our children will come face to screen with questionable online material.

Our kids needn't seek out "XXX" sites to stumble upon a peep show, either. When I was teaching second grade, for example, my class visited the government-sponsored website www.whitehouse .gov in the computer lab one day. That evening I received a frantic call from a parent. "My daughter wanted to show me what she's been learning at school," this mother said through gritted teeth. "And she pulled up a pornographic website on the computer!" It was an honest, essentially imminent mistake. Only three short letters from www.whitehouse.gov, you see, is www.whitehouse.com, where—let's just say—the oval office is hopping.

Some shady websites have even purchased formerly child-friendly Internet domains in order to find their way to an unsuspecting Web surfer's computer screen. When the Girl Scout site www.blackdiamondgirlscouts.com, for example, decided to shorten their web address, they sold their old domain. You can rest assured the buyers weren't interested in selling cookies.

Pornography isn't the only risky content kids are viewing on the Web. There are sites that foster hate crimes (which could prove terrifying for Jewish children); sites that give step-by-step instructions for making bombs and recipes for creating the dangerous drug crystal meth out of common medicines. There are websites that show videos of kids doing downright stupid things, like setting themselves on fire, and encourage other kids to emulate their insanity—and sites that glorify anorexia and bulimia and give tips on how to get away with starving yourself without your parents noticing. There are even forums that discuss the best ways to commit suicide.

If our kids are at risk of coming across inappropriate websites when they're *not* looking for them, imagine what they could find if they were. Googling the word *sex* yields 725,000,000 results, and you can bet that the vast majority of these sites would make *Playboy* look like *Boys' Life*.

I know, I know, we don't even want to let ourselves consider that our child might intentionally seek a pornographic or otherwise objectionable website. But the truth is that kids are curious by design—especially when they have other curious kids around to egg them on. Even "good" kids have been known to voluntarily venture into the darkest corners of the Web, and we have to assume that our children could too.

Since we've already established that banning the Internet from our homes is not a viable solution, we need to take measures to safeguard our children against inappropriate Internet content.

As always, our most effective tool for keeping our kids safe and out of trouble on the Internet is consistent parental supervision. Our primary move in this direction is to NEVER—no matter how much begging and complaining goes on—put an Internet-connected computer in our child's bedroom. Rather, all Web surfing on our child's part should take place in a public, high-traffic area of the house like the kitchen or family room. Assuming there are adults hanging around those high-traffic areas, research shows this precaution will significantly reduce the likelihood of our kids encountering pornographic and otherwise undesirable websites.

Our next stop is tapping into the ever-growing arsenal of technology designed to make the net more family friendly. Here's a rundown of some of these virtual parenting allies:

ISP (Internet Service Provider) Filters
All the ISP big boys offer some kind of optional program for parents to safeguard kids against objectionable websites and unsolicited and inappropriate e-mails. AOL Guardian gives parents a complete rundown of the websites their kids visit and who they exchange messages with. Yahoo's parental controls package allows parents to set different limits for each child using the Internet, and offers one set of controls for kids twelve and under, another for teens thirteen to fifteen, and still another for "mature teens." Yahoo also follows up with a weekly "report card" of a child's online activities. Microsoft's "content advisor" prevents kids from viewing inappropriate content

and lets parents set up an approved group of Web addresses. Their client filtering prevents kids from playing specific Internet games and restricts Web-surfing time. There are also smaller Internet service providers that offer filtering services. Some of note are Family Surf (www.familysurf.net), Integrity Online (www.integrity.com), and Clean Web (www.cleanweb.net). Of course no matter how thorough an Internet service screening program may be, it's always possible that inappropriate material can slip through the cracks.

Kid-Friendly Portals
These free search engines are available to anyone online and produce only G-rated links. Setting your home page to family-oriented portals like Yahooligans.com and Ask Jeeves Kids (ajkids.com), can help ensure your child's safe Web surfing. (That said, a kid could easily call up a more global search engine and all bets would be off, so this tool is best used in combination with other Internet safety measures.)

Blocking or Filtering Software
These programs prevent children from accessing inappropriate websites, while allowing parents to fully monitor their children's virtual activity. They are available for purchase online and at stores like Best Buy. Expert-recommended filtering software includes ContentProtect, CyberSitter, CyberPatrol, and NetNanny.

Lastly, just as our kids are far more likely to stay away from junk food when they have plenty of yummy, healthy options around, they're more likely to stay clear of unsavory websites when they have lots of high-interest, kid-friendly alternatives. While I mentioned homework-friendly websites back in Chapter 5 and playdate-friendly cyberdestinations in Chapter 8, you can never have enough squeaky-clean online options. With the understanding that websites—like any business—come and go and change over time, here are some more websites worth visiting for your little techies:

Family-Friendly Websites

yucky.discovery.com–Kids are drawn to gross things like bees to honey. That's why they'll have a grand time visiting the yuckiest site on the Internet (one section is called "Pimples, Burps, Farts and Funnybones") from Discovery Kids.

www.pilkey.com–Dav Pilkey's Extra-Crunchy Website o' Fun is one of the silliest sites around—from the author and illustrator of the popular Captain Underpants series. See a tongue-in-cheek comic strip biography, crafts, and lots more great stuff (all laced with clean potty humor, of course).

www.gigglepoetry.com–Budding Shel Silversteins can read poetry, learn to write poems, say tongue twisters, and even submit their own poetic creations at the self-proclaimed "#1 fun poetry site for kids on the Web."

www.timeforkids.com–Kids who like to stay up on their current events will flock to this site, which is a scaled-down, child-friendly version of its adult (Time magazine) counterpart.

www.thetoymaker.com–This unique site makes a rare jump to off-screen fun by providing parents and kids with everything they need to make colorful paper toys (i.e., paper dolls, planes, and pinwheels) together.

www.rif.org/readingplanet/–This top-rated website gives Net surfers a chance to write and illustrate their own stories, play reading games, and tap into their inner poet.

www.headbone.com–Fun and educational learning adventures, including Ecology Strikes Back, memory games, and jokes.

www.nps.gov/webrangers–The National Park Service's site for children, this cyber stop is a natural for kids eight and up, and it was rated top of the heap by Common Sense Media.

www.nationalgeographic.com/kids–With weird animal facts, natural disasters, jokes, games, and even homework help, this site is sure to be a hit.

Oy, IM Worried

In case you've fallen behind in your rules of cool, I'll bring you up to speed. Talking on the telephone is perfectly prehistoric, face-to-face conversations pitifully passé, and hanging out at the mall miserably mundane. If you want to socialize in style, there's only one way to go—IM, or instant messaging.

It is estimated that 15 billion IM transmissions are sent per day (a number expected to rise to 46 billion by 2009), and it's probably safe to say that the vast majority of those message transmitters are not of legal drinking age—or even legal PG-13 movie-viewing age.

Unfortunately, many of the unique features of IM that make it such a fave with kids also pose a significant threat to them. Here's a rundown of these features, their potential glitches, and how we can safeguard our children against them.

IM Screen Names

Kids don't use their real names on IM (that would be both dangerous and highly uncool); they use a screen name, like BaseballKing4 or Chatterbox8. An IM screen name is like an e-mail address: anyone who knows your IM screen name—or finds it in the IM directory—can pop in for a cyber tête-à-tête.

The problem: Sadly, there are people out there who comb through IM screen names searching for unsuspecting children to target. Cybersafety experts warn that even innocuous-sounding screen names can pique a predator's interest or give him a big enough crack in the door to fool a child into thinking she knows him.

The solution: When it comes to screen names, the more blasé and nonspecific, the better. Clearly, we shouldn't let our children use suggestive screen names (i.e., anything involving the words *sexy* or *hot*). We should also steer them away from screen names that reveal age, gender, and hobbies (i.e., Soccerboy8 or Dancergirl10). If your child has already signed up for a dangerous screen name, make her change it immediately. Most important, we should remind our kids relentlessly that they should *never* respond to an IM from a screen name they don't recognize and personally know offline.

IM Profiles

The IM profile is meant to provide a glimpse into the person behind the screen name. It generally includes basic stats (name, age, hometown), fun extras like games, cartoons, and movies that can be downloaded from a multitude of IM "accessorizing" sites, and brief personal messages (i.e., "Go, Red Sox!").

The problem: Once an IM profile is submitted, it becomes part of a directory that can be viewed by anyone in the *entire world*—an Internet predator's rolodex, if you will. Kids unknowingly offer up all kinds of dicey information in their basic profiles, from full name and gender to address and phone number to personal photos. They compound their risk by drawing unnecessary attention to themselves with catchy fun accessories and posting personal messages that reveal way more information than we would ever want announced to the world. For example, one of my son's IM buddies (a precious, bright sixth-grader in real life) posted her summer camp address complete with her cabin number and camp session on her IM profile, along with the proud and innocent proclamation "I love being Jewish!"

The solution: The most obvious safeguard against the danger posed by profiles is preventing our kids from filling them out in the first place (they are not required to do so). If your child is intent on having a profile, help him create one that is completely generic. No frills, no facts, just a couple of boring, overused smiley-face icons. Finally, find out your child's password (tell him there will be no instant messaging otherwise) and check his profile periodically to be sure he hasn't made any risky additions.

IM Chat Rooms

A primary reason IM is so popular with kids and teens is that it allows them to gab with oodles of different friends at once. Such cyber social gatherings take place in chat rooms. IMers can enter either a private chat room to socialize exclusively with people they "know," or a public chat room (usually revolving around a particular area of interest) to mingle with, well, strangers.

The problem: Clearly public IM chat rooms are a bad idea. I mean, you might as well send your kid into a truck-stop bathroom alone and let him get to know the folks. But even private chat rooms aren't risk free, as they generally include friends, friends of friends, and friends of friends of friends—also known as strangers.

The solution: We need to make it absolutely clear to our children that they must absolutely, positively *never* enter a public chat room. As far as private chat rooms go, the answer is grayer. If you do decide to let your child participate in private IM chats, tell him to make certain he knows the real-life identity of every chattee. If he's unsure of the actual face behind any of the screen names, he should duck out of the cyberconversation right away. Of course—and I apologize in advance for sounding like a broken record—nothing keeps kids out of public chat rooms and safe in private ones like parental presence and supervision.

Cryptic IM Language

Do you remember that goofy language called pig Latin we spoke with our friends when we were growing up? Well, guess what? Pig Latin has gone high tech. When kids instant message, they use a cryptic code composed of IM acronyms and emoticons.

The problem: All kids who instant message know the IM language. They learn it through osmosis. None of their parents know the IM language. They are still trying to perfect their pig Latin. With modern children doing much of their socializing online, this fluency gap translates into millions of parents who haven't the foggiest idea what their kids and their friends are discussing. Truth be told, most IM acronyms are relatively benign, such as BRB (be right back) or QT (cutie). But some have more bite—such as KOTL (kiss on the lips) and ASL (age/sex/location). Some of the emoticons are kind of creepy, also. For example, ;-)~ translates as "drunk" or "sexy tongue." Worse yet, modern kids—being the bright, resourceful beings they are—have created an entire branch of the IM language devoted to pulling the wool over clueless parents' eyes, such as POS (parent over shoulder), P911 (parent emergency), PAW (parents are watching), and PIR (parent in room). One last IM language–based problem worth mentioning is that researchers are finding that spelling and grammatical skills among middle- and high schoolers are slipping faster than a cell phone on a ski slope—and it's EZ to understand Y.

The solution: Looks like it's time for us parents to start brushing up on the instant-messaging lexicon. The following IM/English dictionary will give you a start:

Popular IM Acronyms

ABT2–about to	AFK–away from keyboard	ADN–any day now
B4N–bye for now	BCNU–be seein' you	BTHOOM–beats the heck out of me
BS–big smile	BRB–be right back	BTDT–been there done that
DK–don't know	E123–easy as 123	EG–evil grin

EL–evil laugh	FF–friends forever	GBH–great big hug
IMO–in my opinion	IRL–in real life	JT–just teasing
KEWL–cool	KFY–kiss for you	KPC–keeping parents clueless
L8R–later	LOL–laughing out loud	N-E-1–anyone
NW–no way!	OBTW–oh by the way	NOYB–none of your business
PRT–party	POS–parent over shoulder	PRW–parents are watching
P-ZA–pizza	P911–parent emergency	QPSA–que pasa?
RLF–real life friend	ROTFLOL–rolling on the floor laughing out loud	TAH–take a hike
TTFN–ta-ta for now	WAD–without a doubt	WE–whatever
WU?–what's up?	WYRN–what's your real name?	XME–excuuuse me!
YKW–you know what?	ZZZ–sleeping, bored, tired	

Common IM Emoticons

Happy Emoticons:
:-)–smile
8-)–smiling with glasses
;-)–winking, I'm kidding

Sad Emoticons:
:-(–sad, frowning; boo-hoo
:-c–really unhappy
:'-(–crying and really sad

Surprised Emoticons:
:O–shocked
8-|–eyes wide with surprise

Affectionate Emoticons:
@–,—'——long-stemmed rose
:-x–kiss, kiss
([hugged person's name]):**–
hugs and kisses

Angry Emoticons:

:--angry

:-@--yelling

:-P--sticking out tongue
(nyah, nyah)

Questionable Emoticons:

#-)--partied all night

>-)--devilish wink

:-Q~--smoking

Goofy Emoticons:

(:l--egghead

:-l--dunce

|-O--yawning, tired

Entertainment Potential

Let's make no bones about it, IM is fun. From a kid's perspective IM is *really, really* fun!

The problem: Many kids find IM so fun, they've become downright addicted. They spend hours a day instant messaging friends and hanging out in chat rooms. Since their parents have yet to catch on that IM makes it perfectly possible to gossip with pals while simultaneously typing a term paper, they instant message during homework time. Kids with cell phones can IM anywhere and everywhere they go. From a cybersafety standpoint, the more a child is online, the greater the chance of predator solicitation. From an academic, social, and emotional standpoint, IM overdose can have far-reaching negative ramifications.

The solution: I once asked a very social sixth-grader in my carpool how much IM time kids should be allowed each day. "Probably about four hours, maybe five on weekends," she replied. Lesson learned:

Don't ask. Children need clear and stringent guidelines regarding their instant messaging privileges. Setting a daily limit (fifteen to thirty minutes works for me) and an egg timer will help you get instant messaging under control in your house. If you notice your child perpetually exceeding his time limits or sneaking in IMs late at night, it's time to temporarily revoke his privileges.

MySpace, Our Problem

Okay, it's time to take a deep breath. Sorry, that wasn't quite deep enough. I meant a *really* deep breath, because I'm about to fill you in on an online danger to our children so monstrous it puts instant messaging in a league with the Muppets.

MySpace.com is an insanely popular, completely KEWL (see IM/English dictionary in preceding box) social networking website. Generally speaking, every teen in America has a MySpace page, and every tween in America wants to have one. As a testament to the website's popularity, the cover story in a recent issue of *Business Week* magazine was titled "The MySpace Generation."

Having heard rumblings about the dangers of MySpace, I decided to find out the true nature of this virtual beast by going undercover as a teenage MySpace member. Here's what I found during my Nancy Drewstein investigation:

An e-mail address and a cyber-oath that I was at least fourteen years of age was all it took to get me into the MySpace network of "friends," which, as of publication time, is surpassing 150 million. Unsure of how to acquaint myself with all my new pals, I narrowed my circle to include only MySpace members living within a twenty-five-mile radius of my zip code. Still overwhelmed, I used MySpace's advanced search capabilities to further limit my scope. Given the choice of searching by real name, screen name, or school, I opted for the latter. Given another choice of searching schools with grades one through twelve, six through twelve, or nine through twelve, I opted for the former. Milliseconds later I had 154 matches from a swanky private prep school in my hometown. Randomly double-clicking on one of the names, I immediately had more scoop on a girl named Rachel than I had on my closest friends. Maybe even my husband.

Based on Rachel's MySpace profile, I know her full name and that—while she claims to be fourteen—her posted graduation date puts her closer to twelve. I know her favorite pizza topping (pineapple), ice-cream flavor (cookie dough), and song ("My Humps," which is conveniently blasting from her page). As far as Rachel's favorite personal physical feature goes, it's anybody's guess because "they are all so good!"

Based on Rachel's MySpace blog (a.k.a. her online diary) I know that as of yesterday, she thinks Nick Lachey is hot, but Nick in her math class is hotter. She's addicted to *American Idol* and text messaged her vote for Ace at least seventeen times last night. Mostly, Rachel can't wait for Saturday night because she and her girlfriends are going to the Hard Rock Cafe.

Oh, by the way, I also know that Rachel is on MySpace right now, so if I wanted to become her friend, I could tack on a picture of myself and pop in to say hi. Of course, I wouldn't tack on a picture of my *real* self (Rachel would never want to talk to someone as uncool and ancient as me!); I'd tack on a picture of someone young, hip, and fourteen—just like her (wink, wink). That way, she might invite me to go to the Hard Rock on Saturday night too! (And thanks to all the pictures Rachel's posted of herself on her MySpace page, I'll be able to find her easily.)

I emerged from my undercover MySpace investigation not only

worried about Rachel's safety but feeling horribly sad for her. Rachel didn't set up a MySpace page because she's an out-of-control tween who should make a beeline to boot camp. She did it because she is a typical kid—short on judgment, lacking perspective, and obsessed with the social scene. A typical twelve-year-old girl who never in a million years would imagine that in fudging her age and displaying every ounce of her personal data on MySpace.com, she'd parked herself smack dab in the middle of an Internet predator's Disneyland and a cyberbullying cesspool (more on this in a moment) and may even be risking her college admission down the road as many universities are now checking MySpace pages to gain the real scoop on applicants.

So how do we begin to safeguard our children against a threat of such scope and magnitude as MySpace.com? We begin by educating ourselves and our kids in the following MySpace Never, Ever, Evers:

- **Never** lie about your age.
- **Never** post personal information that might enable a stranger to find you (i.e., last name, school, address, hometown, or favorite hangouts).
- **Never** post photos that are suggestive or sexual in nature.
- **Never** post photos that provide hints to where you live (i.e., a sweatshirt with your school name, a baseball hat with your hometown team logo, or nearby landmarks).
- **Never** add someone you don't personally know and trust to your "friends" list.
- **Never** arrange a face-to-face meeting with someone you "meet" on MySpace.
- **Never** hesitate to report threatening, embarrassing, or otherwise disconcerting MySpace messages to parents or the police.

To further ensure kids' safety, parents may consider installing MySpace/IM monitoring software like NetNanny 5.1, IamBig-Brother 9.1, and EBlaster 5.0. (Don't think of it as spying on your kids—you needn't scrutinize their every MySpace minute—think of it as parenting.)

Still, in my personal post–Nancy Drewstein experience opinion, the only way we can have a true hope of protecting our children against the dangers of MySpace is to become a part of it ourselves. I know it sounds radical and wholly unorthodox, but the truth is that only by becoming full-fledged MySpace members—better yet, setting up our own hokey parent pages and putting our pictures on our kids' "friends lists"—will we bust the mystique of MySpace (how totally uncool to hang out on the same social networking website as your mom?!) and understand what's really going on in this virtual social underworld.

Mini MySpace Alert

Just because your child is still too young to be interested in MySpace .com doesn't mean he or she isn't involved with virtual social networking. In fact, tens of millions of grade-schoolers have posted personal pages on websites that are—for all intents and purposes—mini MySpace.coms. (Okay, don't freak out. Just keep reading.)

On the wildly popular Club Penguin.com, for example, kids create online penguin personas (complete with screen names and personal igloos), then waddle around subzero chatrooms socializing with other cool penguin personas. On the equally happening Millsberry.com (as in General Mills cereals), kids create cartoonlike "buddies" and custom-built homes, then meander around town so-cializing with Millsberry's bottomless bowlful of citizens.

On NeoPets.com (a site that Com Networks reports had 3.58 million visitors during the month of September 2006 alone), kids create virtual pets and communicate with one another via their furry cyber friends, while Disney's Virtual Magic Kingdom members create cute characters and wander around a—you guessed it—virtual Magic Kingdom park, making cyber friends on all the rides.

Inching closer to primetime MySpace in terms of logistics and curb appeal, MyNick.com (as in Nickelodeon) has kids posting personal pages and profiles, sending Nick Mail to one another, and rocking out to Nickelodeon signature bands (i.e., The Naked Brothers) via exclusive MyNick podcasts.

In all fairness, the forces behind the majority of child-oriented social networking make an honest effort (though some admittedly more than others) toward protecting their young members from the dangers associated with their grown-up counterparts. The vast majority of these sites require parental consent before activating a child's account, forbid the uploading of personal photos, and use content filters to sift out inappropriate material. Some of these sites also employ live adult monitors to ensure conversation remains on the up-and-up, while a select few go so far as to limit kids' communication to drop-down menus of preapproved words and phrases.

Still, save the few websites with supertight security (most of which are considered babyish by tweens and up), worry resounds throughout kiddie cyber-social world.

While parental e-mail consent may be required before activating a child's registration, there's no way for a website to determine whether the e-mailed permission is indeed linked to a parent. While filters can be excellent deterrents to kids making rude or profane remarks to other kids, an older, more seasoned filter dodger could feasibly circumvent them. Although monitors may ban members who engage in inappropriate online conduct, there's nothing to stop an offending party from re-registering under a new identity. Finally, we shouldn't assume cyber-monitors hold the same standards regarding message appropriateness as we do—within milliseconds of submitting my registration on MyNick.com, I received a message from a fellow MyNick member stating: "R U a girl? If U R write me back!" Appropriate by Nick Monitor standards? Clearly. By Mom Monitor standards? Not on your life.

Also of concern is the cyberbullying potential of tons of kids hanging out together in one online location (see the upcoming section). One fourth grader reported that the "mean girls" in her class had banned her penguin from visiting their penguins' igloos on Club Penguin.

Furthermore, like their grown-up counterparts, child-oriented social networking websites are habit-forming. Many grade-schoolers spend hours every afternoon and weekend hours conversing with cyber-pals in these online forums. Also addictive to kids is the gaming element incorporated into many of these sites. The promise of earning Millsbucks, Penguin Coins, or Nick Points (to be used to deck out houses, igloos, and Nick Pages, respectively) is enough to convince any kid to ditch healthy physical activity, family time, and, of course, homework.

Perhaps the most troubling aspect of the cyber-socialization craze currently sweeping elementary schoolyards, however, is its unknown long-term impact. In-the-flesh playdates replaced with virtual-playdates; human facial expressions replaced with penguin facial expressions; neighborhood pals replaced by MyNick pals; chasing fireflies in the backyard replaced by chasing Reese's Puffs on Millsberry.com—such an abrupt shift in the traditional childhood experience is bound to have social, emotional, and physical ramifications. And only time will tell exactly what they are.

What do we do in the meantime? We a) take a deep breath, b) accept that (as we've discussed before) cyber-socializing is part of being a millennial kid, c) impose serious limitations on the amount of time our children can spend hanging out on these websites (thirty minutes a day, after homework and chores, max!), and d) pledge to provide our kids with the same boundaries, supervision, and guidance in the virtual social world as we would in the real one.

The Cyberbullying Epidemic

Do you remember *Lord of the Flies?* You know, that book we read in junior high about a bunch of British schoolboys who get stranded on a desert island. Do you remember how those marooned kids were having a ball at first—basking in the sun and in their parent-free bliss—but after a while they started savagely mauling one another with spears and boulders? Well, I hate to be the bearer of bad news, but *Lord of the Flies* is currently being reenacted right here in twenty-first-century America, where we have millions of modern kids—largely unsupervised in cyberspace—emotionally mauling one another with IM and MySpace.com.

Wow, you may be thinking. That's not nice at all. What a bunch of Jetsonian juvenile delinquents!

But I haven't gotten to the worst part. The worst part is that many of the kids dishing out this virtual social torture are otherwise decent, well-mannered children—kids who would never be involved in such malicious, callous behavior face to face. In fact studies show that the majority of American fourth- through eighth-graders admit to sending cruel, hateful, or threatening messages to someone else online.

The following representative vignettes will provide you with a glimpse into some of the many ways kids are using IM and MySpace as forums for virtual social cruelty:

Cyberbullying Vignette #1: Olivia and the Wannabees

Olivia is the queen bee of the seventh grade, so when she says fly, the wannabees flap their wings. When Olivia commands her followers to log onto IM at precisely 5:15 P.M. for a virtual pow-wow, they willingly abide. Olivia also invites Rachel, a shy new student, to join in the chat. By 5:16 P.M. Olivia is relentlessly pounding poor Rachel with a shower of misspelled but nonetheless cruel zingers. The IMing wannabees follow their queen's lead.

Cyberbullying Vignette #2: Watch Your Back

Michael and David are bored. They've played all their video games a zillion times and have instant messaged everyone they know. That's when they decide to register a MySpace page under their middle-school principal's name, titled "People Who Should Watch Their Backs." They can't wait to see their twenty-five targets shaking in their shoes at school the next day.

Cyberbullying Vignette #3: The Digital Doozie

Best friends Shira and Katie have it out at a slumber party. In retaliation, Shira uses her state-of-the-art picture phone to snap a candid shot of Katie changing into her pajamas. She proceeds to send the digital doozie of her underwear-clad ex—best friend to everyone she knows.

Cyberbullying Vignette #4: Ten Reasons I Hate Amanda

Elana is hanging out with a cool new crowd and wants to make certain everyone knows she is no longer friends with Amanda (uncool personified). So she posts a picture of Amanda on her MySpace page (doctored with devil's horns and a mustache) along with a detailed list of everything she hates about her former pal. She then invites the cool crowd to visit her page and add all the reasons they hate Amanda, too.

Cyberbullying Vignette #5: Sam the Football Cheater

Max is convinced that Sam cheated at football during recess and decides to teach Mr. Rule Breaker a little lesson via IM. Later that afternoon, as Sam instant messages his friends, strange screen names begin popping up on his computer. First comes IhateSam8, next is FootballCheaterSam12, followed by SamSucks88. An hour and twenty-two new screen names later, Max finally wraps up his Sam slam and logs off.

What is it about instant messaging and MySpace.com that bring out the bully in so many modern children? Besides the fact that our kids are all over them like applesauce on latkes while we parents have yet to plug in the frying pan, I'd venture to say the answer lies in some combination of the following fundamental components of IM and MySpace:

They Foster Emotional Detachment and Anonymity

As we've already established, kids are developmentally egocentric. On a good day it's difficult for them to understand the way their words and actions impact people. Through the veil of a computer screen, it's virtually impossible. Consequently, most kids say or do things on a computer that they wouldn't have the nerve to do in person. Since IM and MySpace make it easy for them to go incognito or to pose as someone else, they are able to make cruel remarks with little consequence. In my son's fourth-grade class, for example, a student got hold of another student's IM password and began sending out hateful, inappropriate messages under her classmate's IM identity.

They Breed Impulsivity

Have you ever sent an emotional e-mail only to find yourself milliseconds later wishing it erased from cyberspace? Online communication lends itself to impulsive behavior. If we adults—who have our impulses relatively under control—find it frighteningly easy to make regrettable statements online, imagine how our impulse-control-challenged kiddies feel.

They Promote Cybercliques

Thanks to the IM "buddy" and MySpace "friend" features, modern children hang out online en mass. Charged with social power, they are more likely to send quick zingers to other kids than if they were having a one-on-one chat and, research shows, less likely to come to their defense. Furthermore, the warning and blocking safety features (technically designed to keep Internet creeps at bay) of both IM and MySpace make excluding other kids a snap—or should I say, a double-click.

They Allow for Mass, Simultaneous Communication

Back in our day, rumors were spread using the old "I told two friends, then she told two friends, then she told two friends" technique. Since IM and MySpace enable kids to communicate with zillions of friends at once there's no need to resort to such archaic measures. In fact, a cyberbully with malice in her mouse can easily pulverize her victim's entire reputation over the course of three seconds.

They Are Insanely Popular

IM has replaced phones as the preferred mode of communication among modern tweens and teens. MySpace has a population four times that of the state of New York. The average tween spends an hour and a half per day social networking. Nothing was that popular when we were kids. Not even Scott Baio.

By the way, do you remember how at the end of *Lord of the Flies* the schoolboys are finally rescued by British officers who ruthlessly scold them for their reprehensible behavior? Do you remember what the children do as they receive this tongue-lashing? They weep. Not out of fear of punishment, but in relief of being once again wrapped in the secure and predictable confines of adult-regulated boundaries and direction.

My intent in writing this chapter spotlighting cyberbullying and all the other trouble twenty-first-century kids are getting into on the Internet is not to demonstrate how crass, cruel, and short-sighted modern children can be. It is to help enable you as modern parents to recognize the smoke signals our kids are sending, join forces with their schools and with other parents, and begin to provide adult-regulated boundaries and supervision to the tween/teen cybercivilization.

Jewish Parent 911

Combating Cyberbullying

Combatting the cyberbully requires a group effort.

Parents:
Talk about cyberbullying with your kids.
Tell children they are expected to show the same *kavod* (respect) for others online as off.

Become Internet savvy. Take a course or have your kid tutor you.

Supervise your children's Internet usage as much as possible.

Buy software that records instant messages.

Do not hesitate to approach the school or other parents regarding an aggressor, or to contact the police if your child is physically threatened by a cyberbully.

Kids:

Be wary to whom you give your cell phone number, e-mail address, or IM screen name.

If you get a message from a cyberbully do not respond and log off immediately.

Keep e-mails from the harasser as evidence.

Report cyberbullying to parents and school officials.

Schools:

Amend antibullying policies to include cyberbullying.

Educate teachers, parents, and students about the seriousness of the problem.

Assign a contact person to whom parents and students may report cyberbullying problems.

You can find additional IM safety tips at www.wiredkids.org, www .GetNetWise.org, and www.safekids.com.

Conclusion

One Last Parent-to-Parent Pow-Wow

This can't be the end—we still have so much more to talk about! If we do have to say shalom (the good-bye kind, that is), it's not going to be before we review some key points we've discussed in this book. Ready? Here goes . . .

Enjoy your children for who they are. Modern societal pressure to bring up multitalented offspring can be overwhelming, but as we've established, achievement-oriented parenting is apt to prove counterproductive for our families on about a zillion levels. Rather than constantly sizing up your kids academically, athletically, musically, socially, and otherwise against every other kid on the planet, therefore, give yourself permission to enjoy your children for the marvelous, miraculous, occasionally maddening, one-of-a-kind beings they are. (Be sure to keep your AAA toolbox—*Accept* imperfection, *Avoid* the self-esteem parenting trap, and *Accentuate* your children's unique sets of gifts—close at hand in case of emergency.)

Embrace your Judaism as a parenting ally. Whether you are Orthodox, Conservative, Reform, or anywhere in between, the rich Jewish religion provides you with indispensable backup parenting support in the form of a ready-made curriculum in ethics and morality; a soft place to land when your family takes life's inevitable hits; and a means of anchoring your children close to home through the safety and predictability of our age-old Judaic traditions.

Pay attention to your parent gut. Nobody knows your child like you do—not a teacher, not a pediatrician, not a child psychologist, not the latest parenting guru, not me. So before looking elsewhere for parenting solutions, listen good and hard to your parent gut. You may be surprised how much wisdom awaits there.

Use your child as a guide throughout your parental journey. I've cited the Talmudic decree to "teach a child according to his way" several times in this book, for it is one of insurmountable insight. Parenting is not a uniform, formulaic task. It is a fluid process that must be accommodated to the unique needs of each and every child.

Use the split screen to help you make tough parenting calls. Anytime you find yourself in a bona fide parental pickle, remember to employ the split-screen method. Glimpsing the way your decision will impact not just the child of today but the adult of the future will help you find answers you need no matter what kind of curveball parenthood sends your way.

Stay current on technology. Raising kids has never been easy, but technological advances like the Internet, cell phones, social networking websites, and lifelike video games make parenting all the more challenging. By staying updated on the latest techie tools and the ways kids are using them, you'll be better able to provide your children with the guidance and supervision they need in the twenty-first century.

Remember to stop and smell the bubble gum. Caught up in the hustle and bustle of parenting (homework, carpooling, schlepping, stressing), it's easy to lose sight of what really matters. So every now and then—as you sit behind the wheel of your minivan—tune out the traffic, breathe in the innocence, and give God a little thank-you for the bubble-gum-smacking blessings in the backseat.

Enjoy the ride.

Acknowledgments

Back in my pre–book-writing days, I naively assumed that authors wrote books alone. Never in my wildest dreams could I have imagined how many people sit behind that single name on the cover. I'd like to take this opportunity to thank all the amazing individuals who had a hand in bringing this book to life.

Immeasurable gratitude goes to Caitlin Blasdell, literary agent magnifique, fairy godmother and friend, who saw a spark and patiently, brilliantly helped me ignite it . . . as our seven combined children jumped on our heads.

I am forever thankful to Trish Medved, my Broadway Books dream editor, who believed in this project from the start and shared my vision to the point that she began speaking Yiddish. And to Becky Cole, my second Broadway Books dream editor, whose bright bubble of positive energy found its way to my book. I struck gold. Twice.

Special appreciation to Liza Dawson and Anna Olswanger, who jumped in at the bottom of the ninth and so capably helped carry my proposal through the final stretch. And to Brianne Ramagosa, an awesome editorial assistant who—in addition to countless other feats—can get a package from New York to Atlanta faster than humanly possible.

Infinite thanks to Bob Menaker (ע״ה), who gave me my big break at the *Atlanta Jewish Times*, and Michael Jacobs, who has provided me unwavering support and guidance ever since. To all the editors of

Acknowledgments

Jewish newspapers across the United States, Canada, and Israel who so enthusiastically publish my columns and articles.

Gratitude to Stan Beiner, Roz Cohen, and Amanda Bilek of the Epstein, Solomon Schechter School of Atlanta, who taught me the fine art of working with Jewish parents, and Coleen Lou for all her assistance. And to Rabbis Analia Bortz and Mario Karpuj of Congregation Or Hadash, who generously shared their *halachic* wisdom and insight.

Special thanks goes to Steve Nowicki, who helped me get published for the first time way back in college and is a wonderful mentor and friend. And to Terri Jacobson, Caryn Boxer, Lisa Banov, Sara Fabian, Marla Rich, Beth Marks, and Renee Miller, who read really rough drafts of my manuscript and gave me honest, invaluable insight—not to mention endless emotional support and playdates for my kids—throughout my writing process. To the MEGA Girls— Sara Meyers, Mitzie Goldman, and Barrie Antebi—for friendship and Florida sunshine. And to my courageous little friend Maia Barton, who reminded me just how brave and strong Jewish children can be.

Great appreciation to my sister-in-law Susan Duke, who sent me a steady stream of up-to-the-second news articles that are incorporated throughout this book, to my brother Jon, who understands me on a level that only another writing-obsessed, overachieving Duke child could. And to my grandmother, Eva Bookman, who is always kvelling about my writing and writes marvelous poetry herself.

Loving thanks to my ever-supportive family and friends: Noah, Gabrielle, Rachel, and Shira Duke; Donald, Anita, Mark, Lori,

Laney, Hallie, Neal, Susan, Skye, and Adam Estroff; Abbie Gold; Nancy Harris; Marty, Irene, and Judith Duke; Maggie, Wayne, and Matt Grzecki; Peggy and Herbie Abroms; Kaaren Nowicki; Caroline Adelman; and Adele Glasser.

An immeasurable thank-you goes out to my mother, Sara Duke, who shared her wealth of knowledge; but, more important, gave me my wings and kept my family afloat as I wrote. And to my father, Marshall Duke, who promised me all those years ago that the gift of writing would one day prove more valuable than the (nonexistent) gift of cartwheeling—and kept his word.

Of course this book would not have been possible without the love and support of my wonderful husband, Lee, my partner in this wild, wonderful Jewish parenting journey, who stepped up to the plate (sometimes even willingly) throughout my writing process.

But mostly I owe this book to my children: to Brandon, who helps me find the humor in parenting and in life; to Alex, whose gentle kindness and *menschlichkeit* reminds me of all that is right with the world; to Jakey, who radiates a perpetual smile and wisdom beyond his years; and to Emma—my perfect match in every way—who is, indeed, the exclamation point at the end of my sentence. The four of you provide me with a daily confirmation of God's grandeur. You are my heart, my essence, and my purpose. I love you to infinity and beyond. Oh, and I almost forgot . . . Go Dawgs!

Bibliography

Abramowitz, Y., Silverman, S., and Wiesel, E. *Jewish Family and Life: Traditions, Holidays, and Values for Today's Parents and Children.* New York: St. Martin's Press, 1998.

Aftab, P. *The Parent's Guide to Protecting Your Children in Cyberspace.* New York: McGraw Hill, 1999.

Ahuja, A. "Forget Self-Esteem and Learn Some Humility" *Times,* May 17, 2005.

Baumeister, R., Heatherton, T., and Tice, D. "When Ego-Threats Lead to Self-Regulation Failure: Negative Consequences of High Self-Esteem." *Journal of Personality and Social Psychology* 64, no. 1 (1993): 141–56.

Bennett, W., Finn, C., and Cribb, J. *The Educated Child: A Parent's Guide from Preschool Through Eighth Grade.* New York: Free Press, 2000.

Cline, F., and Fay, J. *Parenting with Love and Logic.* Colorado Springs, CO: Pinon Press, 2006.

Csikszentmihalyi, M. *Creativity: Flow and the Psychology of Discovery and Invention.* New York: Harper Perennial, 1997.

"Cyber911 Emergency: Cyberbullying." WiredSafety. Retrieved January 14, 2006, from http://www.wiredsafety.org/cyber stalking_harassment/cyberbullying.html.

Danan, J. *Jewish Parent's Almanac.* Landham, MD: Jason Aronson, 1996.

"The December Dilemma, December Holiday Guidelines for Public Schools." Anti-Defamation League. Retrieved July 11, 2006, from http://www.adl.org/issue_education/december_dilemma_2004/default.asp.

Duke, M., Fivush, R., Lazarus, A., and Bohanek, J. "Of Ketchup and

Kin: Dinnertime Conversations as a Major Source of Family Knowledge, Family Adjustment, and Family Resilience." Emory Center for Myth and Ritual in American Life. Retrieved April 21, 2006, from http://www.marial.emory.edu/pdfs/Duke_Fivush027-03.pdf.

Duke, M., and Nowicki, S. *Helping the Child Who Doesn't Fit In.* Atlanta, GA: Peachtree Publishers, 1992.

Duke, M., and Nowicki, S. *Teaching Your Child the Language of Social Success.* Atlanta, GA: Peachtree Publishers, 1996.

Duke, S., and Duke, M. *What Works with Children: Wisdom and Reflections from People Who Have Devoted Their Careers to Kids.* Atlanta, GA: Peachtree Publishers, 2000.

Elkind, D. *The Hurried Child: Growing Up Too Fast Too Soon.* New York: Perseus Publishing, 2001.

Faber, A., and Mazlish, E. *How to Talk So Kids Will Listen & Listen So Kids Will Talk.* New York: Quill, 2002.

Gallo, A., and Gallo, J. *The Financially Intelligent Parent: 8 Steps to Raising Successful, Generous, Responsible Children.* New York: NAL, 2005.

Gardner, H. *Multiple Intelligences: The Theory in Practice.* New York: Basic Books, 1993.

Gardner, H. *Intelligence Reframed: Multiple Intelligences for the 21st Century.* New York: Basic Books, 2000.

Greenberg, G. A. *MitzvahChic: How to Host a Meaningful, Fun, Drop-Dead Gorgeous Bar or Bat Mitzvah.* New York: Fireside, 2006.

Greenspan, S. *Playground Politics: Understanding the Emotional Life of the School-Age Child.* New York: Perseus Books, 1994.

"Helping Your Student Get the Most Out of Homework." National PTA. Retrieved February 10, 2006, from http://www.pta.org/archive_article_details_1118088722562.html.

Hughes, D. "Instant Message & Chatroom Safety Tips." ProtectKids
.com. Retrieved March 22, 2006, from http://www.protectkids
.com/parentsafety/imchatips.htm.

Iovine, V. *Girlfriends' Guide to Parties and Playdates.* New York: Peri-
gree, 2003.

Kearsley, G. "Operant Conditioning: BF Skinner." Theory into
Practice Database. Retrieved April 2, 2006, from http://tip
.psychology.org/skinner.html.

Lansky, V. *Birthday Parties: Best Party Tips & Ideas.* Minnetonka, MN:
Book Peddlers, 1995.

Latane, B., and Darley, J. *The Unresponsive Bystander: Why Doesn't He
Help?* New York: Appleton-Century Crofts, 1970.

Magid, L. "Child Safety on the Information Highway." SafeKids
.com. Retrieved April 17, 2006, from http://www.safekids.com/
child_safety.htm.

"Making Parent-Teacher Conferences Work for Your Child." National PTA. Retrieved January 20, 2006, from http://www.pta
.org/archive_article_details_1118085766734.html.

Mintz, S. *Huck's Raft: A History of the American Childhood.* Cambridge,
MA: Belknap Press/Harvard University Press, 2004.

Mogel, W. *Blessing of a Skinned Knee: Using Jewish Teachings to Raise
Self-Reliant Children.* New York: Penguin, 2001.

Mogel, W. "How to Choose a School." *Jewish Journal of Greater Los Angeles,* August 24, 2001.

"MySpace Safety Tips for Parents." MySpace.com. Retrieved February 23, 2006, from http://www.myspace.com/Modules/Common/
Pages/SafetyTips.aspx#.

Pomerantz, E. "Mother's Affect in the Homework Context: The Importance of Staying Positive." *Developmental Psychology* 41 (2005):
414–27.

Salkin, J. *Putting God on the Guest List: How to Reclaim the Spiritual Meaning of Your Child's Bar or Bat Mitzvah*. Woodstock, VT: Jewish Lights, 2005.

Samalin, N. *Loving Each One Best: A Caring and Practical Approach to Raising Siblings*. New York: Bantam, 1997.

Shepard, L., and Smith, M. "Synthesis of Research on School Readiness and Kindergarten Retention." *Educational Leadership* 44 (1986): 78–88.

Stearns, P. *Anxious Parents: A History of Modern Childrearing in America*. New York: New York University Press, 2003.

Teluskin, J. *Book of Jewish Values: A Day by Day Guide to Ethical Living*. New York: Bell Tower, 2000.

Twerski, A., and Schwartz, U. *Positive Parenting: Developing Your Child's Potential*. New York: Mesorah Publications, 1996.

Vail, Kathleen. "Homework Problems: How Much Is Too Much?" *American School Board Journal* 188, no. 4 (2001). Retrieved March 14, 2006, from http://www.asbj.com/2001/04/0401coverstory.html.

Weinstein, M. *The Surprising Power of Family Meals: How Eating Together Makes Us Smarter, Stronger, Healthier and Happier*. Hanover, NH: Steerforth Press, 2005.

Zill, N., Loomis, L., and West, J. "The Elementary School Performance and Adjustment of Children Who Enter Kindergarten Late or Repeat Kindergarten; Findings from National Surveys." Washington, D.C.: US Dept. of Education, Office of Educational Research and Improvement, National Center for Education Statistics, 1997.

Index

Topics and Questions for Discussion

Topic 1: Focusing the Big Picture of Jewish Parenting
   (related chapters: Introduction, 1, 2)

1. Describe the first time you caught yourself sizing up your child against other kids (i.e., in baby playgroup, at a pee wee soccer game). Describe a time in the past *week* that you've caught yourself doing this. (Come on, you know you have!)
2. Beginning with babyhood, list all the extracurricular activities and enrichment classes outside school that your child has participated in. Which activities have had the most impact on your child? Which—if any—do you view as less beneficial? Now make a list of the extracurriculars you participated in as a child. How do the lists compare? What are your thoughts on this difference?
3. Imagine your child as an adult. What qualities and achievements—both Judaic and general—do you hope to see in him or her? How are you fostering these goals in your daily parenting practices? How might you inadvertently be hindering them?

Topic 2: Educating Our Children According to Their Way
   (related chapters: 3, 4, 5, 6)

4. What do you think the Talmudic rabbis meant when they said, "Educate a child according to his way"? Do you think this statement holds true in contemporary times?
5. What type of teacher comments does your child consistently receive on his or her report cards and progress reports? Are these assessments in line with what you know about your child? What do you think this recurring feedback says about your child as a learner?

6. Using the Multiple Intelligences framework in chapter 4, what do you see as your child's natural areas of strength? What opportunities does he or she have to foster them?

7. Reflect on the nightly homework drill at your house. Do any of the parental mistakes in chapter 5 ring especially true to you?

Topic 3: Sailing the Social Seas (related chapters: 7, 8)

8. How would you characterize your own social experiences as a child? How do you think these experiences impact your feelings and/or level of involvement with your child's social life?

9. We discussed the importance of ritual and repetition in giving kids the stability they need to survive the treacherous terrain of the childhood social existence. What Jewish and secular rituals do you regularly incorporate into your family life?

Topic 4: Celebrating with Jewish Values (related chapters: 9, 10)

10. What do you hope your family will gain from your child's bar/bat mitzvah experience? How do you plan to keep these goals throughout the process?

11. Brainstorm ways your school, synagogue, and grade-level parent population can help ensure appropriate behavior at b'nai mitzvah.

Topic 5: Nourishing Our Children's Jewish Soul
(related chapter: 11)

12. Our rich Jewish heritage offers year-round opportunities to strengthen and sustain our children. Share some of your favorite family-friendly traditions for Shabbat, Rosh Hashanah, Yom Kippur, Purim, Passover, Hanukkah, and other Jewish holidays.

Topic 6: Raising Children in a Materialistic World
   (related chapter: 12)

   13. Think about conflicts you've had with your kids over purchases and material possessions? How would the Spend/Save/Tzedakah plan help circumvent these situations?

   14. How do your own consuming/shopping behaviors manifest themselves in your children's attitudes and values?

Topic 7: Parenting in Cyberspace (related chapter: 13)

   15. Do you know what your child does online? (Are you sure?!) Do you have parental monitoring software in place? What other measures do you take to ensure your child's cyber well-being?

   16. How do you think the Internet impacts your child—and modern children as a whole—both positively and negatively?

Sharon Duke Estroff is an internationally syndicated Jewish parenting columnist whose articles address contemporary and traditional parenting issues within a Jewish context. Her columns appear in over fifty publications that reach nearly two million readers. She is an educational consultant with Perimeter Educational and Psychological Services in Atlanta, co-creator and co-director of Epstein Summer Adventure Day Camp, and an award-winning Jewish educator with nearly two decades of experience in both public and private schools. She lives in Atlanta, Georgia, with her husband and four school-age children.